WHAT PEOPLE ARE SAYING ABOUT "FINDING HIS TIMING"

"Holy revelations!!! I realize this was written from Jen's perspective but more often then not it felt as if she was telling my story! Not that I experienced the same trauma of losing a father to suicide, but I did experience the trauma of losing my mom to cancer at a young age. Prior to reading this, I had little understanding of the degree to which this trauma had affected every aspect of my life! As I read through each chapter, there was a revelation Jen described in her journey that literally, with a few changes in words or characters, also described exactly where I was in my journey. Revealing how lack of identity is such a stuck point for SO many and then showing, through very relevant stories, how aligning with our Creator helps us to realize exactly who He has designed us to be! Jen's unique sense of humor, her analogies to everyday things, and her selfless transparency help make this a must read for everyone who has struggled with truly understanding who you were created to be."

– MELISSA NEUMAN

"Jen's journey of discovering God's perfect timing is positively inspiring. Truly, the depth of her insight regarding God's alignment and synchronicity just "oozes" out of every page!! I absolutely love how she beautifully ties her life events and lessons learned to the Hebrew calendar and scripture. The sincerity of her humility and teach-ability is so refreshing. Throughout the book, Jen's personality shines through with endearing 'Jen-isms' that often made me chuckle! More notably, however, her passion for helping others, especially those who are hurting and confused, is undeniably evident. The coach in her doesn't leave them there, but instead she unites the readers with their Creator to reflect on their own lives and seek that divine alignment. Readers will find Jen's personal stories captivating, filled with hope, excitement, and encouragement. With the perspective that Jen consistently demonstrates throughout the entire book, I believe those who read this book will be transformed from feeling fear and doom and anxiety to embracing the revelation that their life journey is a divinely orchestrated adventure! This is more than just a book; it's an invitation to embark on a thrilling spiritual journey of self-discovery and divine connection. I highly recommend this to anyone seeking to uncover the hidden treasures in their own life story."

– DONNA LUCORD

"Jen's second book "Finding His Timing" is even more compelling and powerful as she walks you through the next steps of her overcoming journey of faith: listening to Yeshua's voice, following the thrilling roadmap of her Heavenly Father, and seeing how He intertwines her path with the Jewish calendar and feasts! I was once again captivated by her sense of humor, vulnerability and practical Biblical wisdom and applications. Yeshua has been using her book to speak personally to me about my present journey giving hope, inspiration and encouragement to follow and trust in His goodness and mercy as I too adventure with Him! Discover your own personal roadmap and treasure as you journey with Jen through her autobiographical reflections!"

– KERRI THEWLIS

"Finding His timing kept me on the edge of my seat. This book is raw and real about finding yourself at the right time. 'There is power in your story. There is power in the word of your testimony!' It is a blueprint to harness your own power to move forward with the hard things. It is a must read if you are looking for encouragement to become more in this life."

– MISSY BOWMAN

"Your book struck a chord with me, capturing the full spectrum of human emotion in a way that felt both familiar and profound. The humor sprinkled throughout the narrative had me laughing out loud, reminding me of how laughter often serves as a lifeline during tough times. As I navigated the themes of real life struggles and growth, I found myself reflecting on my own losses, struggles and growth. Your exploration of mourning resonated deeply, validating my own feelings of sorrow and confusion. Similarly, the raw portrayal of anger reflected my struggles with life's injustices, offering a sense of camaraderie in the face of frustration. Accomplishments, both big and small, were celebrated in a way that inspired me to acknowledge my own victories, reminding me that every step matters. The struggles depicted were achingly relatable, reinforcing the idea that resilience often emerges from our toughest moments. Overall, it is a beautifully woven narrative that resonates with the complexities of life. It left me feeling understood and connected, reminding me of the shared human experience we all navigate. I highly recommend it to anyone seeking a heartfelt reflection on life's highs and lows."

— DELYNN MARIE

"I am not a big reader. I do not always finish every book that I start reading. I had a very hard time putting down Jen's first book! I felt honored that she invited me to be a part of the preview of her second book and had a hard time putting it down also! I love her openness, honesty, choice of words, sincere vulnerability and expressions! Even if your life experiences, traumas and challenges are not exactly the same, you can still relate and grow from her sharing her story. Anyone who reads "Finding His Timing" will be blessed with peace, clarity and hope! It is so real and relateable, every emotion you truly feel with her!"

— JUDY MENZIE

"In her rawness and vulnerability, Jen exposes the inner workings of a child of God, who is shedding herself of her fears in this, her second book, 'Finding His Timing'. Most of us don't notice the changes in us overtime, the things that make us who we are and the timing that God uses to put all of that together into one single person. In Jen's book, we get the luxury of seeing or learning just how it is that God has made Jen in His timing."

— BILL YAICH

"'Finding His Timing' is an impactful journey that had me crying at various moments, deeply moved by Jen's raw honesty and vulnerability. Her exploration of faith and timing is not only powerful but also incredibly relateable, inviting readers to reflect on their own lives. Jen masterfully intertwines her personal experiences with the richness of the Jewish calendar, offering insights that resonate deeply. This book is more than just a narrative; it's a blueprint for finding strength in struggle and understanding God's perfect timing. I wholeheartedly recommend 'Finding His Timing' to anyone seeking hope and inspiration. It's a must-read that leaves you feeling seen, understood, and uplifted."

— BROOKELYNN KASKI

"This has been both an emotionally tense and uplifting read, that I highly recommend! If I compared our stories side by side, there would be few similar life events. Yet as she writes about her processing during those events, Jen describes reactions and perceptions that I have experienced, as well, under totally different circumstances. At times, I found myself thinking, 'wow! I know exactly what she's feeling!' Jen exposes her own vulnerability yet maintains a sense of humor as she shares feelings of fear and doubt. She vividly describes dreams and situations as the precursors to revelations and deeper understanding of her Creator's plans for her. As she puts His plans into actions, Jen realizes that her success is intrinsically tied to scriptural timing, God's timeline! Jen has taken raw, personal, painful, and joyful moments of her life and masterfully woven them into a tapestry only God could have designed!"

– KATHY TORKER

"'Finding His Timing' helped me to hear Yahweh's voice in my own life. There are so many things that Jen writes about that I needed to hear or be reminded of, such as: Shame and pain may be preparation for what God has next; I need to look beyond myself. It's not about me, it's about Him; Look for Yahweh in every little thing - in everything! That's what Jen does, and SHE FINDS HIM! Suffering is allowed so we can know what grace is; We don't need to look perfect. It's okay to fail; I only need to be what He designed me to be; Yahweh never left Jen alone on her journey, and He's never left me; It's worth it, even if you are only able to help one person; God is not the author of confusion; Pay attention to nudges from the Spirit; Only God's voice is always the voice of truth. There are these and so many other golden nuggets to collect along the way as you read this book. You'll have an entire treasure chest full of wisdom, encouragement, hope and peace by the time you finish it. She shares these things with the reader by being authentic, and vulnerable. I truly believe she is putting the needs of the reader before her own. She shows, by example, how to have faith enough to surrender everything to Him, then shows how He replaces despair with joy, pain with hope! It is all tied together with a map (which you find out about as you read) that lights the way, and demonstrates that everything is in His perfect timing. Throughout the book, Jen is cheering us on and assuring us that she believes in us. I believe in her! I think this book will help so many people who are searching for meaning and for peace."

– KAY VANDYKE

"This book helped me understand God's immense love for me in ways I hadn't before. Jen's words reminded me to give myself grace when I fall short and to trust that God is not only a good Father but has beautiful plans for my life. Reading it gave me renewed hope for a future I can't yet see and faith to trust in His perfect timing. It's like Jen's story reached into my own, showing me how to move forward with clarity and confidence. Her writing is encouraging, uplifting, and left me feeling closer to God and more secure in His plans for me. Since finishing the book, I've experienced real breakthroughs. I've forgiven myself for past mistakes and reconnected with God in powerful ways—I'm journaling again, reading my Bible, worshiping, and even writing letters to seek and extend forgiveness. The depression I was carrying has completely lifted, and I'm creating healthy boundaries, saying no when needed, and leading my boys in prayer and communion every Saturday. If you're seeking clarity, grace, and hope, this book is a must-read. Thank you, Jen, for sharing your heart and helping me deepen my faith and trust in His timing!"

– JAX CARDENAS

"I cannot contain my excitement about this book! 'Finding His Timing' is a revelation—a powerful, life-changing journey that will ignite your faith and awaken your spirit! Jen first introduced me to the concept of Biblical timing through Chuck Pierce's 'A Time to Advance', but nothing could have prepared me for the depth, wisdom, and divine insight she pours into 'Finding His Timing'. This is not just a book—it's an encounter with Yahweh's perfect plan! From the very first page, Jen's raw honesty and bold storytelling pull you into an adventure of faith, surrender, and discovery. She doesn't just tell a story; she invites you into the very heartbeat of Yahweh's timing! Every triumph, every struggle, every moment of divine alignment leaps off the page, reminding you that Yahweh is always working, even in the waiting. What makes Finding His Timing truly unforgettable is how deeply it resonates with anyone searching for clarity, purpose, or a deeper relationship with the Creator. Jen doesn't just share her experiences—she reveals how Yahweh's voice has guided her through some of life's most pivotal moments, unlocking identity, destiny, and purpose with every step. One of the most powerful aspects of this book is Jen's courageous vulnerability—she doesn't shy away from the hard questions, the struggles, or the ethical dilemmas. Instead, she lays it all out, showing that grace and redemption are always within reach. If you've ever wrestled with doubt, felt stuck in the waiting, or longed for deeper intimacy with Yahweh, 'Finding His Timing' is your roadmap. It's not just words on a page—it's a divine invitation to trust Yahweh's perfect timing, step into your purpose, and embrace the unknown with unshakable faith!

– TIMOTHY SAIPRAMUK

"'Finding His timing', is such a great reminder to surrender, pray for His guidance and let everything fall on the arms of our Creator. More than anyone He has the prefect plan for us. Psalm 46:10 'Be still, and know that I am God...'"

– LEILA STOCKWELL

"If you are human and have ever been through anything tough in life, you won't regret reading this book. Jen's words are so relateable and inspiring. This is the story of a woman that is not shy in talking about the hard things while at the same time screaming from the mountain tops that it's all for God's glory. I love the way that she transformed her life by simply giving it all to God and choosing to live for him. She is living proof that the hardest battles we face in life can be the exact thing that God uses to make us the Overcomer He calls us to be."

— **STEPHANIE MURDOCK**

"'Finding God's Timing' is an inspiring, faith-building book that meets you right where you are in whatever season you're in. For anyone seeking a deeper connection with God, hoping to find renewed purpose, or seeking clarity in uncertain times, this book is for you. So go ahead, stop reading this review, open up chapter one, and let the journey begin!"

— **CHRIS OSMORE**

FINDING HISTIMING

AN OVERCOMER'S JOURNEY FROM CONFUSION TO CLARITY

JEN HORLING

Copyright © 2025 Jen Horling
All Rights Reserved. No part of this book may be reproduced in any form or by any electronic or mechanical means, including information storage and retrieval systems, without permission in writing from the publisher, except by reviewers, who may quote brief passages in a review.

Thank you for your honor in helping protect author's rights.

Finding His Timing
An Overcomer's Journey From Confusion to Clarity

ISBN: 978-1-7349204-1-3
Printed in the United States of America

Cover Design by: Sponge Designs, Inc

www.theovercomersmovement.com

An overcomer's continued journey.
The secret was not so secret at all. It had been there since the beginning, in appointments planned before time for us to meet.

DEDICATION

To the Great Designer, my Yahweh-Nissi! My banner of victory in it all. The One who designed it all, in great detail. This book is dedicated to You. May You use it for far more victories than I could ever imagine, every single day, month and year, as You equip so many more hearts with clarity to overcome.

ACKNOWLEDGMENTS

Dani J, there's not a single day that goes by where my gratitude for you doesn't rise up in my spirit. The deposits you made—and the deposits He made through you—echo endlessly. As I put pen to paper for this second book, your name was the first He dropped into my spirit to include once again. Why? Because you gave it all—all of your journey with Him, all of your wisdom, and all of your heart. You love your Creator with all that you are, and who you are is living proof that His promises are true. Even the promises I had yet to experience, the ones I was still holding out hope for. Through you, He showed me what was possible when we seek Him fully and trust in His perfect timing. Your hunger for the Creator and your relentless pursuit of discovering more of Him didn't just inspire me; through you, He beckoned me for more. More of Him, more faith, more surrender. Had it not been for your generous and passionate sharing about your own discoveries of His timing for so many years, I would never have begun my own dive into it. I wouldn't have been on the hunt for uncovering so much more, and this book would not exist. Your obedience, passion for the Creator, the hearts hungry for Him, and boldness to share it have sown seeds that will bear fruit for generations to come.

Finding His Timing

Timothy, Mai-Thai, wow—is our Creator epic. Epic in His timing, His plans, and in leading me to you. HAH! Who knew I would be writing to a MAN, when the stories of book 2 began! Only He could have written the timing of you so perfectly. Your presence in this story has been a reminder of His perfect love that exceeds anything I could have imagined. Your mutual surrender to the Creator has made this journey even more profound. It's not just who you are but whose you are that makes sharing it with you so beautiful. You truly love Him with all your heart, mind, and soul, and it reverberates into everything you do. The ripples of your love for Him, your willingness to walk this path in alignment with His plans, and your teachable spirit continue to illuminate so many discoveries together—about the One we love most and how to better love the hearts He places before us. You truly love people. Thank you for living out the second commandment to love others fully, with so much compassion, acceptance, and encouragement. It is a gift you give so generously. You are a reflection of His grace, a reminder of His promises, and a partner who makes every step of this journey more meaningful. Your discipline, strength, and lion-hearted identity are a force to behold. You carry yourself with a boldness and courage that reflects His character so powerfully. It is who He created you to be—strong, steady, and relentless in pursuit of what matters most. In every word, action, and moment of leadership, you wave the banner of our Yahweh-Nissi before us, declaring His victory and His name with your life. I'm so grateful for your love, intentional words, and focus on truth that continue to point us forward. Thank you for being an unwavering champion of me, of The Overcomers, and of the vision He has placed in my heart. You are a gift that reveals more of His glory each and every day.

Mom & Dad, thank you for who you both are and were. You exemplified love in every sense, reflecting the Creator's design through the depth of your epic love for each other, for me, and for everyone around you. Your love has been generous, endless, and steadfast—even during the seasons that have been challenging or hard. Every day, I carry with me the beautiful example you set: a love that endures, that uplifts, and that never fades, even beyond the grave. Your unwavering commitment to one another, and to me, is a reminder that even in our most imperfect moments, love is what remains. It is a light that continues to shine and light the way forward, no matter what yet lies ahead. Mom, your continued support and love since dad's passing in every season has been a constant anchor in life's seas. No matter if things ever went perfectly, you have been perfect for me—because your love was secure.

To every single person who has attended our *Monthly Hunt for Gold* calls, what a journey it has been! Oh, how I have loved being on this hunt with you! Your stories inspire me. Month after month, year after year, as we've gathered to align ourselves with the Creator's timing I have been amazed by the glimpses of Him in your journeys. The stories you've shared—the ways you've experienced Him, heard from Him, and seen His hand in parallel with Biblical timing—have been nothing short of awe-inspiring. Thank you for your authenticity, your courage, and your vulnerability. Thank you for your boldness to say yes—yes to the hunt with your Creator, yes to a crazy idea, and yes to diving into the unknown. It wasn't just a yes to the journey; it was also a yes to a pink-haired, passionate hunter, and I am so grateful you chose to join me! You've shown what it looks like to pursue Him wholeheartedly, even in the waiting, the unknown, and the challenges. Your willingness to open your hearts, to share your highs and lows, has created a space where His truth shines brightly and His love meets us every single time. Your faith, hope, and pursuit of His timing have made this journey even more meaningful. I am so proud of each of you—proud of the ways you've leaned into His timing, trusted His leading, and allowed me and so many others to walk this path with you. Thank you for your belief, your stories, and for seeking Him with such passion and devotion. I look forward with great anticipation to what He will continue to reveal as we keep meeting, seeking, and discovering the treasures He has placed before us. You are a gift, and this journey wouldn't be the same without you.

To the entire Overcomers community: Where do I even begin? You have been with me since 2019, when the launch of my first book marked the beginning of something extraordinary. Your belief in what we started—the idea that if we showed up authentically with our stories, sharing what we had been through and what the Creator had done to help us overcome—would inspire others who were still hurting, those who desperately needed hope. And oh, how you have inspired so many! To every single one of you who has courageously shared your overcoming stories with us on YouTube, thank you. Your vulnerability, authenticity, and willingness to speak truth into the lives of others have created ripples of hope that reach farther than we may ever know. To those who have said yes to joining one of our many panel discussions, covering deeply personal and powerful topics, thank you for lending your voice and perspective to these conversations that continue to uplift and inspire. To those who have stepped into coaching, bravely saying yes to continuing their own journey of overcoming, you embody the heart of this community. Your choices, your courage, and your growth are the very essence of what makes this message come alive. And to those who have submitted the names of family and friends who lost someone they loved to suicide so that we could send them an Overcomers Kit, thank you. Your compassion and love for others ensure that hope reaches even the darkest places. To everyone who has given generously to the

Overcomers Kit fund, enabling us to send even more kits to those who need them most, thank you. Your generosity fuels this mission and reminds us of the power of community. You are the heartbeat of The Overcomers. Your belief in this message, in the Creator's redemptive power, and in the hope we're bringing to the world is what makes this movement possible. Together, we've made an impact—and this is only the beginning. Thank you for your stories, your courage, and your faith. Thank you for being The Overcomers and for inspiring me every single day. This journey would not be the same without you, and this movement will continue to grow because of you.

TABLE OF CONTENTS

Introduction — 29

Chapter 1: *The first light of the map and the Red Sea* — 37

Chapter 2: *See the whole globe as the adventure begins* — 47

Chapter 3: *Truth or the lie? Which will you bite?* — 55

Chapter 4: *Say yes to surrender—the key to overcoming* — 69

Chapter 5: *Discover the entire map* — 81

Chapter 6: *Reset the foundation of the journey—claim your identity* — 93

Chapter 7: *Shavo't—find freedom from suffering* — 105

Chapter 8: *The stamp for a new beginning in the fifth month* — 117

Chapter 9: *Trust His presence in the lights* — 129

Chapter 10: *Align with your identity* — 143

Chapter 11: *Embrace the torch of true identity alongside Esther* — 155

Chapter 12: *Marked from birth for the journey* — 165

Chapter 13: *A light that leads others out—transition with the Israelites in the wilderness* — 175

Chapter 14: *Focus forward—on the coming victories* — 185

Chapter 15: *Believe in the unseen and gifts from the other side* — 193

Chapter 16: *Moses, Mt. Sinai and Pipeline Beach Oahu —a God who beelines to you* — 203

Chapter 17: *Shift into an enormous fruitfull future* — 213

Chapter 18: **The gift of timing in your birthday, His design, and** 229
who's behind you

Chapter 19: **Your blessings are on the way, stay in line—the** 243
month of the new year of trees.

Chapter 20: **Your blessing is on the other side of the transaction** 249

Chapter 21: **Hold up truth and embrace the waves with humility** 265

Chapter 22: **A date with Him for your identity** 275

Chapter 23: **The light that leads you out, the manna amidst Sukkot** 287

Chapter 24: **Declare victory and overcome the internal giants** 301
with each light from the map

Chapter 25: **New beginnings everywhere—the fruit you're** 319
designed to bear

Chapter 26: **Feel, process, and heal—the Feast of Esther & Purim** 329

Chapter 27: **Fix your eyes on the Creator and face the waves. It's** 341
just a choice

Chapter 28: **War for your blessing, your destination** 357

Finding His Timing

Finding His Timing

INTRODUCTION

Have you ever thought to yourself *"I wish I understood why this is happening right now,"* or *"What am I not seeing that I should be seeing?"*

I know similar questions have swirled in my head, many times.

If I could go back to any of those moments in my life—when I was drowning in uncertainty, desperate for clarity, and questioning everything—I would want to tell myself exactly what I discovered next. I too would question what I'm about to tell you. But honestly? I probably wouldn't have believed it. I would have scoffed, laughed, or rolled my eyes and said, *"That's not what we've been taught!"* or, *"That sounds too good to be true."* Maybe even, *"Okay, Hollywood, when does the movie come out? That can't be real."*

But what if it was? What if the questions themselves—the longing to understand the timing of it all, His timing—wasn't just wishful thinking? What if it was an invitation?

A call to discover something deeper?

I believe that's precisely it. In fact, I would tell myself:

"YES! These questions have the potential to lead you to so much more than you ever imagined. Don't settle if you don't hear an answer. There is so much more in store for you, waiting for you to find it. Waiting to show you your design! Waiting for you to show you even more about that Voice and all that He designed! You were designed to discover it! Keep asking questions, continue the hunt, because he who seeks, finds."

Friend, what if that longing, that desire, is a cry from the very core of your being? A signal that there is more—that you were designed for something intentional, purposeful, and divine?

A great woman I admire, Dani Johnson, once said, *"Our desires reveal our design; our designs reveal our destinies."* Could it be that your spirit is simply yearning for what the Creator KNOWS it was made to experience but has not yet discovered?

The answer is a resounding yes!

As you turn these pages, I'm going to take you on a thrilling adventure. Not just my journey, but one that can launch you into your own. A adventure where I discovered that not only does the Creator have a plan—but it's a plan so intricately designed that it defies randomness. A plan that operates on an orderly, systematic timetable, and as you discover it be overwhelmed by how faithful it's designer is.

What if I told you that time itself—the very years, months, and days we live by—was originally designed like a map? A divine schedule filled with appointments set by the Creator Himself? To meet with you! A framework that, if followed, could bring clarity, alignment, and even answers to the questions you've been asking?

I know how this sounds. Like I went skipping down a yellow brick road and got lost in a land of flying monkeys. But that's just it—this journey I embarked on wasn't fantasy. It was real. And the deeper I dove, the more I realized that what had been hidden from plain sight was, in fact, written into the very fabric of creation. It had been there all along, waiting for me—waiting for us—to see it.

Genesis 1:14-15 says, *"And Elohim said, 'Let the lights come to be in the expanse of the heavens to separate the day from the night, and let them be for signs and appointed times, and for days and for years, and let them be for lights in the expanse of the heavens to give light on the earth'".* (ISR 2000)

Little did I know, the key to it all was right there—right at the very beginning.

His timing.

At the conclusion of my first book, *Finding His Voice*, I stood at a crossroads. I had found freedom, yet I was walking forward into a dense fog of uncertainty, confusion, lack of clarity and a new awareness that a whole new audience knew the truth about my past—the truth of me. Ew.

I couldn't see through it; all I could do was walk forward, praying I wouldn't be choked out by it's overwhelming enormity, even with the new freedom I had found.

I had no clear direction—only His whisper, reminding me that

He was with me. He was my compass guiding me at the most pivotal moments of life, letting me know it was OK to walk forward, reminding me I wasn't alone and that He was with me wherever I went.

That compass pointed right to the truth obscured in the murkiness of life; a design grander than I ever imagined possible. Full of details so intricate that would I have known beforehand the journey I was about to embark on next I would have believed this new fog I was emerging through was part of a fairy tale.

What happened next would change everything.

I discovered something ancient yet revolutionary. A timeline woven into the fabric of creation. A rhythm designed by the Creator, guiding us through every season of life. A pattern that, once recognized, could bring clarity to the very things that once felt like chaos.

How could this be? An adventure woven with so many moments that seem to transcend our own grasp of reality. As if the lives we're currently living are running parallel to an illuminated path we simply are not seeing. But if we did open our eyes to it, it would blaze a trail before us full of illuminated steps that, one by one, led us through our own life experiences with all the answers we so desperately seek. Lighting up, one by one, as blaring road signs amidst the murkiness, telling us where the fire-breathing dragons lurked, which poison apples not to partake of; and that told you you are the most fairest one of all the land as they displayed in all their glorious array.

Answers that every year, every month, and every day were designed to not only tell us who we are, but who the great designer

Finding His Timing

is?! Kinda sounds like we're off to see the Wizard (of Oz).

Let's consider Dorothy for a moment—how different your life might have been if you did have a map that transcends time, given at the start of history itself to be used not only to help guide us as we navigate through the uncertainties of life, but to equip us with the very things the Creator knows we'll need every single month of our lives, before we even need it.

I know how I sound right now—like I absolutely got lost down that golden road and the flying monkeys wreaked their havoc. But friend, that's precisely what I found (the map, not the monkeys). And I fully believe that map not only exists but has been intentionally removed from the fabric of our daily lives by eyes that didn't want us to know of its existence. It's been stolen from our time. I guess we know there's a villain in this tale now, too (more on that later). They used it in the beginning, but somewhere down the line it was removed from the everyday man's use. Now it solely exists for those daring enough to find it and continue the hunt for it's treasures meant for us to find. Meant for us to meet with it's Designer at pre-determined and perfectly appointed moments in our lives.

Can you hear the singing? It's where the sing-a-longs are. I'm not singing, you're singing. Well at least it's how you'll feel in such moments, whether you can sing or not. Your life IS a fairy tale.

He loves you that much. And it was never His heart for you to have to do this alone.

So friend, as you embark on the adventure that lies ahead within these pages those are the very stories of which you'll read. The stories that as each illuminated step from this map made it's appearance in my life, lit up and revealed another step as I sang. Not...I definitely didn't sing. I hummed. I'm a hummer.

But that map I found wasn't just meant for me. It was also meant for you. How do I know? Because like He said back in the beginning: *"let them be for signs and appointed times, and for days and for years".*

His gift of creation, His design of it all, was for those very appointments with YOU, to sing or hum, together. It was all laid out in an intricate design, a lighted journey that would lead us through our lives with great detail and perfect timing.

You were worth it.

You were designed to be aligned to this map. Aligned to His timing. And there's so much He wants to show you, just as He has shown me.

I can't wait to see what He shows you on your adventure! We'll finally get to hear your life's symphony. Let me show you what I mean.

Finding His Timing

Finding His Timing

CHAPTER 1

The first light of the map and the Red Sea

It all started with a crazy dream.

It happened right after I delivered my first book, *Finding His Voice,* to a list of pre-readers who had graciously offered to be the very first to learn the first part of my story and share their experiences with it. What brave souls! What poor, unfortunate souls. Wait. Sorry, wrong script, I'm not the Little Mermaid.

In the dream, I was sitting at a table with six women—five I didn't know and my mentor. One of these women clearly needed to be set free. I stepped in to help—not my mentor, ME! It seemed crazy to me at the time, because after all, who was I to help her? After the woman was freed from what was oppressing her, she came over and said, *"Jen, I see you so differently now, you're like a completely different person."* If I WAS the Little Mermaid, this would be the part where I have legs. But I knew her comment contained a much deeper meaning.

Finding His Timing

Later, I was in a car and a really attractive man was driving (Now I really know I was dreaming). I had just come out of the water wearing my bright coral wetsuit and my hair was drenched and slicked back. We went to a hotel and I exclaimed, *"I really don't think I should be here; I need to go."* Instantly, I was in the hotel lobby. A fatherly figure in my life appeared and said, *"Jen, I think you should stay."* Okay, King Triton, I did love all my dinglehoppers and my pet Flounder who I call "George" (my cross-eyed Siamese cat) but maybe I will embrace this new future. These legs are kinda nice.

As I tried to process the dream, a close friend shared her thought that maybe the first half of the dream was me no longer letting fear stop me, while the second half of the dream was a message from a Father, saying *"you're going to be okay; you're turning a new leaf."* Maybe this "father" was just trying to comfort me as I was in turmoil about being so transparent in my first book. All my guts were out there for the world to see; guts with all kinds of digestion issues (so you can imagine the "mess.") And in a sea? Goodness. I'll stop. But that was the truth of me.

If I could go back to that day and let the person I am now talk to the person I was then, I would say:

> *"You're not going to believe this until much later, but His TIMING was so perfect. His timing IS perfect! Your Creator knew exactly the transition that was happening in your life, within your soul, and He also knew what lay ahead of you. He also knew the thoughts that would creep in and was helping you fight them! Take every one of those thoughts captive! Fight! Fight for the voice of truth within you!*
>
> *Keep walking forward! Each step you take will get more*

secure. He's prepared every step. As you hit them, you will start to learn what He's done. Have faith! He goes before you! And He has so much MORE to show you!"

As the list of pre-readers worked their way through all my guts, my insides spilling all over their souls, the second book was already being written. The lights of what would illuminate the entire next season of my life started flickering on.

A particular pre-reader by the name of Jax just so happened to be reading the book of Esther in the Bible the morning before she sat down and read my entire first book (in ONE sitting). She said she couldn't put my book down. Crazy. She had only meant to read a few chapters that day, but ended up reading the entire book in one day. I was stunned! She was the fourth person to say that to me, as they embraced all my ugly truth.

She called me sobbing after finishing the book. She went on to share the correlations that were hitting her spirit between my words and the Creator's words: how sometimes promotion comes in unlikely, painful, and even embarrassing ways.

Where there is shame and pain, promotion follows. Embarrassment in front of everyone brings promotion.

Esther went through a year-long preparation before she was promoted that included bathing in oils. Okay I like that oils part, I don't know about the year of shame and pain.

These things are necessary to position you so you can save a bunch of people. There was so much intention in preparing Esther as there was for me. Could He have been preparing me? I think I'm gonna need a lot more oils. Well, that was certainly her conviction as she continued on. The character of Haman wanted to cause harm on the people, especially Mordecai.

She said, *"you're like 'OK, I'm gonna go to the king and if I die, I die. At first you didn't want to do it. Then Mordecai was like, 'listen woman, if you don't go people are going to die!' Can you imagine how scary that must have been for Esther? Could you imagine being at the table with the King, you're talking about the person who is causing harm to the people - and the person is sitting RIGHT there next to them - Haman. She had to have a lot of faith to open her mouth! This kind of injustice is happening. My people are dying. It must have taken amazing courage for her to speak. Esther unqualified herself. Mordecai had to shake her, like Dani-your mentor-shook you! You worried about if you'd die, but there's a whole world that might die if you didn't! Just like in the story of Esther, when Mordecai passionately pleaded with Esther "if you don't' speak, your Father's house is going to be destroyed! Who knows who cometh to the kingdom for such a time as this. You really are an Esther!"* (Esther 4:14)

Her words lit me like a lantern that was trying to flicker on but needed the kerosene to shine through what would become the darkest and longest of nights. OK, let's be real; it felt more like a bolt of lightning. I was electrified from head to toe. Which answers the question everyone always asks me, *"Jen, how do you get your hair to do that?"*

This is exactly the pattern those lights were beginning to turn on, reveal and then lead me on a path where He showed me the correlation of His timing and my timing as I continued the discovery.

But those lights of that lantern had been silently waiting for me.

Waiting for me to look to their glow and follow the path each flicker unveiled the further and further I was willing to swim.

Jax shared a little-known fact about the guy who wrote the song *"I Can Only Imagine,"* a song which held great meaning for me in the aftermath of the loss of my father. Before he wrote the lyrics he had been saying the words *"I can only imagine"* over and over and over again, everywhere he went, but it wasn't until his dad passed away that the song came pouring out of him: *"Like the song was always there for Him, waiting to be revealed, your first book had been waiting there for you. But it wasn't ready to come out yet. It was ready to come out, to be as impactful as it is because of what else you've been through. You still had obstacles to overcome, now it's a complete book."*

Little did I know the lantern had turned ON and the path forward was about to illuminate with so much light.

The day I released my first book to this group of pre-readers (the very first group of people who were going to truly know everything about me, and all the secrets I carried) just so happened to be the Wednesday after Passover.

Why is that so significant? Well, my mentor, Dani, did a live recording on social media to talk about the significance of the day, not knowing I had just released my book to this first group of readers. She shared that the Wednesday after Passover was the very day our Creator parted the Red Sea during the exodus of Moses and the Israelites. The day He freed them from what had been oppressing them.

WHAAAAAAT?! Wow! Now, that is crazy! Could it be a

'coincidence' that I would release my first book on that day, a book that told the world the dirty secret that had held me in bondage? Could it be that my oppressor was taken out ON THIS DAY?! I knew my Creator did things in His timing and His fingerprints were all over this! As Dani exclaimed in her live video, *"Your Red Sea is being parted,"* I knew...THAT DAY WAS MY DAY. The path forward was being laid bare before me. I saw dry ground between the raging waves inside.

I commented on my mentor's Facebook live recording, *"Oh my gosh, unplanned by me I had released the first draft of my book to a group of pre-readers ON passover to start gathering testimonials to use in it when it gets published. I figured my Creator was up to something with that timing. Because I didn't know it was passover when I did that. Watching your LIFE now, it hit me, the red sea was being parted with the 'release' tied to this day, and the 'release' that's in this book. I got chills through my whole body when you said "your red sea, is being parted". He is such a good Father! Thank you for your passion coach, and for sharing this!"*

That's the truth; I couldn't have planned any of that, but He had. I can't tell you how many times in the previous years, learning absolutely everything I could from this mentor, that I pondered the thought: *"Man, it is SO cool that she just knows the timing of Biblical events and their timing TODAY in our calendar throughout the year! HOW does she know that?!"* Thanks to my mentor's passion for sharing her journey with her Creator and what He had been showing her in such detail, it too beckoned to me.

So why am I choosing to share all this with you? I mean, let's be real, the stories you will find within this second book are even more scary to tell.

Like the Israelites walking through the Red Sea on the dry path before them, I can't imagine the thoughts that were hitting them...

"Wait, how long is this giant wall of water next to me gonna hold?"

"Uhhhh, anyone else see this SHARK swimming in the water next to us?"

"I touched the butt!" (wait sorry, that's Finding Nemo). I might be the only one thinking that one.

In my first book I laid all my struggles out there, and I said that I didn't know what was going to come next. I honestly didn't know what I was going to choose, but I did know that I was going to be listening for His voice wherever I went; the Voice that had guided me through everything.

As you'll soon discover, I'm still struggling with some of the very things I struggled with in the first book. This is a first class ticket to humiliation. So why do it? Because I have to.

I know there are people out there desperate for answers in the same way I was, still stuck in the murkiness themselves. They are worth it. YOU are worth it. I would have given anything to have found the answers I'm sharing with you, when I was stuck. I wouldn't trade anything for the peace and clarity that I have now, friend. If you're struggling, I want that for you, too. It's time for you to get your legs and walk, too. *"Ahahaaaahahahahaahaa"* (sorry, Little Mermaid just came out again). But just as a quiet hum.

Laura, another one of my pre-readers, said it best (and by that I mean I cried when she said it to me. I'm a crier.): *"No greater love has anyone than this, than to lay down his life for another. It doesn't mean you have to die physically. You are willingly letting yourself be FULLY seen. You're willing to lay your life on a line socially, and how other people might view you. You're showing God's love by laying that down. You're saying, I love you so much, that I'm willing to tell you all my stuff. That's you, Jen"*.

Tears filled my eyes at the truth of her words. His words spoken through her had just hit depths within me that I had not yet known; a depth that revealed the beauty of true surrender.

An emotion echoed through the responses from the pre-readers that poured in: *"I think I need to revisit this idea of God, and how I had taken that out of my life...I read your book and I want that. I want that relationship back. I could cry."*

What?! A heart that I truly cared for got back that gift of Him, simply from reading my book?! Oh, hell yes, surrender is worth it! Oh hell yes, putting all my mess out there for the world to see is worth every anguishingly painful moment of it. Another friend got tears in her eyes just reading the acknowledgments, she had never been an emotional person. She had outlawed emotions, avoided them. Just the embrace of the acknowledgment section alone, the floodgates opened. I knew my Creator was at work, not just in my own life, but in others lives as well. Every word I had written had been worth it.

So I can't stop. There are more stories to tell and these stories are even more powerful than the first. Just watch as more lights turn on as you read.

If I could go back to that day, I would say:

"This is only the beginning! Keep surrendering in it all. Even you don't know what's ahead as you begin this next season. It's all for a reason. Trust Him! He's still got you! I can't wait for you to experience every step, every surrender, every illuminated step as it makes its appearance on the map, and see what's on the other side. Not just for you, but for them; for the hearts around the world that you care most for!

I bless you with continued surrender! I bless your heart with leaning not on your own understanding, but acknowledging your Creator in every step! With trusting Him in everything that's yet before you!"

Finding His Timing

CHAPTER 2

See the whole globe as the adventure begins

Then came the global pandemic.

It was April 2020. The mentor who had been a vessel of radical change in my life had to pivot. Like much of the rest of the world I had to adapt to attending her conferences virtually when I had preferred to attend in person. Thankfully, the conferences had the same impact on me. I was glued to my screen, as if it were the final episode of a hit series, but all the more, because I was a part of the story—it was my season finale! Would I have a happy ending, or would I succumb to circumstances? Surely, I would at least drop some witty one-liners that would have the stuffed animals sitting beside me in an uproar. I glanced at their fuzzy faces...nothing.

Emotions ran high for me as this conference ended. I shared with them how excited I was in the middle of all the fear and hopelessness engulfing the world, here was a place where people could enjoy, hope, joy, laughter, community, and freedom! What was most the world using to fill their minds and hearts with?

My mentor, Dani, said it best: *"None of us reach our full potential without pressure or fire."* She shared about how kind people had brought about so much healing in her life, and it hit me...that's what was happening to our world. Our world was going through pressure and fire, but lacked the willingness to be refined by it or learn from it. If He allows the pressures and fires of life to refine us to our full potential as mature, loving people, we can bring kindness to a hurting world...if we can remove the fear, and lead them from fear to hope. We could help people arise from that season stronger. In that moment, I knew we could do it. I looked at my stuffed Baby Yoda sitting next to me on the couch, gave him a head nod, and said, *"This is the way!"*

But what's crazier is that, as that virtual event ended and the cameras turned off (as did my television), I sobbed. My heart was heavy because I wasn't physically present with all the faces that I knew in the community of friends. I wanted to run around the conference ballroom hugging every one as I had so many events before. I wanted to be surrounded by the life I had found in the community that had truly become a family to me. But as I sat there alone on my couch, letting the tears pour down my face, it hit me that my tears were revealing something greater. Baby Yoda didn't care.

For a moment, I felt selfish for those tears. I knew many people had experienced breakthrough—including me—during the conference because of the commitment of the organization that put it on. No excuses, just commitment. One of them was my friend, Elissa in Las Vegas, who had also been tuning in. She texted me right away saying, *"my eyes are swollen from crying."* We jumped on the phone and she exclaimed, *"When Dani was saying someone is on their knees crying in pain, I think she was talking to me!"*

She had a mass the size of a football in her stomach. It was not cancerous, but she was resisting having surgery. I was blown away; she had been attending these conferences with me for an entire year, and I had never known her to be an emotional person. She had even confessed to me that she felt weird that she never cried. Now, at home watching the event remotely, she was finally so broke down that her eyes were swollen with tears. *"I feel like I need to embrace Him more,"* she sobbed as raw emotion found it's voice at last. I encouraged her that when she felt like our mentor was talking to her, she could trust that it was Him—her Creator. He knew what her heart needed and He was speaking to her, as He was me in that moment.

I stared, sobbing, at the blank screen, realizing He was showing me to continue seeing beyond myself. To take myself out of the equation. He did that with my first book, prompting me to give all the profits from my pre-reader's orders to a non-profit organization that frees kids from sex-trafficking. I knew He was teaching me something powerful with this moment and all the tears that were releasing. Through that whole conference weekend, He had been working in the hearts of every participant, no matter where they were watching. He was present with each of us, all over the world, and His presence was all that was needed for freedom to come. He was all we needed.

My mentor had gone to great lengths to help people gain more freedom, including me. Suddenly, I felt acutely aware what that first book was about to do, the hurting hearts around the world that it was going to reach. The hundreds—if not thousands—of hurting hearts that might have died if it had never been written, especially now. The ripple of rescue from the Creator through my mentor, to me, to the countless people the story would reach.

All this awareness made what happened next so much more wondrous. It was as if my heart was being led on an adventure, being prepared for the next treasure to make it's appearance from just beneath the surface of the sand. Thankfully, there were no dogs in sight, so I knew such treasures weren't going to be the stinky kind.

I went to the post office to set up a mailing address for the back of the first book.

The clerk handed me a globe keychain and said with a smirk, "*And you get a cheesy keychain,*" and continued on with filling out paperwork. I could not stop staring at it, I was transfixed.

"*No, seriously, this is great. I love it,*" I stammered.

She laughed and said, "*I just gave you the world!*"

"*Oh my gosh!*" I blurted. "*OK, now I'm tripping. I'm setting this address up for my book. I'm about to release it to the world.*"

She snapped up from the papers and peered inquisitively at me. "*WHOAH! Wait, really? What is your book about?*"

Still dazed, I said, "*It's my life story...so far, anyway. Trying to inspire people that they can overcome really difficult things.*"

She smiled softly and said, "*Well I would love to read that!*"

I felt tears rise to meet the beauty of what felt like an appointed moment and a message from the Divine. I was blown away by how much my Creator was making Himself known in every single step of the process. He was seeding me with the exact nuggets designed for me to experience, hoping I would notice. Hoping I would see Him and a whole new world. He was building just for me.

Oh, I saw Him, alright. Not literally Him, but I began to see His fingerprints on the pieces falling into place around me, showing me another glimpse of the grandeur map.

I was talking with several friends with whom I had traveled to Israel and we pondered the story of Adam and Eve. It's so crazy how He keeps bringing me back to the beginning, back to His design. As we reread the Genesis account I exclaimed, *"man and woman, made in His image...I want to experience the fullness of HIS image!"*

Have you ever said something spontaneously and thought, *"Whoah! Wait...why did I say that?"* This was one of those moments. I let something slip out that my mind wasn't quite ready for, but my heart was, way deep down. This release didn't make me jump, as the gaseous kind do.

Oh, how I wish I could go back to that moment and tell myself to pay way more attention to that nudge than I did. But there was still so much confusion within me, I couldn't align to my own words and embrace what He was seeding within me.

If I could go back to that day, I would say:

"Let that light in there! He knows your design. There's so much more He's going to show you. You're on the right track. Things are awakening within you. They've always been there.

It's your design. It's His design within you! He knows your soil.

Take courage! There is so much more to discover! You won't believe what that fullness will look like and feel like, years from now. Just keep walking, keep hunting! It IS there for you to discover! Continue the hunt! It is worth it! But remember, you were NOT designed to be perfect. Only He is perfect.

It's going to be OK, Jen. It's all right there, back at the beginning. In creation. His design. Eve took a bite of the apple when the lies presented themselves. We would not know grace without what happened in the garden. Sometimes suffering is allowed so we can experience what grace is; so new things can grow and old things can die. Adam and Eve knew they were naked, and felt shame, but it was not His design for them to carry that shame. That's why He sent His son. Remember, it's not about being perfect-it's not even about right or wrong. It's about discovering truth and recognizing the lie. It's about discovering Him!"

These words are important for me to tell myself, because the next chapters include the hardest parts for me to share. This is where the great waves of suffocating shame come crashing down.

Finding His Timing

Finding His Timing

CHAPTER 3

Truth or the lie? Which will you bite?

So much was going on inside of me, way more than I was willing to admit at the time. Major indigestion—I didn't want to see it (yuck). Who wants to see that? With the pandemic forcing us into virtual conferences, I was desperate for community and the joy of simply being face-to-face with people.

I was invited to take a surfing trip to the Florida coast, with two female friends, one of whom I had only recently briefly met. But SURFING?! How could I say no? It had become my new love, despite the fact that I really wasn't that good at it (unless of course your description of "good" includes being really good at posing as professional photographers are taking epic photos of you falling off the board, not actually leaning into the waves...but falling. I was good at that).

I just loved the feeling of being in the waves. I felt the presence of my Creator so powerfully in it. It was euphoric, and the few times I did catch a wave, it felt like a major personal victory over my past. Those waves and that water represented so much more, they embodied all the tears of sorrow and heartache I had cried, but now conquered. Those struggles had been so hard to overcome, but man, were they worth it! I wasn't just riding a wave, I was riding over it all in victory! I reveled in these little moments with my Creator.

Off I went, with great intentionality. I took the time to pray before the trip (as I always had) that He would not only reveal what each of these friends needed to hear, but that He would show up powerfully that week. Of course, He exceeded that request. It was a week overloaded with revelations, deep conversations, inspiration, and true joy in real and vulnerable friendships. We wrapped the last day with surfing and I shared the meaning of a Biblical Mikvah, which I had learned in a previous trip to Israel—an act of cleansing, surrender and intimacy with the Father.

And then I had a Mikvah moment—right there, on that beach, walking through the waves. Wave after wave crashed over me, plunging me under the roaring, watery turmoil, and I surrendered to each. Seven times I felt the chaos of the waves all around me, and I became aware that whatever life hurls at you, you simply try to keep your suit on and keep your head above the surface.

After that surrender and submersion, I walked back toward the shore, with the waves subsiding and my feet reaching more stable footing. As I neared the beach, He reminded me that His presence meets us at those moments when we realize we can't do it without Him anymore. When we simply decide to surrender to Him, He brings us closer and closer to the safety of the shore. Then we are ready for the next adventure and the next waves that this life will bring.

And it's a good thing, because the next wave of adventure was about to break.

In fact, these waves were about to rip my suit right off.

If I could go back to that day, I would say:

> *"What you just experienced in those waves is truth. He will be with you in the loud, crashing, and intense waves that feel so enormous. Be ready. More are coming. It's OK. He will lead you safely to shore as you surrender. You will feel like you are struggling to swim through it and not drown. It's going to be intense—others will capsize, you may feel like you're going under—but you will NOT drown. It is not your design. You will walk out, cleansed from the beating of the water and the things that will be washed off of you."*

Have you ever been on a beach when the red flags are posted? It's a sign that danger is brewing, even if it's hidden under the surface of the water. As much as I didn't want to acknowledge them, red danger flags had been popping up in my spirit through that whole trip. Just like most beach-goers, I ignored them. I pretended they weren't there.

But those red flags were out on the shores of my mind and there was no way I couldn't see them. I had just spent a whole week getting to know one of the most vivacious females I had ever experienced. Her spirit was so full of life and a joy that bubbled over in the tiniest of moments all throughout our trip. She carried a personality that just overflowed, bringing so much energy wherever she went. It was effortless for her, and it was intoxicating.

That intoxication spilled over the tipping point the night we all decided to glam up and have a night on the town. For the first time in my life, these friends gave me a personal makeover, even carefully attaching fake eyelashes. I was astounded at my own reflection in the mirror. There was a vamp of beauty that seemed to mirror a part of me on the inside that I had been afraid to embrace. For the first time in my life, I felt truly beautiful. Look at me!!

But that reflection was nothing compared to the sight that walked into that bathroom as a friend was adhering my lashes. The second she turned the corner into the bathroom, I was electrified. I was glued to her eyes like a moth to a flame, and I knew she noticed. I couldn't look away. I was figuratively throwing off my own bikini, ignoring the danger flags, and running head-first into the dangerous waves. I don't need the water to take this off; I'll gladly do it!

I returned home to Las Vegas, and spent the following weekend completely alone on my couch. The friends I had just spent a week at the beach with both lived in Texas. They texted me, *"Don't let yourself get depressed between conferences, just move here already!"* As I pondered their message and how alone I felt during the pandemic, I reflected back on the end of that virtual conference; the moment the cameras had turned off and how my tears had flowed, I was truck by how much I needed to address the need for more community in my life. Baby Yoda wasn't cutting it.

As I started to seriously consider their invitation to uproot my life in Nevada, I put out a post on social media simply asking how many people I knew that lived in Texas. That one post garnered over 160 comments! People were cattle calling me to move, and I hadn't even mentioned I was considering it.

Finding His Timing

The message seemed to be clear: Texas was the answer to find much-needed community. I Moo'd (I mean I moved). After all, so much had been happening as my first book was getting prepared to release. I was beginning to understand just how many people needed the message of the first book, like my hairdresser who had suicide running through her family, having lost 13 family members to suicide, including one who had just died two weeks before as a result of the pandemic.

The final file was ready for a printer test on Father's Day weekend of 2020. It was going to release on my 37th birthday. I was so grateful to a friend who pointed out that chapter 37 of the Biblical book of Ezekiel is about a valley of dry bones coming to life.

I kept hearing stories from people that confirmed how God's timing for that book was perfect. I could never have planned it so precisely. The waves within me started to crest. I felt myself struggling against it; *"I am not worthy, of any of this..."*. He whispered in response, *"It's not about your worthiness, it's all about Me, and what I will do!"*

The water inside me kept rising and swirling; I struggled to swim. I made the decision to move to Texas. Those red danger flags were flying in my heart! Rather than caution, I felt excitement! I ignored their warning and dove head first into the water and officially threw off my bikini.

Swells of conviction and humility raged within me. The battle for control of my mind was on. Was it going to focus on truth or the lies that were swimming along with me? Relief from the storm and the safety of shore felt far away. Would I cling to His design for my life or give myself over to the lust of the flesh? I gave in. His design was still in chaos in my mind.

I ignored the red danger flags in my spirit. Like Eve in the garden of Eden, I took bite after bite of the poisonous apple, trading the truth of who I was created to be for the urges of my physical desires. Each bite plunged me deeper into feelings of failure, unworthiness, and chaos. My spirit pleaded with me to swim back to safety, and back to His Voice who wanted to remind me who I truly was. But I felt so undeserving of the future that was ahead of me—so much shame.

Lifeguards yelled from the shore, *"Look up Jen! Focus! Watch your step! You're going to run right into that barricade in your life! Be aware! Go around that thing, and knock down that other thing so you can walk down that path He has called you to walk."* Who knew lifeguards could be so exact? The Creator put lifeguards in my life, who shouted out exactly what I needed to do with this woman, who had become a source of poison in my life. *"The road is narrow already, and as the book of Matthew describes it, 'you can enter God's Kingdom only through the narrow gate. The highway to hell is broad, and it's gate is wide for the many who choose that way. You gotta keep your eyes on God, but you also need to focus on where you're going. He doesn't want you to get distracted and bump into too many obstacles that deter you and cause you to go down a wrong path. They may seem right but lead to destruction. At the end of the day, none of us is worthy, but He has called us for greater things and much better than we can even fathom. But we need to humble ourselves like Job, David, and the prophets did, so that He can do that amazing thing that He does. We have to get out of the way. Jen, you are worthy of reaching this amazing plan He has for you, because your heart reflects His character. You know deep down in your heart of hearts that you are nothing without Him and that*

Voice, and because of Him and Him alone, you are worthy. He sees you. He has collected every tear you have cried in a vial close to his heart, on a necklace around his neck. All those tears will reap an amazing harvest simply because you chose to quiet your voice and listen to His."

As these words swirled further within me, they revealed deeper roots: the fear of failure and the fear of looking perfect that were deep within. I was so afraid that I could mess it ALL up.

That was the barricade he was warning me about. I was beating myself up as I looked back on every bite that I had taken with this female, and my swimsuit was nowhere to be found.

The messenger's words continued:

"If you think you need to look perfect, or you think you have to not fail at times, you will run into that barricade. Knowing that you are not perfect, and being okay with imperfections is exactly the Spirit He wants you in. No matter what, you pressed on. You decided to chase after God, no matter what, even though there was WAR all around you. That was David. He felt like he was unworthy, like he wasn't good enough because of what happened to Absalam, and what happened with Bathsheeba. But he's known as a man after God's own heart because He humbled himself every time he made a mistake. He knew he needed God. Is your appetite for God greater than your appetite for something else? This is how you can gauge it. Matthew 5:5 shows how our Creator blesses those who hunger and thirst for righteousness."

So, who is the messenger unloading all these revelations on me? You can't guess. I surely did not. It was the very female I had dove into those waters with (and was still trying to find my own suit, which had flung off). How could this be? The one with whom I ran into the waves, ignoring all the red flags, is the one who deposited truth into me that led me out to safety.

You can imagine how difficult it also made it to navigate everything going on inside my mind amidst these waves. She, too, was in love with her Creator and had been through her own overcoming journey (for which she had given Him the glory) so the words she poured into me helped me navigate back to shore. She partnered with me so many times as I almost went completely under. She kept my eyes on Him.

But the storm inside me wouldn't let up. I knew what I was doing was not healthy, simply because of the chaos it was creating inside. Deep down, I knew it was only a matter of time before this delicate balance of navigating those emotional waves attempting to take me under and the physical things I was doing in secret would reach it's limit. I could feel it coming...the wave that would one day take me out.

Perfect timing revealed itself again. It was time for another virtual conference with my mentor. Those conferences have a way of re-centering me. Truth of what I needed to do rang in my ears. I needed to shut out the voice that said I wasn't worthy of all that He wanted to do in my life. As His Voice whispered, *"It's not about you, it's about ME. There is nothing you could ever do to separate you from My love. It's about Me, not about you, and that's why I'm going to use you."*

As my mentor shared how she couldn't believe where she had come from and what God allowed her to do, the cascading tears came.

I knew He was telling me He was about to do the same with me. Did I know what that was going to look like? No. Absolutely not. But I saw myself in her. I had seen it the first time I attended one of her conferences and now, many years and countless conferences later, I saw it again. His words rang louder: *"Be comfortable being imperfect. Be comfortable with being uncomfortable."*

Then I got a breakthrough I couldn't have expected. The fear of failure and the fear of looking perfect had revealed themselves and I finally got the answer to get them out for good. Dani said, *"If you carry unforgiveness, you carry fear!"* I saw my freedom.

There was fear, so I needed to finally forgive someone for something I had been holding onto. I needed to forgive ME.

I said, *"I forgive you, Jen, for holding a bar over your own heart. I chose to feel like if I ever made a mistake, failed, or didn't live up to it, that I was a failure and I had ruined everything. But that's NOT the message You have for me. I release you, Jen. You owe yourself nothing! And I bless you, Jen, with the assurance that you made it. You made it, because I made you and make you NEW again every day!"*

This time, the freedom rippled out beyond the end of the conference. I had been treading water so hard. I dove in when those red flags had warned me not to go in, and I couldn't seem to get out of the water.

Another wave attempted to take me out:

Me: *"Do you think you could ever block your own blessings?!"*

Creator: *"Why are you asking that?"*

Me: *"Well, I'm worried that I'm not good enough or that I could ruin what He would do."*

Creator: *"Why?"*

Me: *"Because I'm not strong enough. I'm not perfect, I mess up. I lust. I wanna try things."*

Creator: *"Do you think you have to be perfect?"*

Me: *"Yes."*

Creator: *"Why?"*

Me: *"Because why would you love me if I'm not? Why would you want to use me? Why would the world believe me if I failed?"*

Creator: *"Why? Because it's not about you, it's about me. Because this is who I am, and what I do. And this is who I use. Why do you hold this bar over your head?"*

Me: *"Because if you messed up, you failed. At least, that's what I believe."*

There it was. My fear of failure.

A second wave came, swirled with the desire to try things.

Creator: *"Why?"*

Me: *"Because I want to deal with this curiosity, I don't want to *wonder the rest of my life what if?"*

Creator: *"Why?"*

Me: *"Because I don't want to not be fully committed later down the path."*

Creator: *"Why?"*

Me: *"Because I don't want to hurt someone like that."*

Creator: *"Why?"*

Me: *"Because I want to be fully committed."*

Creator: *"Why?"*

Me: *"Because that's a marriage I want."*

Creator: *"Why?"*

Me: *"Because that's a marriage that's healthy."*

As the internal conversations continued, the waters raged. I shared my fear of my heart being torn if I never dealt with the waves, because I was afraid. I didn't want to let others down, especially my Creator. I loved Him more than anything because of what He had done for me. I knew He loved me, had made me to set people free…like me. Because I knew I wasn't the only one.

As the waters continued to crash around me, the thoughts were at war. Being with a woman looked enticing to me; they were truly beautiful, and now I had experienced one in a way I never had before.

I was also alone, and it looked safe, despite all the chaos I felt inside. I asked myself why it looked safe, and I suddenly realized it was because I was deep down in the depths of that storm...it was simply because I was afraid of being with a man.

His Voice then calmed the storm, whispering *"I MADE IT,"* with the softest of reassurances I wasn't yet ready to embrace. How could I be afraid of something He had made?

I had a new opportunity for freedom laid before me. It was time to put another fear to rest through forgiveness. I whispered to myself, *"I forgive you, Jen, for thinking you have to be perfect. I forgive you, Jen, for thinking you could do something that would thwart what He will do. I forgive you, Jen, for beating yourself up, for getting foggy, distracted, and lustful. I chose to feel unworthy, not good enough. I chose to feel like I had done something wrong and that I had messed up. I release you, Jen. You don't owe yourself anything. I bless you, Jen, with being everything you're designed to be. I bless you with influence. I bless you with VOICE. I bless you with peace."*

The Voice then wrapped His arms around me and whispered, *"It's just another part of your story, My daughter. Let Me use it!"*

If I could go back to that day, I would say:

"He will use it! Just keep taking it one day—one step—at a time. He is with you in those waves. Let Him wash over you— it's who He is. Trust the process. Trust Him! He's got you! He's always had you! And He is not done!

I bless you with courage! I bless you with faith! I bless you with forgiveness! Receive it! Let it seep to the deepest parts of you. Let that take root! Let Him cleanse and renew it all!"

CHAPTER 4

Say yes to surrender —the key to overcoming

I moved to Texas. So many things conspired (or came together) to lead me there, although I couldn't see them working.

I was still settling into my new apartment, with a roommate I barely knew, when she invited me to join a Zoom call with her two spiritual mentors. As she describe them to me, I began to feel very anxious and vulnerable I was sweating inside, thinking that these spiritual people had ways of seeing the things I was so ashamed of. "Could they see in the spiritual realm the season I'm in? What I'm engaging in? Can they see that I'm naked and my bikini is missing?" Conviction hit my spirit heavily as I prepared to be exposed.

I took a deep breath and joined the call. But as I got to know these sweet, tender people, my spirit was lifted in another way. In their words, I found my answer to freedom in this meeting. Despite the fact that they were just meeting me for the first time, they had a message for me that I knew was from the Creator. Oh boy! Little did they know that my first book, *Finding His Voice*, was one week away from release to the whole world. They went on to share that, if I gave the Creator everything, He would give me everything in return. In that moment, I knew it was Him in those words. I saw Him extending His hand to me, inviting me to give him my shame and pain. All of it! Inviting me to take what He had to give. Even the things that would be a sacrifice for me.

Why? Because deep down, in that moment, I believed that I loved the woman I had been seeing. I didn't want to let her go; I didn't want to give her to Him. I was at a crossroads that offered me the known on the left, and the unknown on the right. On the left, I knew I had enjoyed my relationship with her but by the same token, it had also brought confusion, battles with shame, fear, and regret. If I were being honest, none of the pleasure was worth it. Those weights were far too heavy to carry (despite my enormous muscles, which I could be pretty proud of.) When did I even choose to pick up those things? *"Hey! I'm shame. Wanna pick me up, and carry me for a while?!"* Lovely. NOT. Don't be ridiculous. Who would want to say yes to that? But here I was, willingly carrying all the unnecessary weight around.

But over here on the right, what would that even look like? I surely didn't have the foggiest idea, but for the first time, I was beginning to feel something inside me that wanted to dare to find out. I knew that continuing down that path on the left wasn't going to bring me the freedom, clarity, and peace I wanted for my future. I had experienced it and those things weren't there. It was time to stop carrying around those unnecessary weights.

I wasn't the only one at a crossroad, it turns out. The woman

Finding His Timing

I had been with came over to do a Mikvah with me, and as we listened to *WorshipMob* on YouTube in the pool, suddenly, the singer started speaking and sharing a vision of a dam of water. God was showing us that the singer in his own life was the dam. He was the only one holding back what God wanted to give him, and the Father desperately wanted to burst the dam and give him His overflowing spirit. But first he had to give God everything.

By this time, I could tell that the Voice was asking, **"Are you ready now?"** Inviting me to surrender what I wanted as He had so many times before. Inside I knew the thing I wanted was going to drown me, but it was so incredibly hard to let go. It was like tearing off flesh. I chose to make a huge personal sacrifice. I said yes. I gave up what I loved.

How was this even possible? I could have been face down in the pool, floating in my own sadness, while attempting to feed myself soggy Oreo's for comfort, but I wasn't. Because I wanted Him–that Voice–more, and I knew He wanted me to surrender it to Him. There was no more denying the message. Surprisingly, I wasn't emotionally defeated this time in giving it up. Instead I felt great anticipation of what He was going to do next in my life.

As the song went on, the worship leader spoke of how the Father (the Voice) looks at us with pure hearts and pure eyes and remembers things no more. I looked at the woman and tears were streaming from her eyes. She needed to hear that message as much as I did, with everything she had been through.

That following Sunday morning, I was in church. It had been one whole week since my first book had been released. The pastor did a demonstration of two jars: both jars had been broken, but one of them had been glued back together. He observed how beautiful it was when the light shined through the cracks of the mended jar. A friend leaned over and said, *"Jen!! God just hit his church with YOUR book! You talk about this very concept in it!"*

Could this really be happening? It was too big to be a coincidence. It seemed like the grandeur map was revealing itself again, with impeccable timing—divine timing.

Little did I know I was about to have a direct encounter with this parallel path where I would find and enjoy greater freedom. It hit me like the entire night sky just fell right into my lap.

In the first week after it's release, my first book garnered just under $1,000 in profits, which I directed to my favorite charity, *Kings Ransom Foundation.* I made sure to thank all those who purchased the book, because in turn they helped us rescue kids from the sex trade, while housing and feeding orphans and widows around the world.

I was floored as the first wave of numbers rolled in. Something big was developing. It was as if this time, the waves weren't meant to wipe out, but to renew, to usher in freedom, and for more than just me. Plus, everyone got to keep on their bikinis.

Our new Facebook page reached over 54,375 people, with over 5,000 engagements on posts. We recorded a video for the release, and shared it within 15 different groups we carefully selected about suicide prevention, awareness, and help for those who have lost someone to suicide. It reached 21,346 with over 5,100 views and counting at the time. We had researched and targeted countries with the highest suicide rates around the world, and people with names I couldn't even pronounce were "liking" the video. I knew He–that Voice–was up to so much! I knew this was just the beginning.

I also knew, with all these new eyes looking in, I needed to be ready. Ready for questions like, *"How DO you overcome?"*

As I journaled and researched, I found my answers, and so much more truth was revealed.

We overcome by faithful commitment to Yahaveh and by declaring His goodness in our lives. Our testimony is what we believe about who Yeshua (Jesus) is, what He did on the cross, and who we are in Him. We enforce Yeshua's victory by exercising our authority in Him and refusing lies in our life, whether those lies are from the enemy, our own mind, or voices around us.

He had literally just been walking me through this.

There is power in your story. There is power in the word of your testimony! That's what an Overcomer is all about. You don't think your story matters? Read Revelation 12:10-12. Your story is what triumphs over the enemy. He was showing me how my story (with His) was doing that very thing.

Revelation 12:10-12 (ISR) says, *Then I heard a loud voice in heaven say: "Now have come the salvation and the power and the kingdom of our God, and the authority of His Messiah. For the accuser of our brothers and sisters, who accuses them before our God day and night, has been hurled down. They triumphed over him by the blood of the Lamb and by the word of their testimony; they did not love their lives so much as to shrink from death. Therefore rejoice, you heavens and you who dwell in them! But woe to the earth and the sea, because the devil has gone down to you! He is filled with fury, because he knows that his time is short."*

We can make the choice to overcome. I was choosing it in many ways. Will you choose to be an Overcomer and step out of the past?

You may ask, how is that possible?

2 Corinthians 5:17 says, *If anyone is in Christ, he is a NEW creation; old things have passed away; behold, all things have become NEW.*

How can I be in Christ?

Romans 10:9-10 says, *If you confess with your mouth the Master Yeshua and believe in your heart that Elohim has raised Him from the dead, you will be saved. For with the heart one believes unto righteousness and one confesses with the mouth and so is saved.*

How can I move forward?

Matthew 16:19 says, *I will give you the keys of the kingdom... whatever you bind on earth will be bound in heaven and whatever you loose on earth will be loosed in heaven.*

As I continued my digging, pondering questions I knew I would need to answer on the path ahead, it was like bright lights illuminated a path and continued to get brighter. I searched for answers about overcoming all the more.

1 Corinthians 15:54 says, *Death is swallowed up in* **OVERCOMING.**

Revelation 2:7 says, *To Him who OVERCOMES, I shall give to eat from the tree of life, which is in the midst of the paradise of Elohim.*

Revelation 2:11 says, *He who OVERCOMES shall be no means be harmed by the second death.*

Revelation 2:17 says, *To Him who OVERCOMES I shall give some of the hidden manna to eat. And I shall give him a white stone, and on the stone a renewed name written which no one knows except him who receives it.*

Revelation 2:26-27 says, *And He who OVERCOMES and guards my works until the end, to him I shall give authority over the nations. and he shall shepherd them with a rod of iron as the potters vessels shall be broken to piece, as I also have received from My Father.*

Revelation 3:5 says, *He who OVERCOMES shall be dressed in white robes, and I shall by no means blot out his name from the Book of Life, but I shall confess his name before My Father and before His messengers.*

Revelation 3:12 says, *He who OVERCOMES, I shall make a supporting post in the Dwelling place of my Elohim, and he shall by no means go out. I shall write on him the Name of My Elohim the renewed Yerushalayim, which comes down out of the heaven from My Elohim and My renewed Name.*

Revelation 3:21 — *To him who OVERCOMES I shall give to sit with me on my throne as I also overcame and sat down with My Father on his throne.*

That's when the lights really came on for me. He was showing me that the prerequisite for overcoming was a genuine commitment. *"We overcome by faithful commitment to Yahaveh and by declaring His goodness in our lives."* I became acutely aware of my own need to commit—to draw a line in the sand and say I will never go back from here. His words echoed, ***"Are you ready now?"*** He was leading me to get off the fence, and commit to that surrender.

In October I was back tuning into another virtual conference with my mentor, Dani. The word *commitment* rang loud in my ears. That Voice was looking for my commitment and I could sense a major shift coming in my spirit. It was like the fresh smell of an ocean breeze was hitting my nostrils. God was about to usher in a new wave of freedom with so much more redemption.

And boy, did it smell good.

Friday night, as that virtual conference was about to start, I was in conversation with two friends who had been on my first trip to Israel. One said, *"Man! Isn't it crazy that one year ago, we had zero idea that coach—our mentor—would be retiring? What would we have missed if we hadn't been all-in, not knowing this was our last chance?!"* I echoed the statement, saying, *"exactly! I'm so glad I was all-in, not only with every conference, Israel last year, but Nuclear Coaching, too! I can't imagine how much I would have been kicking myself if I hadn't taken every opportunity, knowing now that she was going to retire!"*

But that was exactly it. We didn't know until then. This friend said, *"It almost feels like we were chosen! Chosen for a special time, and a special season."* I was reminded of our trip in Israel where we noticed there were huge flocks of sheep everywhere we went. At the time, it seemed odd, especially the one standing at the bus stop. People pointed it out: *"There's something to all the sheep we're seeing, because that's not normal."*

"OMG!" I thought, *"What if the season that's coming—the change that's coming—has to do with the sight of the sheep we saw back in Israel? What if it was foreshadowing? What if He—that Voice—was showing us what was about to come? What if He was showing us what He was about to do? All the people that would be coming as the seasons shifted! And that we were a part of it?!"* We were at the end of an era for this mentor and my spirit knew things were changing. It could sense a major shift that was coming. We started jumping up and down, hugging in excitement, like little children. We knew something powerful was happening; that the Father was going to show whether our speculations were correct or not.

The next day, we started to hear rumblings that a major announcement was coming from the trainer and her company. I had no clue what the announcement was, but knowing it was coming soon, I sat there in my seat and closed my eyes and shot up a quick prayer. I assumed, based off my years of conferences, that it would be an opportunity of some sort. I prayed, *"Father, whatever is coming, if I'm supposed to take up whatever opportunity is presented, I pray for clear confirmation and the finances to do it."*

Five minutes later, the trainer announced a brand new, first—ever, coaching program in the company's 30-year history. Then he chuckled, *"I wish I could see Jen Horling's face right now!"*

Wait, what?! Did he just say my name? Maybe it was a good thing he couldn't see my face at that exact moment, as I probably looked like I had just been tazed. After my immediate shock wore off,

I laughed out loud. But as elated as I was, what hit me in that moment was how quickly the Voice answered. I looked to the sky and said in my spirit, "HAH! Okay, that was pretty epic confirmation. He just said MY name!"

But the truth was, I couldn't have been more excited in that moment. Another one of the speakers that weekend said, *"We have been especially equipped and trained for such a time as this! We carry the spirit of freedom! It is not you who chose Me, but I who chose YOU! We are striking down strongholds and will strike hard showing them our boldness, our courage, and our love. We will use our freedom to serve one another in love. Freedom WILL grow because we have been equipped. We have been trained. And we will do it because we know how to take action, thanks to our coach and mentor who led the way. Coach is not done, she lives on; the message lives on. The Creator lives on inside all of us! And together we will do great things! Together, for freedom!"*

Back in my new home in Texas, the shifts continued.

I was sharing with a friend the story of when my father died, and I remember when my mother said, *"It's just going to be me, you, and your brother now."* My friend Trina, asked, *"Wait...where was your Heavenly Father?"*

And suddenly for the first time I realized that orphan spirit had taken root in my relationship with the Creator. I had felt helpless, like He had orphaned me, too.

She asked me what the truth was in that situation. That was simple. My Creator was also there in that moment. He had been there and had promised to never leave me or forsake me. Whether I was aware of it or not.

If I could go back to that day, I would say:

"YES!!! You know the truth. And that truth will continue to set you free! Even as your mentor retires, you can trust your Creator! Rely on truth; it will not lead you astray! He is the way! He has always been there and will always be there. He is doing a new thing! Keep walking. Keep trusting. Keep the faith! Keep surrendering it all! Where He will lead will blow you away.

I bless you with perseverance. I bless you with protection. I bless you with knowing you are not abandoned! It will get tough, but you are tougher. He is with you! He is behind you. Press on! The lion of the tribe of Judah is behind you. The strength of a lion is behind you! The Voice of a lion will come out of you! The heart of a lion is inside you! And the mind of a lion is within you! Go forth! And take ground for the Kingdom!"

Finding His Timing

CHAPTER 5

Discover the entire map

Looking back, I could see that my Creator had known what was coming next, and had been gently guiding me to surrender for so many reasons, including my own protection. He knew it was going to be a process, and He made sure that process started. You never realize things when you're going through a season of change; you only see them in the rear view mirror.

Had I not surrendered the woman I had been with to Him, surely my life would have capsized with the waves that came next.

One week later, for the first time in my life, I had to call 911. I was witness to her first psychotic break, and it was terrifying. I went through so many emotions so quickly. First, I was afraid of her, as the mental break occurred, then I was afraid for her, and then I was afraid I had lost her, or at least who I had known her to be up to that point.

For 48 hours we couldn't see or talk to her. I didn't know if I would ever truly get my friend back. Even though I had surrendered her, I still loved and cared for her.

A close circle of friends were helping me process through what was happening. One of them reminded me that oftentimes, a break can be a good thing because it can cause a reset. Sometimes, broken things need to be taken apart in order to be healed—to be built again better. Another friend reminded me that the Creator is the Master of resets, a true miracle worker. We believed for a miracle and broke any spiritual agreements with any mental health labels on her family line. At the same time, I was still scared I had lost the person she had been. Would she ever be the same?

My friend, Trina said, "I know He's going to lead because you're listening, Jen. You're like Esther; it's not easy to love someone, and what if God was like, 'I know who I'm going to put in her life for such a time as this - Jen - because I know it's not gonna be easy, but Jen can do it, for such a time as this." Tears welled up inside me. The Creator had brought me through some tough seasons and difficult moments to equip me to be His ambassador to whomever was in front of me.

Knowing the training company had announced they would be offering coach training, I knew it was vital for me to get that training, as a matter of life and death. I had just witnessed it. I wanted to be better equipped to help the helpless—people who are desperate for answers. While it was terrifying, the breakdown stoked that desire even stronger within me to fight for people and to receive any additional training I would need. I had to be all-in.

The more I pondered my responsibility and my role in people's stories, the more overwhelmed I felt, like the waves of anxiety were merging into a tsunami inside. It wasn't just my story anymore, not just hers, it was an ocean of stories and I felt responsible for them all! Just as I wanted to scream, *"HELP! What can we climb?! Will it be high enough!? Where's my bikini?!"* here it was. Like a lifeguard, my Creator sent a messenger running right to me with the oxygen I would need to still breathe (and to give me back my suit).

He breathed in to me, *"This doesn't have to be hard, because I'm right here beside you, helping you. People need someone to hold space for them, to hear their stories and encourage them to share them. Our stories are painful and traumatic. It can feel so weighty when you go backwards in your journey, but it's not it's just there."*

As I wrapped my mind around how to help people tell their stories without stepping in as a counselor (which I wasn't), Trina shared about Van Gogh and how he lived a super-traumatic life. When you hear the story behind each painting, you see glimpses of his faith, but it's so moving to see what came out of the brokenness of his life. *"Telling or sharing your story is like walking around his paintings on the wall and going back to see the full story so you can experience the full glory. You don't have to go fix it. He's already redeemed it. We see our relationships, our family, our career, on the canvas of our lives, and they add their own beauty to the painting, but it shimmers so much more when you read the backstory. Going back, is simple a 'hey paint the room for me, put me there'. That's how you tell the story, and how it's so powerful. That's when the connection happens for someone else when they realize, 'Hey! I felt that way, too'.*

What is a story without the backstory?! When we've done the work to write our story, then God gets to use it whenever He wants."

Phew!! I found my tree to cling to in that tsunami. Being all-in with people didn't mean I had to have all the answers, or be the healer. That was the Creator's job. It simply meant I had a responsibility to listen and encourage them to share their paintings—their overcoming stories—so others could experience their full glory.

That is His design. Once again, He was back to gently reminding me.

I often listen to audio books while driving, because I don't read. I was listening to the audiobook of Johnathan Cahn's *The Harbringer 2*. He talked about the significance of the rainbow in scripture, as a symbol God used to represent His promise. Even His very throne is covered in a rainbow. Yet, in our current culture, the rainbow has been stripped of it's meaning. Whoa! Wait a minute. The rainbow is His throne, yet we, in modern culture, use it for our own thrones of identity?! Ah! Scary thought! I wouldn't want to be sitting on it if He were here...oh wait. He is. How must He feel?!

I had, just months prior, decided to wear a rainbow watch, because to me it symbolized what I loved most—the promises of my God. Nevermind that I also was obsessed with Rainbow Bright as a kid. I wanted to be a part of redeeming that symbol that meant so much to the One I loved the most. And here I was, a few months later, reading about how that symbol was becoming a part of the judgment on our nation. No wonder! It was then that I knew how serious it all was. What my Creator had lovingly designed for good was being vandalized, turned against His design.

Such powerful words that revealed a part of His backstory. It's crazy now to look back at how He led me from one thing to the next, step by step toward the grandeur map He was illuminating for me to walk forward on. Why? Simply because I was seeking Him, hungry for Him and for answers. I wanted more of those lights that kept flickering on, pointing the path forward.

The more they did, the more grandeur they revealed. The lights and the aura around them spilled over into my life, becoming that much more captivating and irresistible to my spirit. I wanted nothing more than to turn more of that light on. BEAM. ME. UP. I am one ready Padowan, chomping at the bit to become a Jedi. (Please don't hate me for mixing a Star Trek reference with a Star Wars one. It's all the same, right?)

I picked up a copy of Chuck Pierce's book, *A Time to Advance*, thanks to a referral from a friend. I was startled by what I read in the dedication.

"This book is dedicated to all those who are determined to become one new man. May I encourage you to continue celebrating Yeshua as the King of the universe. If you give Him your best, He will bless all the rest. He is bringing us out and into a glorious new dimension. When He brought Israel out, He brought them out by armies. He is bringing us out as a triumphant, OVERCOMING people."

I was struck by the Creator's timing again, because I had been directed to this book at the same time I was affirming over myself, "I believe I will always know the next step to expand my business, because He has promised to never leave me or forsake me," thanks to my friend, Trina.

Little did I know that I had just been given the key to everything. I had been given the introduction to the actual map that housed all these lights that had been flickering on further and further. This was it! My Luke Skywalker that would save the entire galaxy.

This book is all about coming into alignment with His timing and the Hebrew calendar. In the modern world, we operate on a Greek calendar (January, February, March etc.) The Hebrew calendar has slightly different timings and names. It was about honoring the Creator and going back to His design.

I started writing down in my planner special Hebrew days to pay attention to, like the first day of each Hebrew month (Rosh Kodesh) so that I could study the significance of each month as we entered into it; what stories in Biblical history happened during that month and how His timing worked.

So here I was, writing all these days into my calendar (and most assuredly pronouncing all of them incorrectly), when it hit me that I was doing this as I was saying, *"I believe I will always know the next step to expand my business because He has promised to never leave me or forsake me."* I knew something powerful had just been revealed. I could feel in my spirit that something epic had just been made known to me. This was the cord that connected all the lights for the path forward—that parallel illuminated path that ran in conjunction with our own; that existed on the other side of reality.

If I could go back to that day, I would say:

"YES! You've been on a hunt for Him your whole life! You know who He is, and this is Him! It is His design! It is His Time! It is your time to align, in greater detail! Just wait until you see, hear, and experience Him on a whole new level. It's about to get even more epic, because that's how much He loves you!

Finding His Timing

He loves you epically! Dive in! Dive into Him! Don't stop the hunt! This is only the beginning of so much more that is in store! You are ready for it! Keep saying YES!"

At this same time I met a new friend at church who quickly started loving everything we had going on at The Overcomers. Knowing he had a powerful story, I asked if he would be willing to share his own journey in an interview. He wasn't just willing, He was ready! He said, *"God told me, I want you to do this because this is going to be huge!"*

During that service, as the Pastor was speaking, more of my Creator's words hit so deeply. My Creator had been revealing to me His original design of the calendar and now, it was as if He knew I was ready for more. *"God is NOT the author of confusion!,"* the pastor exclaimed. My spirit knew deep down it wasn't just someone's opinion; it was truth. Another huge light turned on within me. *"That means He never intended for us to be confused about the way we were made! That means, this confusion is not of Him. He didn't do that. OMG!"*

The pastor went on:

"Light destroys darkness; Satan is darkness. What you're willing to walk away from will determine what He can bring you to!" I saw more lights turning on, showing The Overcomers was going to be huge—just like that initial interviewer had spoken over it—because it wasn't just about one light, it was about thousands! Thousands of lights turning on, as we find Him...and find ourselves.

The next day, I had to pop back to Las Vegas to complete my taxes. Boring, but what can you do? While I was there, I visited one of my favorite spots, Red Rock Canyon. When I lived there it was just across the street from my condo. I liked to think it was my backyard, but in reality, it was everyone on that side of the city's backyard. I didn't own the mountain.

It's epic beauty and bright orange surfaces were absolutely breathtaking. Ironically, sights like this surround the city—breathtaking mountains on every single side—but no one talks about them. I mean, before I lived there, I had no idea it looked like this. The focus is on all the scandalous and scantily-clad things the city swims in. I mean dehydrates in. It's a desert.

Interesting, right? Can't tell you how many times, as I walked, hiked, or adventured through various parts of those mountains, the Creator deposited something in my spirit. It was where I went to breathe, to be still, and to hear Him speak.

There was such a stark contrast between the marvelous, sculpted beauty of the mountains, formed in the Creator's hands, and the mean, man-made scar of the Vegas Strip in the distance behind me, crazy what we miss when we don't focus on Him and what He has done, even though it's all around us.

I could sense a poetic rhythm between the even pulse of the Hebrew calendar and the beats where He introduced each new revelation into my heart. His design had been all around me, but it was up to me to choose to look at it, to dig in, to dive in, and to take a deeper look. To turn my attention away from the distractions of downtown and to discover more of His unfolding design and what might be found within it.

I had an opportunity to interview a man I met at church who

Finding His Timing

had become part of The Overcomers, so he could share his story of overcoming with us. Three significant things happened.

As he was talking about surrender and how that was the key to everything, it hit me that surrender was the key to my story, too: everything changed when I surrendered, and every single time that I had.

Second, as he talked about the amazing peace that he felt after surrendering, it reminded me of how I felt after my surrenders. I told a few people how crazy peaceful I felt, no longer wondering about same-sex attraction feelings—not even a little bit. I wouldn't trade that peace for anything. If I had known what that would feel like, I would have surrendered sooner. I would have wanted this peace that truly passed understanding.

Yes! I said it! I was getting excited about my future, and about getting married! My confusion was gone. I knew I would no longer struggle with "what-if's" in a future marriage. Pretty unbelievable for a woman who used to have zero interest in ever getting married. Of course, you could say that was always there and I was tuning it out—I did after all, attend a marriage seminar in 2018, which ended up being one of the catalysts for all this change. So there's that. That seminar helped me surrender so much.

During the session on conflict resolution in marriage, as I sat there asking myself how it applied to me (at the time single and interested in women), it suddenly dawned on me that I was already married to my Creator...and I was in conflict with Him. I hadn't been honest with Him about my struggle, even though...of course, come on...He absolutely knew it was going on inside me. He knows everything. Silly me. But I came home from that event and collapsed in my shower, bawling my eyes out with my Creator, as the water cascaded over me. I exclaimed, *"Please help with this! I know I haven't talked to YOU about it, and I'm finally coming to you with it, and asking for help."* Surrender had been everything.

Third, I had just read earlier that night in Chuck Pierce's book, *"A Time to Advance,"* about what I believed to be my own tribe–the tribe of Dan! They were meant to be Overcomers.

WHAT THE?!

I'm a part of a Hebrew tribe?! I felt connected to their leaping anointing. They were supposed to leap from idolatry, but they didn't. I thought, *"Whoah! If I chose to leap from anything that might misalign me with His design or get me out of His timing, I would be doing what my tribe was born to do, but had trouble doing in Biblical times."* It filled me with an even bigger desire to be a "leaper" on behalf of my identity, on behalf of the blood that runs through my veins, put there by my Creator!

I could feel the propelling of my spirit the more I aligned with His design. The map was in my hands and I couldn't wait to continue following it to where it's lights might lead.

If I could go back to that day, I would say:

> *"YES! He is showing you where to look! Keep your eyes on Him and His design! It's been there from the very beginning. It's meant for you to find! Turn your eyes from the things of the flesh, the things of this modern world, no matter how they make you feel or how enticing they look. Feelings often lie, but your Creator brings truth! Truth will set you free!*

Finding His Timing

He is your helper and He will lead you to so much more than you even think is possible. Let go of the old and embrace the new. Step into the adventure before you! That peace you are experiencing will pass understanding. Just wait till you see what is still before you!"

Finding His Timing

CHAPTER 6

Reset the foundation of the journey—claim identity

Here's where it started to get eerie, but in the best of ways. Have you ever felt like you're living another life? Not one in the here and now, but one that echoes in eternity?

Echo. Echo. Echo. (Don't tell me you didn't do it, too.)

I'm not trying to get all spiritual with that statement; I'm simply pointing out that the stories that started to happen from this point forward not only began to suggest that parallel story line running just out of sight, but I could pinpoint it's existence with crazy precision. It's almost as if we were meant to find it, because it was so clearly there—like looking into a mirror, you see your reflection! You can't not see it! It's simply there. Now, if you're a ghost...well...I'm not talking to you. Bye, boo.

The Hebrew calendar was becoming a daily focus for me. I had fully engaged with paying attention to the Hebrew, so I knew this particular day was Rosh Kodesh, the first day of that Hebrew month, a day meant to be set apart. As things unfolded that day, I knew it couldn't have been an accident. Not like that day I drove right past the intercom in the Freddy's Burgers drive-through and opened my window expecting to receive my meal at the pickup window...that I never ordered. I was paying attention this time. I knew what day it was, because I had just recently chosen to write every single Rosh Kodesh into my planner for that following year. The morning of each Rosh Kodesh, I would set time apart to seek my Creator, to find out the themes at work within that Biblical month. I asked Him, *"What do YOU want me to see?"*

I spent the middle of the day interviewing another story for *The Overcomers* YouTube channel. I was blown away by all that the Father had done in this man's life. After the interview, I spent the afternoon sharing coffee with a friend, talking about our Creator. I completely lost track of time, enjoying the sweet fellowship and the nuggets of revelation He dropped on us. I neglected to pick up my phone at all. (We were weren't quite suction cupped to our phones yet.)

Later that evening it suddenly hit me, *"Oh my gosh, I was supposed to meet someone about a mattress I had for sale!"* I felt horrible for my tardiness. Naturally, I started to beat myself up for treating this woman so dishonorably. My phone was littered with "missed call" notifications hours after we were supposed to meet. To add insult to the injury, it was her birthday. Of all the days I could have wasted, I wasted her birthday. Naturally.

Finding His Timing

I messaged the woman apologizing up and down. Sheepishly preparing for the worst, I asked if she were ready to meet. Feeling horrible, I turned to my friend and said, *"I feel like I should do something for this woman. I feel horrible. I'm not like this. I can't believe I did that! ...but I also know I was honoring our Guest, and staying in the moment with him this afternoon...so I just don't understand what happened today, Was I wrong in that?"*

I struggled to process everything that was happening. The friend looked at me and suggested, *"Give her your book!"* It seemed so absurd, so self-promoting, I chuckled and said, *"Wouldn't that be weird? She doesn't even know me! 'Here, read all about this woman who just dishonored you all day.'"* But I listened to my friend, and brought one with me.

Had I met this woman at the time we were originally supposed to meet, it would have just been a sale—nothing more. We probably wouldn't have stood chatting in the parking lot for over 30 minutes, like we did that evening. I started by saying how sorry I was that I had missed the earlier appointment, and the conversation grew from there. Would you believe this woman not only had seen that I had written a book, but asked about it in the first few minutes?! I handed her a copy and said, *"Whoah! Yes...Here, I was told to give this to you! Happy Birthday!"*

This incredible woman shared her story with me. She passionately raved about the redeeming work the Father had done in her story. She pulled up her pant leg and showed me the tattoo on her leg which said "CONQUEROR" in Greek, referencing how we are more than conquerors in Christ.

I was stunned. I had been beating myself up all evening for missing our appointment. Meanwhile, the delay had allowed the Father to do more with that connection, to be more than a quick sale. All day, He had been trying to show me something.

We get all caught up in planning our days, thinking how we can't just be in the moment with the person in front of us. That day He said to me, *"Hey, I'll work it all out! Stay in the moment and trust me!"*

It was all about connection–a set-apart connection. Just like Rosh Kodesh is supposed to be. Just as our lives are meant to be, if we let Him. Set-apart. Are we trusting in our timing or in His?

Later that night, I received a message from this woman. She was already reading the book I gave her. *"Been reading your book!"* She shared. *"It's great! My son died when he was 23 of unknown causes. In 2008. 'I can only imagine' was played at his service and is a song that I dearly love. The other song by Chris Rice and the part you mention is the one that I read the lyrics to and released balloons! Fly to Jesus! Wow! Both songs we both had connections to with!"*

Man! To think I could have missed out on such a special connection and gift of a moment with a total stranger if I had gotten caught up in my own thoughts of what the day was "supposed" to look like. Then it hit me...could there be more I'm missing out on?

I felt like I had taken a peek on the other side of reality–a reality that seemed to beckon and invite me to look further; to embrace the Alice within and fall down further the rabbit hole. Looking ahead was going to take great faith, and there's no doubt in my mind that the Creator knew I was going to need that where we were headed. Was there even gravity?

That very next Sunday at church, as I sat listening to the sermon, it was so clear I was being prepared with faith, if I listened;

"Great faith is the product of great fights!"

"God's provision is in His promise. Not one of them will work until you have faith. He SAW their faith, and they were healed. He SAW their faith and the lions' mouths were shut. He SAW their faith and they were kept safe in the fire. He SAW his faith and his son was spared. He SAW their faith and the walls came down."

"Barriers to your success are broken by faith."

"By faith, Noah built an ark. The Titanic was built by experts; the ark was built by an amateur with faith in his God."

"Faith cometh by hearing, and hearing by the word of God. Are you reading it?!"

These words were so timely. I couldn't fathom their importance at the moment they hit my ears. But deep down I knew the fights that lay ahead of me were going to take the kind of faith He was describing: faith beyond anything I might see or experience. Faith that would defy gravity.

"Great faith." What perfect words to have mulling within me as I headed into my next First Steps to Success seminar and the coach training I was scheduled to attend immediately after. He was hitting me heavily with the message of "more than you can possibly imagine" as I was preparing for the training. We were instructed to do a 10-year audit of our past and future in preparation. I reflected on how, 10 years before, I had had dreams and visions on my heart, but here

I was, actually living 10 years later...WOW! It's so much more than I could have imagined it would be back then, ...in only 10 years' time!

The Pastor dropped one more truth bomb: *"Are you preparing your mind to be ready for the dreams and visions you have right now to be more than you can possibly imagine 10 years from now?!*

Throughout the First Steps To Success event, I kept thinking how inspiring it was to fully grasp the ripple effect of just one life, in this case, Dani's life. Dani dared to believe and took action, and look what He did through her! Her ripple had changed countless lives and was continuing out forever. At the end of the event, we celebrated Dani's retirement after 30 years of training people. They played a video made by her son that included a song with the lyrics: *"This is not the end, but the beginning."* They rang in my ears as good tears flowed. The kind that just burst out of me that Friday when Dani surprised all of us soon-to-be coaches by bringing us all on stage to pray for us. As she prayed over each of us, I saw each person's story unfold. Knowing each of their journeys and what He was doing brought another set of tears. The whole time we were up there, I was so moved by how powerful of a moment this was, because of what it signified. He knew the desires of my heart; to help the hurting, struggling hearts of others after losing my dad 17 years prior. Here we were, stepping further into our purpose on this earth. You could see how good He is, and that He does redeem.

Another powerful shift happened during that same conference. Someone asked the question, *"What needs to change in you?"* I wrote in response, *"Where there is still fear I have not leapt with enthusiasm in it with the gift He gave me! He's out there. I believe it. I have faith He made someone just for me. To experience more of the Father and what He not only wants to show me but also give me! I have faith that He exists! And that I will say YES! Enthusiastically! Not full of fear but full of elation, joy, adventure, and everything the Father originally designed for me to reach out and grab! To dance with Him in the rest of this life together!"*

I forgave myself for not using the faith He gave me as a child to embrace how He had designed me and what He had designed me for. I fully forgave myself for not remembering what He had given me... FAITH TO BELIEVE WHO I WAS!

I entered into a vision—a sea of people was before me, each wearing a different-colored band representing one of the 9 areas of life where they were experiencing pain. The colored bands were visible to everyone, showing to the world, *"I Have OVERCOME* (fill in the blank). It encouraged total strangers who were stuck in their pain to come up to them and ask them how they had done it. As they shared their stories, connections formed and the hurting found hope to overcome. The Voice whispered, *"THIS is how I will redeem the rainbow: they will see ME and all I have done in these stories, and they will be reminded of who I designed them to be!"*

During this same conference, He took that message deeper within me. One exercise breaks the audience up into personality groups so you can learn more about who you are and what makes others tick. I had felt a major nudge in my spirit to sit with a personality type that I normally didn't sit in.

This time I sat with the people who are usually organized, structured, on time, and diligent. Despite not wanting to ever come into agreement that it could even be possible I might be this particular personality (how boring!), several people who knew me thought there might be a chance I belonged with that group. How preposterous! I always sat with the fun, spontaneous, disorganized, chronically late, and bright-colored folks. That's where "I knew" I belonged and you couldn't tell me otherwise. But I remember my mom saying, *"Jen, you didn't grow up that FUN personality"* – the one I desperately wanted to be. I knew she was right: I was the quietest kid ever, I was never late to anything, got straight A's in school, NEVER got in trouble (not even with my own parents) and I'm super-organized! But I knew something traumatic obviously had to have happened to me because I identified so much with that fun personality, even though I grew up more straight-laced.

I sat in the "diligent" section out of my own curiosity, to see if maybe I was missing something everyone else could see. As I sat there, it finally hit me (maybe because I was ready for the full meaning of what He was trying to show me all weekend): I needed to fully accept the way He made me. It was time to finally embrace the diligent, organized, truth-seeking, black-and-white personality He sculpted inside me. I needed to embrace my true identity!

All of a sudden, while Dani was talking, I flashed back to when I lost my dad. A young woman, Laura, with that opposite, fun personality saw me hurting and had compassion on me. She became my best friend, walking alongside me through those dark years. She was so full of life and joy, and I was in such a dark, painful spot. I wanted to be like her. She not only helped bring me out of that dark place, she also helped me bring out the fun that was in me! She helped fan it to flame, until it exploded years later; so much so that years later I had convinced everyone (including myself) that I was this fun personality. That was the power of the fun personality. That is the power of learning and appreciating people who have personalities opposite your own.

I realized in that moment that I was the diligent personality who simply loved to operate in the fun one, the opposite one, because I had seen what it can do, and how it can impact another life. It could, quite frankly, save a life.

As the vision faded and I sat comfortably with the diligent, organized people around me, I saw the fun ones across the room. I pictured myself standing in the center of the room, where Dani was teaching, with arms outstretched toward them, exclaiming, *"WE NEED YOU!!"* Of course, this was just a vision, I just sat there quietly in my seat.

But as I sat there processing the light that had just came on, it permeated into my spirit. He had just led me to fully accept who I was and how He had made me. With tears running down my cheeks, I looked to the heavens and quietly asked my Creator for forgiveness for not accepting how He had made me. I had rejected the identity He built into me.

In the first night of the event, Dani called all of the coaching trainees to the stage and prayed over each of us. She gripped the sides of my face with her hands and proclaimed, *"THIS is what it's all been for: all the pain, all the questions, asking God WHY?! You're going to literally be pulling people back from the edge, from the pit of hell! Run, daughter, run! Run into the camp of the enemy! You're going to set people free."*

But the next thing she said seems prophetic now: *"People will be coming up to you!"*

Indeed, they did. The very next morning, a woman I didn't know grabbed both my shoulders and said, *"I need to talk to you!"* She shared how she had considered suicide coming into the event. She had been battling with it for some time, but had never told anyone. I spoke life into her, with words the Voice gave me to say in the moment. Her face lit up. I told her I had something for her and to find me the next day.

The next day, I gave her a copy of my book. I told her there was no pressure to read it; I just wanted her to know that she was not alone in her struggles. If it helped, great. And I knew how hard of a battle that was.

The last day of the event we hugged goodbye and she thanked me for being a light to her. When I wasn't looking, she slipped a card into my bag which I found when I got back to my hotel room.

The moment I read it, I gasped and collapsed on the floor, tears flowing. The very night my mentor had said people would be coming up to me was the very night this woman committed not to kill herself.

There are no words. Only He–That Voice–could have orchestrated things so precisely. Although I felt the grieving for my mentor's retirement, here was proof that this was not the end; this was just the beginning. The beginning of so many more lives being redeemed; so many more people accepting who they are and who He designed them to be; so many more seeing Him and all He has done, and all He will yet do! So many more finding freedom!

Friend, do you know who you are? Do you know that you were born with specific gifts designed into you by your Creator?

As Dani Johnson says, "*You were born with the gift of enthusiasm—you were made in His image! You were born as an adventurist, but we have substituted Netflix for adventure! You were born with the gift to 'get over it'—think how quickly you got over things as a child. You were born to think and live like a 2%-er, but were trained to live like 98% of the population. You were born with the gift of persistence—you were born a winner, but were trained to lose! You were born with the gift of faith and freedom, but we traded it for fear and judgment! You were born with the gift of love, which we traded for fear of rejection!"*

Where you have faith, you take ACTION! Where you don't take action, there is fear!"

I don't know about you, friend, but I wanted to get back to what I was born with. We were all given gifts back at the beginning. Anyone else wanna go back? It's time to claim who you ARE; who He designed you to be from the very beginning!

If I could go back to that day, I would say:

"YES! It is a journey of identity-your identity! His identity in you! He makes all things NEW. He is resetting the foundation, showing you who you truly are! Receive it! Believe it! Walk in it! The road ahead is paved with so much more truth of all the things He meant for you to find! It is solid and secure! It is made with gold!

Keep running to Him! He knows who you are! He designed you! He's refining you! Let Him do what He does best! And the rest will come! People will continue to come! Just watch what He will do! And who He will save!"

CHAPTER 7

Shavo't—find freedom from suffering

I began to realize that the purpose of seeing this lighted path was not just so that I would see it, but so that I would draw near to it and embrace it, that I would let the lights lead me and shine through me. Sing it with me; *"This little light of mine, I'm gonna let it shine!..."*. Yea, that's right, don't blow it OUT on your birthday (your literal day of identity). That would be so dumb. We'll get back to that later.

The more they flickered on, the more I ran toward them and the more exciting the future became. So often we believe the lie that stepping into that light isn't going to be fun—you might feel exposed or uncomfortable—but my experience was completely the opposite: I wanted to set myself on fire! Well, not literally.

Remembering this next story still leaves me stunned today. Looking down at my calendar, I quickly realized the day I had surrendered the woman to Him was Shav'ot—the Feast of Pentecost. Of course it was.

Shav'ot represented the attainment of spiritual freedom from the bondage of our passions, bad habits, and the pursuit of unlimited pleasure.

SAY WHAT NOW?! I didn't plan that. But perfect timing was making itself known again. The invisible map and path was making itself obvious yet again.

As exciting as it was to surrender, I guess I should have expected the waters to be turbulent afterwards. I wasn't the only one swimming; there were others in those waters with me, each on their own journey. But do you know what else was in those waters? Imagine the deadly jellyfish called the Portuguese Man of War–so full of color and life, breathtaking to look at, but touch it and you'll regret it. That's what this woman had become for me.

Unfortunately, as I surrendered this woman, things spiraled into quite a mess. Sure, I had let her go, but it doesn't mean my affections for her just instantly stopped. But that's when she stung me, and the pain of that sting burned for a long time. Almost instantly this female was chasing hard after a male, and flaunted it right in front of me. She treated me horrifically with so much dishonor, disrespect, blatant usury, and manipulation. Any attempts to hold onto our friendship brought accusations of selfishness. I felt so stupid to even consider that a friendship anymore. Her new man even called her out on how horribly she was treating me. She wanted him to approve of her, so she manipulated me, to try to make it look like she had made things right between us.

Finding His Timing

But I was furious; how could she call me selfish when I had surrendered her? To me, that was the most unselfish thing someone could ever do—let go of someone they love, let them swim away, and not have them in your life anymore.

I learned some deeply painful lessons and quickly realized how much I needed to separate myself from the situation. The friend who once saw me with such compassionate eyes was now casting heavy judgment, completely misreading my heart.

Watching her intense chase after this man was one of the most difficult times of my life. I wasn't over her yet, despite the decision I had made. I couldn't handle it. Nightmares and panic attacks repeated through that weekend. I was capsizing in those waves, paralyzed from the sting. Deep beneath the surface, gasping for air, I realized that I didn't like the friend I had become through all this drama. I had allowed someone in my life, who I knew was not honoring to the people around her. I didn't like the dishonor I was seeing. I had to be better; I had to surround myself with better, but I needed help. I hadn't just let someone I loved go...I had lost my friend, too.

I was invisible to her, as was my pain. I was being used and manipulated, as were others. I finally got to the point that weekend that I had simply had enough. By the end of the weekend, I completely moved on. It was time to take care of me and concern myself with no other agenda than His.

If I could go back to that day, I would say:

"He sees you! He sees the pain you're going through. He sees every single tear that you've cried, and He cares. Intimately. He is close to the brokenhearted and saves those

who are crushed in spirit. I know your spirit is crushed. Take heart! He knows the depths of those tears, and the weight of every single one. He is not done! You are not done! You will rise out of this moment!

I bless your heart with healing. I bless you with courage to continue on. I bless you with new strength. I bless your spirit with new joy and a new beginning in this ending. I bless you with new friends who will see your heart and understand. I bless you with new life! I bless you with giving life to others, and seeing others! I bless you with being surrounded by those who truly honor others, too!"

My soul was still stinging, though. Thankfully, my deeper cries did not go unanswered. Another friend, Donna, called that day. I didn't tell her anything about the drama I had just been through, but I fully believe my Creator came to my rescue as the words slipped from her lips: *"Jen, I just have to tell you I'm so proud of your journey."* I bawled. *"You have no idea how much that means to me right now and how much I needed to hear that today,"* I sobbed. He knew.

We talked about the importance of being in community, and how we need to put on barriers of protection against the enemy who wants to keep us from what we were each designed to do. She said, *"YOU were designed to do great things, Jen. Make sure you are surrounding yourself with your own 'secret service'...don't let the enemy or anything tear down those walls."*

I knew it had been my fault for letting my walls get weak, leaving my heart vulnerable. I gained a renewed awareness of the need to protect myself from the dangerous creatures lurking around me in the sea. I had just been witness to their dangers, and I couldn't just sit on my floatie in the ocean, completely naive to the enemies beneath. I knew He wanted to take me much farther and I couldn't go with Him when my walls were weak. I needed the walls of my heart to be made of impenetrable steel, like a military grade submarine complete with secret recruits inside, not a paper-thin plastic tube full of my own hot air.

I was having to fight through more than I should have been then, but I knew I had to win, so I fought on. I had to put those guards back up, and start building that submarine. I couldn't let my feelings win. My future required it. The mission required it.

Donna wasn't the only messenger the Creator sent to speak to me. Around the same time, I received another call from a friend I had worked with on a short film more than seven years prior. Keep in mind, I probably only spoke one or two words with him those few short days we worked together, and hadn't spoken since. But he had been following my journey. We chatted for a long while—surely the longest conversation we had ever had—and he shared about numerous people he had known that had died from suicide. I had no idea all the loss he had seen.

At the end of the call, I asked, *"How can I help you? You obviously have such a caring heart."* He responded, *"Oh, I was just wanting YOU to know that what you're doing with The Overcomers matters, and it's awesome!"* Tears immediately started welling in my eyes. What a message to heart in the midst of the waves churning inside of me.

Never give up on your dream, friend, and never for one second think that, just because no one is commenting or responding, you're not having an impact. You never know who is watching. It could even be people you've only ever said two words to! Keep doing what you are called to do and the right people will find you. I don't care how big the ocean might feel, your buoy of rescue will be like a beacon to them!

Little did I know how quickly those walls would start going up, and how solid they would be! Just as one season was ending, a new one was beginning.

As I embarked on my new journey of being a personal development coach, I was overwhelmed with everything it took just to get started. My mind was racing, trying to figure out what to do, where to do it, and what system to set up. I was like a chicken with it's head cut off. That's such a weird phrase, especially for me, since I know nothing about farming. Or chickens.

I knew I needed to get a hold of my feelings and center my mind. I looked to the sky, exasperated, and exclaimed, *"SHOW ME HOW TO DO THIS!"* I went to take a Mikvah to clear my emotions. I knew I needed to talk to my Creator more than just yelling at Him (not that He couldn't handle my outbursts). I filled the tub with bath salts, added in essential oils of peace, calming, and stress relief...I was serious. I thought, *"what else can I throw in here?"* I grabbed the wine and headed to the tub. George, my Siamese cat, was spared.

I sat down in the tub and chose not to stay in that overwhelming head space (or lack of a head space, if I were that headless chicken). As I was still in that water, He spoke. One phrase dropped into my spirit: *"set apart"*. If I could be anything—a friend, a woman, a business owner, the starter of a movement, an author, or a coach—I wanted to be SET APART first. Set apart to Him. I wanted to operate according to His timing, His calendar. I wanted to invite my Creator into every part of my life and work; for it to be all about Him and what He wanted to do.

That's when He gave me the next idea: *"So do that!"*

Duh, Jen.

I sent out an open invitation on social media for anyone to join me one evening a month to look at His timing, and to tell their stories of what they saw their Creator do in their own lives. Over 25 people signed up for that first call.

As I write this book, we've been meeting for over three years. The stories shared on those calls are much of what you will be discovering in the rest of this book. The hunt for Him hasn't stopped, and neither has the grandeur of the illuminating lights that have turned on along the journey.

I was on the phone one night, catching up with my friend, Jenn, who was living in another part of the country at the time. She asked if there was anything she could pray about for me. I was transparent with how ugly my financial life had become. I had gone three weeks without even one new client and I was scared. In my whole personal development journey, this had never happened before. The first week, I was starting to worry. The second week, I was starting to not sleep.

By the third week, it was no longer funny. *"What the heck are You trying to show me?!"* I exclaimed to my Creator. *"What am I supposed to be learning right now?! It's SO uncomfortable. I'm sweating in all the wrong places and I don't even sweat. Pale people don't sweat."* My design business went from swimming in new clients to none in under a month.

My heart really wanted to get a coaching program off the ground and spend time on stuff for The Overcomers, but there was no income coming in there, either. I was also frustrated because, despite being ready to coach—and feeling like I had got the hang of it—I failed miserably coming out. I couldn't get anyone signed up for months. I asked myself for weeks, *"What am I doing wrong? What am I not doing that I should be doing? What do I need to fix? What are You trying to show me?!"*

What makes all this turmoil seem crazy is that I didn't technically have to be worried. I had been following directions from my coach for the previous few years, living off 70% of my income and investing, saving, and paying off debt with the rest. So even if I went months with no income (which I knew it wouldn't), I was going to be just fine! I had the largest pocket of wealth and savings I had ever had in my entire life up to that point. But I was still freaking out. I had this core belief that, if I wasn't always working, I was in trouble.

There I was, beating myself up, and maybe (just maybe) there was a set-apart purpose for what I was going through. It wasn't for lack of effort—the effort was there! But friend, I was talking to my Creator more than I normally do. I was reaching to the sky and exclaiming to Him in angst, *"SHOW ME HOW you want me to do this!"* One night, He finally answered: it was all about alignment. Curiously, that's the very night this new Overcomers group started, which has met monthly for three years. Interesting, right?

Back to Jenn. Remember Jenn? On the phone? Talking about my financial woes? We both sensed that things were going to change, it was just a matter of when. Suddenly, I remembered a quote I had just seen: *"The times where we are about to birth into something new* and absolutely beautiful...come right after when things are the MOST uncomfortable. You have to be put in a place of uncomfortability, for you to move. For you to move where He wants you to go!"

Jenn shared the analogy of a butterfly she had just watched in a documentary, and we joked around as if we were the dang maggot still stuck in the cocoon because that's how we currently felt:

"It's so dark in here!!!!!"

"I'm so hot!!"

"It stinks in here! Am I sitting in my own crap?!!?"

"When am I going to be able to get out?!?"

"Will I be in here forever?"

"Hello? Is anybody out there?"

"I think a part of my body just fell off!"

"I'm seeing colors...am I hallucinating?!"

When we're in a dark cocoon season of life, we can't see the changes that are happening to us. We can't see the process. We can't see what's just ahead. But the time in that cocoon, undergoing traumatic change, is required for new birth to happen—and not just a normal birth, but an epic birth, like a dang butterfly! Complete transformation. Of course, if you're like me and don't like bugs at all, this analogy may be harder to grasp. But hang in there.

I didn't want to be a normal coach; I wanted to be a set-apart coach. Well...how does that happen and what does that look like, Jen?! Hellooooo! I'm going to have to go through a set-apart process in order for that bug to bloom.

What a message! And once again, impeccable timing. All this was happening in the Hebrew month of Tammuz. The new online group I had started took time to look at the months and the Biblical stories that happened during each month.

This was the month in the Hebrew calendar where the Israelites had just left Egypt, been freed from slavery, and they sinned in the desert by building a golden calf.

I asked myself what golden calf might be in my life and this thought dawned on me: what if one of our golden calves could be our mindsets and ways of thinking? Could we worship a thought to the point that it makes us sick? Could we be stuck in areas of our lives because we're worshiping a mindset that we shouldn't even have, through how much attention and belief we're giving it? What if that was what He was showing me—that I needed to stop believing some old mindsets I had, like:

I have to work every day or I am going to be in trouble.

I'm not good enough.

I'm going to fail.

There's something I'm not doing that I should be doing.

I should be living in Hawaii, married to a Polynesian, sitting on a surfboard and drinking Mai-Tais while people throw money at me from their boats.

What am I doing wrong??

I needed to stop my own mind from spinning in old mindsets and beliefs. Maybe we'll keep that one about living in Hawaii, though.

He was transforming me. He was giving me exactly what I wanted. Does that mean it was easy? NO. Where does beauty come from? Ashes! Embrace the dirt, Jen. Be the yucky bug.

If you are in a place where it feels incredibly dark, it stinks, you're sitting in your own crap, wondering if you're ever going to get out, you even lose some limbs or start hallucinating, remember: sometimes it has to get that way in order for you to move—in order for transformation to happen!

He speaks through all creation, friend. Even bugs.

Finding His Timing

CHAPTER 8

The stamp for a new beginning in the fifth month

So there I was, closed up in my own cocoon, sitting in my own crap. But like I just mentioned, that's where transformation happens. And that cocoon was about to crack.

The 4th of July came and freedom hit me in a new way. Not literally, like my mom when she got hit by a firework as a kid. This went so much deeper. All it took was one line: *"You shall know the truth and the truth shall set you free."* Clarity suddenly rushed into my brain, as if my eyes were opened to see the brightest blue sky above me. Prior to this day a blue sky, would cycle into the darkest overcast filled with rain and thunder, creating powerful storms.

"You shall know the truth and the truth shall set you free."

Why does the truth set you free? It is all tied into being set apart.

What does that mean, Jen? What does it mean to be set apart? You keep using that phrase.

Back in Israel in 2019, I learned that being set apart simply relates to talking to your Creator, aligning with Him, and constantly laying down whatever you need to on the altar, as they did in Biblical days.

Going to an altar to sacrifice used to be a daily or weekly thing for Israelites back in the days of Moses. Altars were located in specific places, like the tabernacle. Nowadays we can go to an altar anytime, anywhere. Pause. Not a literal altar. Let's not go that dark. I mean figuratively, in your spirit. Man, how lucky are we that we don't have to do it literally anymore. We don't have to carve up live animals every week, month, or year anymore. So messy.

Approaching the altar in our heart with a sacrifice sets you free from condemnation, guilt, and shame: we sacrifice the way we have always done things, recognizing that our old thoughts, habits and patterns had become a trap that enslaved us. It means freedom from our own minds and hearts, from the storms inside us that beat us up week after week, saying we're not good enough, we're failing. It's not about "we," it's about Him and the freedom we receive by continuing to come to Him, align, confess, burn our old ways on the altar, and begin a new day. That's what being "set apart" means.

Freedom comes from aligning with Him: freedom stays by aligning with Him every day. For the first time, that year of July, freedom meant so much more to me—it meant:

Freedom from me.

Freedom from guilt.

CHAPTER 8

The stamp for a new beginning in the fifth month

So there I was, closed up in my own cocoon, sitting in my own crap. But like I just mentioned, that's where transformation happens. And that cocoon was about to crack.

The 4th of July came and freedom hit me in a new way. Not literally, like my mom when she got hit by a firework as a kid. This went so much deeper. All it took was one line: *"You shall know the truth and the truth shall set you free."* Clarity suddenly rushed into my brain, as if my eyes were opened to see the brightest blue sky above me. Prior to this day a blue sky, would cycle into the darkest overcast filled with rain and thunder, creating powerful storms.

"You shall know the truth and the truth shall set you free."

Why does the truth set you free? It is all tied into being set apart.

What does that mean, Jen? What does it mean to be set apart? You keep using that phrase.

Back in Israel in 2019, I learned that being set apart simply relates to talking to your Creator, aligning with Him, and constantly laying down whatever you need to on the altar, as they did in Biblical days.

Going to an altar to sacrifice used to be a daily or weekly thing for Israelites back in the days of Moses. Altars were located in specific places, like the tabernacle. Nowadays we can go to an altar anytime, anywhere. Pause. Not a literal altar. Let's not go that dark. I mean figuratively, in your spirit. Man, how lucky are we that we don't have to do it literally anymore. We don't have to carve up live animals every week, month, or year anymore. So messy.

Approaching the altar in our heart with a sacrifice sets you free from condemnation, guilt, and shame: we sacrifice the way we have always done things, recognizing that our old thoughts, habits and patterns had become a trap that enslaved us. It means freedom from our own minds and hearts, from the storms inside us that beat us up week after week, saying we're not good enough, we're failing. It's not about "we," it's about Him and the freedom we receive by continuing to come to Him, align, confess, burn our old ways on the altar, and begin a new day. That's what being "set apart" means.

Freedom comes from aligning with Him: freedom stays by aligning with Him every day. For the first time, that year of July, freedom meant so much more to me—it meant:

Freedom from me.

Freedom from guilt.

Freedom from shame.

Freedom from condemnation.

Freedom from my past.

Freedom from yesterday.

Thank you, Father, for freedom from me.

His truth set me free.

Freedom rippled through my life in many ways. By this point, I had my own flag. It was His! He was my banner of victory.

I was in Orlando, Florida when the lie that I had to do things perfectly was ripped apart right in front of me, without me even trying. No ninja moves required (this time). I met a new friend at the water fountain inside the hotel. I went to shake her hand but because of my horrible timing, she let go of her water she was filling, and it splattered all over the floor. I exclaimed, *"Well, we're always going to remember the way we met, aren't we? Haha."* Inside, I was mortified at my own greeting. Ninja Jen's dreams, dashed.

The following day, this new friend overcame her fear and got up in front of the whole conference and described a massive change in her mindset. She got a huge standing ovation. I took a moment to speak life into her afterwards, and edified who she was.

The next day, all of us new coaches got a quick two minutes to come on stage and share who we were there to help. As I gave my pitch, I shouted that I was an OVERCOMER. She found me after and was interested in hearing more about my coaching. So crazy—all this training I had received, and here He was showing me that you can completely ruin a first impression and can still get the sale. Maybe I am a ninja after all?

Maybe that's precisely the point. People crave authenticity, not perfection. Yet we tell ourselves that we have to be perfect. Be free, friend. It's amazing what that freedom can do inside of you and through you for others.

I found a new courage that day, and with that courage I hosted our very first panel discussion at The Overcomers, focusing on loss. I put out a public request for those who had suffered loss and had a heart to help others in this area. I was shocked at how quickly people jumped up and offered to help.

I hosted the panel with these three other panelists. We felt it was tremendously successful. But afterwards, I just sat completely frozen, so moved by all that had happened and how powerful it had been. I was overwhelmed by how present the Creator was. He was doing a new thing and I could see it unfolding right before my eyes.

Our panelists shared so many awesome nuggets, as well as their stories. We asked them very pointed questions, with the goal of helping anyone who was struggling with overcoming loss that might be listening.

One answer I had never thought of before dropped into my spirit as I was preparing the questions for our speakers: *"What is the best thing a person could say to show support and show that we care when someone is grieving? Are there phrases that should be avoided? What should we say instead? Or is the right thing to say nothing at all?"*

Finding His Timing

I shared that, looking back, I honestly wished I would have shared more about my dad and how amazing he was. I missed him. I just wanted to talk about him. He was physically gone, but the memory of him didn't need to be. I recommended that people ask what the person they lost was like. For example, *"What did you love about the person you lost? What did they do for a living? What did they like to do for fun?"* Man, if anyone would have asked me those questions and then edified what they heard about him to me, I would've bawled. I can't imagine how it would have felt for someone to celebrate who he was like that; and to pour that into me. Little did I know that years later, a new friend would do just that, without even hearing this.

That was just one nugget shared from that panel discussion. That night, I stepped into so much more courage. I stopped worrying about needing to be perfect. Who's perfect? We had three other speakers who showed courage, too: a mom who had lost her 18—year—old son two years prior and a man who had lost his dad to suicide when he was nine years old. This is why The Overcomers launched: to connect those who had been through hard things with those who are walking through a similar journey and need help.

I was floored by the impact I was seeing in other people's lives. I was free, and I knew I was being me. *"This is me!"* (sorry, inside my head Jen just broke into an amazing dance routine. I love the film *"The Greatest Showman"*).

The more I stepped into it, the more the reminders of that identity came…as did my costume. Kidding. This is reality, not a circus musical. But I definitely would have been wearing a top hat, and a cane. Definitely a cane. I had a point to make, and they are so pointy! Great for emphasis.

Finding His Timing

It was September and I was back in another business conference, this time without the mentor who had so epically changed my life. Three new trainers had taken the lead. Thankfully, I saw the same heart for people pouring from the stage. My Creator's heart for people was still there, because He was still there. During the session about personality differences, the new trainer named Carmen stopped right in front of me, looked me dead in the eyes, and said, *"Jen! What you are doing is so important and is going to be so freaking huge! Keep going!"*

I could feel the fuel being added to the flame, making it brighter. I didn't even have to light this flame to get it to turn on brighter! Shortly after that event, I was on the phone with a coaching lead and I could feel her need. She wanted to hear from the Creator specific directions to live as a single mom. She had left her spouse years prior, for good reasons. She mentioned the spiritual sections of these conferences were her favorite, so I invited her to our monthly Hebrew calls about the Creator's timing. I shared what the current Hebrew month was all about and what happened in Biblical history during that month. I told her about the story of the ten spies in the book of Numbers and how we are either in the camp of belief or unbelief, when she gasped *"Oh! He just said to me, 'how long do YOU want to wander in the wilderness?"*

Unreal. I didn't tell her to do anything or even give her any advice. All I told her was the story of the Israelites. I didn't need to know what to tell her. All I had to tell her was what month we were in, and He spoke to her what she needed to hear! I mean, what do I even know about marriage or being a mom? He gave me the perfect picture of how He will show people the answers they need. Again, it was never about me. It was about Him! His timing!

Finding His Timing

As all this was happening, I was reminded of all the drama that played out when I fully moved on from the woman I had been obsessed over. All that had transpired in the fifth month of the Hebrew calendar.

Why is that so significant? Well, it's described as the month you either metamorphose or disintegrate. Remember the butterfly? Our choices either bring a curse, break a curse, or believe God's promises and enter blessing. It's the month the Creator allows things to be destroyed so they can be rebuilt. Things had surely been destroyed, and I was being rebuilt. The fifth month is all about OVERCOMING.

In *"Numbers that Preach,"* Troy A. Brewer says:

"Grace from God gives us the ability to overcome 'the valley of the shadow of death'. We're given the authority of Christ to conquer any situation the enemy would use to take us out. I know grace is traditionally known as unmerited favor, but it's also more than that. When it is, God likes to stamp the number 5 on it.

"The ultimate of all overcoming power is the God-given ability to get back up out of the grace once you've been buried in it. Yeshua has given us that ability. He marked that ability when He was pierced in 5 places on the cross: both hands, both feet, and His side. He overcome the cross and the grave."

Consider this:

About Genesis 15:9, Troy Brewer says, *"God established His covenant with Abraham by five sacrifices, a bull, sheep, goat, dove and pigeon."*

About Exodus 13:18, he says, "*Israel came out of Egypt, ranked in fives, proving it was God's power that brought them out. The number 5 is marked all over the Exodus account, preaching there's no bondage God's grace cannot bring you out of.*"

About 1 Corinthians 14:19, he says, "*Paul writes of speaking clearly in the church and the Holy Spirit marks it with the number 5.*"

About Exodus 30:23-25, he says, "*The holy anointing oil was made of five ingredients. This precious oil was the symbol of God's power to set things, and even people, apart for His purpose and use, and to mark them as His holy territory. For the Christian, God's anointing is on our life. It is still marked by the number 5 and grace.*"

About John 5, he says, "*the pool of Bethseda had 5 porches. It was there that the lame man was healed and made able to walk.*

"*Even our very own design, all the way back to the beginning once again reveals His design for overcoming.*

"*We have 5 fingers, He has given us the grace and ability to overcome with our hands!*

"*We have 5 toes, He has given us the grace and ability to walk and progress forward into His promises no matter what we walk through in life.*

"*We have 5 senses, sight, hearing, taste, touch and smell. It is by His grace and ability we can perceive!*"

As I read that the fifth month is all about overcoming, and choosing whether you're going to believe in the promises of God

Finding His Timing

or stay in doubt and fear, after over a year of waiting, I received in the mail the official notification from the US government that The Overcomers trademark had finally been officially registered.

WHAAAAAAAAAT?! You can imagine my face looking at the envelope (especially those who actually know me, as I've been told I'm highly animated despite not having any idea at the time what that even meant).

You read that right, and I had to check it again. Sure enough, there it was, finally registered in the fifth month, and the fifth month is when our Creator likes to stamp things that are all about Overcoming?!

Unreal timing, once again. Perfect timing. Timing I wouldn't have even noticed had I not been looking at the Hebrew months and their meanings, and starting to see the parallels within my own life. There it was again, a peek at the other side of reality and the map.

What a gift to see this! To receive this! To know this! And to think, I would have missed out on recognizing this impeccable timing (and the Creator's stamp on all of it) had I not taken the time to look. All I could think was, what else might I be missing out on?

I certainly didn't want to miss anything, so before the month ended, I set apart time with my Creator, and Mikvah'd in my bathtub once again. This time, I cleansed away everything from the previous month, submersing myself beneath the waters six times. Right before the seventh submersion, I uttered *"Let everything die that is supposed to die this month. I give it all to you; it's all yours. My time. My words. My mind. My heart. My very life. I give it all. Let it all die that needs to, and may it be rebuilt as you desire."* I hadn't planned to say

Finding His Timing

that, but as I aligned myself with my Creator, it just poured out of my spirit, marking completion.

If I could go back to that day, I would say:

"Yesssss! You've found the key. It's all about surrender! Letting it all go. Letting every part of who you are find freedom, and rest at His feet. Watch Him work! Just watch what He will do to restore. To rebuild. To begin again with Him! He makes all things beautiful in time! He has truly set you free! And you are learning how to see it and trust it!

He is so proud of you! You were born with the ability to overcome hard things and you are! You are His design, in His image! He is the great designer! Keep running to Him! He's got you! And He's got this! He's even stamping it as His design! You are official. Because He is!"

Finding His Timing

Finding His Timing

CHAPTER 9

Trust His presence in the lights

As the next few months progressed, the flame that lit the path forward burned brighter. Interestingly, the next month was Elul, which the Hebrew calendar described as *"a haven, like a city of refuge from the ravages of life."* It is a month where the Creator supposedly surprises you with His presence.

That month, I was in Kauai, Hawaii. Before the trip, I prayed over everyone who would be on the trip by name. I prayed that whatever each person needed to hear, the Creator would deposit into their spirits in some way on the trip. We had eight people, including six who knew each other, from our First Steps to Success conferences, and two new friends from Las Vegas. There was enough diversity of lifestyle, and perspectives that there could have been conflict. But there was none and that was so beautiful. I knew the Creator had brought this group together. I can't tell you how many times every single person was in tears because of the conversations we had and from watching what God did all week among us. These two new friends from Las Vegas cried because they felt so seen and encouraged. They felt their deepest visions celebrated. And this was just in the first couple days.

One in particular shared how much she wanted to have a mentor who used Biblical stuff as the foundation of their material. I was so honored to get the opportunity to speak life into her vision. She was so overwhelmed by the experience that she wept.

Toward the end of the trip I decided to Mikvah in the ocean. I knew once I returned home I would immediately be driving up to Las Vegas for another month-long television gig.

But such gigs come with chaos, and I knew it. The last time I did one of these shows at this level, it was the hardest thing I had ever done; it challenged everything in me. So this time, I swam out into the waves and prayed over the upcoming gig for what felt like more than 30 minutes. I took spiritual authority over the gig and I declared peace over it. I declared that nothing would be able to penetrate the peace that my Creator had given me in my spirit, mind, and heart. Nothing! No matter what chaos was around me. I also prayed that the job would be easy, fruitful, and much more.

In the book, *A Time to Advance,* Chuck Pierce said, *"What part of my life can I put completely in God's hands? What have you been worrying over that you can just entrust to Him? Look at the cares and anxieties that have drained your strength and cast those cares totally on Him. Then allow Him to shine His favor on you!"*

Even though there was total chaos around me on that gig, I

entrusted my life and cares to Him and He showered His favor around me. The people who had hired me quit the gig the day before I got there, without even telling me. I had driven up from Texas to Las Vegas for it! Imagine my shock. Where are you guys? I just got here. They were my connection to the project, and now I was surrounded by strangers.

But His favor was absolutely upon me, despite all the chaos. It was one of the most peaceful, high-level entertainments gigs I had ever worked, developing a brand new show with a mainstream network and name. Those prayers back in Kauai had done something; my Creator had done something. Peace was present in circumstances where it didn't even make sense for peace to be possible. The entertainment industry is complete insanity. The Creator was making His presence known in me and around me. I'll never forget what He did next.

I found this passage in *"A Time To Advance;"*

"If you will celebrate in the Rosh Kodesh of each month, you will acquire the blessing of each month, which will penetrate the loss. Otherwise, you will just stay in the loss, and some people will do that. If you process through the blessing of each month, the Lord will enable you to bring many people through the process of death, into healing. You will be like a skilled nurse, full of mercy, who brings mercy. Your weeping will turn into joy."

It suddenly occurred to me that He had given me the idea to start the monthly calls as a platform for people to share stories and go through the Hebrew months together under the umbrella of The Overcomers, which is all about helping people who want to overcome hard things. He had literally given me the exact tool to help people do that by helping them experience the monthly Rosh Kodesh's and the resulting blessings, and I had no idea the significance or the depth of it. Could He really be this epic? I felt like Moses as the Red Sea parted before me. All I had to do was walk.

But what makes it crazier is that light of the invisible map had once again flickered on, revealing another perfect timing. This revelation came in the same exact month in Biblical history when Moses received the ten commandments. In the month where the Creator made Himself known to the Jewish people with great mercy, He made Himself known to me. Called it! I was spot on with that epic feeling, like Moses. Can't wait to fist bump Him in eternity.

After the gig in Las Vegas, I stayed for another two weeks and spent some time with my old roommate. One night, she and I sat outside on the patio and chatted, and when she asked me, *"How do you cleanse yourself, Jen? How do you get rid of anything that's in you that might need to come out? What script do you use?"* She was smoking weed at the time (which I found so comical considering the topic of conversation) and knowing she wasn't asking for soap or body wash recommendations but rather was speaking spiritual terms, I explained the Mikvah process to her. *"WAIT! You're going too fast!"* She interrupted. *"I need to write this down!"* I suggested, *"How about you just say it right after me now? I'll text it to you after so you have it."*

I walked her through taking authority over her mind, spirit, heart, and body; cast out anything that wasn't of the Creator; and then I blessed her with what she did want. She repeated each line back to me. I was so proud of her for being so teachable (she was hungry for truth) as I saw my friend take another step toward freedom.

These two extra weeks in Las Vegas crossed over from the Hebrew month of Tishrei to the Hebrew month of Chesvan. Would you believe that Hebrew month we were in is the month for new beginnings, the month to digest what you've heard and to "war with words"? It's traditionally the month to be looking for deliverance; to take authority and stand in it.

During those extra two weeks, yet another light of the map made itself known. My old roommate had two other guests during my visit. One was a traveling nurse—a total stranger to me. During one late-night chat, I walked this new friend through the steps of forgiveness from a wound that we identified was there from her mom when she was just three years old. This wouldn't have happened if I hadn't stayed an extra two weeks and this new friend hadn't been there.

The next day, she and I hung out by the hot tub together and chatted for a long time about her life, her kids, and her hopes and dreams. She shared about her intense desire to provide true healthcare for people in the LGTB community. She hated how humans treat each other. No matter whether we agree or not, they are still human beings that need help.

I spoke life into her vision and observed how it had felt like it wasn't an accident that we ended up at my friend's place at the same time. She shared how she never stays at strangers' houses, and this wasn't like her, but something felt so peaceful when she made the decision, she knew everything was going to be okay. By the end of our conversation, she bought my first book, *Finding His Voice*, from Amazon and asked if I wanted to grab dinner with her.

At dinner, I learned that she had been diagnosed with a serious health condition and had been given three to five years to live. As you might imagine, that took the conversation to a much deeper place. I asked how she was handling it, how her family was dealing with it, and what plans she had for the next few years. She expressed her excitement for the trips she planned to take.

Suddenly I realized, this was one of the reasons my Creator brought me here for the TV gig—to be here for this complete stranger, because she mattered that much. Every human mattered that much.

That night, I encouraged her to ask her Creator for the things she wanted. She was stunned, like it had never crossed her mind before. She had always asked for healing for other people when they needed it, but never for herself. There had been a block. Later during my visit, she told me how, for the first time, she asked her Creator for her own healing. Tears welled up in my eyes as I witnessed my new friend's newfound freedom and faith like a child to believe.

The light from the eighth month—a month marked by new beginnings because of dealing with roots—was beaming. I saw both stories so perfectly parallel to the history of this month from thousands of years ago—His timing on display.

As we entered the ninth month of the Hebrew calendar, the lights of the map only got brighter, making themselves known more clearly. It was the beginning of Hanukkah, a Biblical festival I knew pretty much nothing about and had never celebrated. Come on, I grew up Baptist. I barely even knew they existed! But as I dove deeper into the meanings and stories from the month, it spoke to my need to examine my heart and break out of old patterns of mistrust, to enter into new levels of rest. With perfect timing, my Creator was making that need known within me.

Finding His Timing

I attended another First Steps to Success seminar, this time virtually. As I tuned in, I realized that I had developed a belief that, if I made a mistake it meant I wasn't trustworthy. As I dug deeper, I realized I had a mindset that everything had to be perfect or that I had to be perfect.

This dialogue came up in my spirit:

Creator: *"Why, Jen?"*

Jen: *"Because I have to figure it all out, because so many are struggling. I can't make a mistake, because they won't trust me if I do. They won't believe it will work for them."*

Creator: *"Why?"*

Jen: *"Because when you make mistakes, people stop trusting you."*

Creator: *"When did you feel like people didn't trust you, Jen, because of a mistake you made?"*

I identified the root of this belief and remembered the last time I felt that way. A memory flashed for me of a time in my journey that I had felt misunderstood during one of the toughest seasons of my life, I made a series of relationship mistakes that caused others to misunderstand my heart, my motives, and my character. I had developed feelings for someone and didn't want it to be known. But it left me acting very awkwardly.

Tears flowed freely as I realized where this blockage began. That was one reason why I continued to be afraid of being transparent with my mistakes, despite having already been so transparent, facing my biggest fears by writing my first book.

Dani's words echoed in my ears: *"Your desire reveals your design."* I had a desire to be fully transparent to help people, and my own mindsets and beliefs were still holding me back. When does it end?!

That day, I chose a new belief. I forgave myself for that moment in my past and I chose to believe that I was trustworthy, even when I made mistakes.

Like a great woman once said, *"The things we let our minds believe either birth or destroy our dreams."* If you're like me, they can beat you to a pulp inside in the very thing that your heart yearns to do more than anything else in this world–in my case, helping people who are hurting–all while knowing the importance of vulnerability and transparency to do that very thing.

If you don't like what is destroying you, friend, I have good news and bad news. The good news is you can change it, the bad news is you're the only one who can change it. It wasn't until I stopped letting my past dictate my future that it all changed. I had to change the labels I wore: Abandoned, Invisible, Confused. Instead of labels of who I have been, I chose to wear labels that reflected where I wanted to go.

Choose your labels, friend. If you need someone to believe in you, I do! I am already holding your banner of victory high in the air, yelling to you to run towards me! Run toward Him! Run toward your future and all that He has for you! Run! Run, Forrest, run! (Or whatever your name is, if you're not Forrest.)

Finding His Timing

Life can hit you with so many things. Believe me, I get it. If there's a curb, I've probably hit it—just look at the dents on my car! But you and I can choose the labels we will wear. My label is I am an Overcomer. But I also bought an off-road vehicle...for the curbs. So when one wheel's up on the sidewalk when I park at the bank, I don't let it define me. I overcome.

The day I chose to step into that new belief and own that label, I publicly shared this story on social media. A Production Designer that I know from the film industry immediately texted me and asked if he could hire me to work on a 5-million-dollar feature with Bruce Willis (or maybe it was because he saw my skills with those curbs and knew I would be perfect to work with an action star.) I was stunned. The Creator was helping me enter a new level of trust in His perfect timing, as I was seeing the crazy, epic things that happen on the other side of vulnerability and transparency.

That same month, I was given a new support system, a couple that profoundly impacted me, Bill and Jacqueline. He was a professional counselor who had read my first book. While reading it, he emailed me notes about each chapter because he was so impacted by what he read. He was so honoring to me, and fully accepted me immediately. I was so overwhelmed by their kindness that I poured out my heart in a 4-page letter. I met him in person later that year, and he said something to me that I honestly didn't know how to respond to in the moment: *"If you ever need another fatherly figure in your life, Jen, I know my wife and I would be honored to be that for you."* I was speechless. No one had ever said that to me.

Many months later, I ended up rooming with Jacqueline at a First Steps conference. It was a weekend I will never forget. I had been so impacted by him, and was getting to know Jacqueline as well, and watching the two of them together renewed my excitement for marriage. Observing how she talked about him to others, and talked to him on the phone, I saw my own spirit enter into a new place of peace, rest, and trust, in more ways than I could express. I moved from friendship to an incredible new support system, to a renewed excitement for marriage–and it all happened in the month where trust can be renewed and support systems are reviewed—Kislev. I couldn't wait to find someone to ride up on curbs with me.

The lights kept flickering on. It was also the month in Biblical history in which the rainbow appeared after Noah's flood. In that moment, the Creator made a covenant with us so that we would not have to struggle with old patterns again, which was the symbolism of the rainbow. I was sure ready to be done warring. I was ready to let that Portuguese Man of War jellyfish dry up on the shore and suffocate. Of course, I didn't want that for her...well, okay maybe a little. I was pretty angry with her. I'm just being honest.

In the same month of Kislev, when the Creator renewed my excitement for marriage to a man, I spent three straight nights chatting into the night with Jacqueline. Each night, around 3:45am, we looked at the clock and said, *"yea, we should probably go to bed now,"* not just because she passed out mid-sentence in front of me (and I mean mid-her-own-sentence). It was eerie, but in the best of ways.

After I returned home, I took out my Bible and studied book-by-book on the inkling that He might be trying to tell us something. Sure enough, in nearly every book, chapter 3, verses 4-6 described something being "set apart." For example, Joshua 3:4-6 said, *"Set yourselves apart for tomorrow Yahaveh is doing wonders in our midst."*

The month ended with the celebration of Hanukkah, and for the first time, I felt I understood something about it's significance: *the message that the light will not go out. In the midst of destruction, God will find a way to impart mercy to you.* No *matter what aspect of destruction you are dealing with-whether external, internal, physical, or spiritual*—God *has a way to impart mercy to you, to build the future.* That's precisely what I saw Him do.

At the same time, I was going through another round of emotional destruction, as the Portuguese Man of War (I mean, the woman I had let go of) was throwing her deadly tentacles of anger through text messages, trying to get them to stick. I had gone through so much hurt and needed joy again. Not only did He impart mercy amidst the attack by giving me new joy, but He did it while building toward my future.

The lights from that that illuminated map were continuing to flicker on and lead me forward towards greater freedom.

If I could go back to that day, I would say:

"Yesss! Keep trusting Him! He never expected you to be perfect. Only He is perfect! But He is perfect for you!

Keep allowing Him to work inside you, to free you! You are trustworthy because of who He is! He died for you and for them! Show Him to them! Show what He has done for you. Show the mess. Show the cleanup. Show the victory!

Keep those walls up and watch what He will do! What He will do through it and through you! His mercy will never end! This is not the end! The light will not go out! The light will not go out within you!

I bless you with authenticity. I bless you with transparency. I bless your mind with knowing how you were designed! I bless you with being set-apart! I bless you with being a light that never goes out!"

Finding His Timing

Finding His Timing

CHAPTER 10

Align with your identity

Vulnerability was becoming a thing. I boldly spilled my guts to the public about another dark story on social media. By this time, so many people knew so much about my insides, they probably could have described in detail what I had for dinner that day.

This time, it was about the things that we tend to beat ourselves up for. It's crazy how we can be our own most brutal critics, dishonoring to our own minds, our thoughts, and our own progress. We are often the ones keeping ourselves from everything that we've ever wanted. But how many of us give time and space to work through those things?

Unless you do, they gnaw at you, taking bites out of everything you're supposed to be, and you may not even realize it.

Have you found yourself wishing that the "thing" that is beating you to a pulp could be erased? I surely did. I wanted to take that internal bully and show him my giant biceps (kidding, I actually wanted to douse him with kerosene and light a match and then bury him 10 feet under...but unfortunately, I would've gone down with him, so I didn't).

Instead, I realized I had to forgive myself. Forgiving myself has always been the hardest thing.

I was on the phone with some amazing friends in our community who regularly attend these conferences, when something came out of me that I wasn't expecting. With tears streaming down my face, I shared how I was having a hard time forgiving myself because I loved my Creator more than anything else in this life and I didn't want to disappoint Him! But what's beautiful is that Yahaveh, my Creator, had seen me and met me where I was in that thought.

Just a few days prior, another friend who had never had me in their dreams had a dream with me in it. In the dream we were on the beach, looking at our shadows and writing in the sand, but there was just one word, written in big bold capital letters..."FORGIVEN." Hmmm...I wonder what it meant? Kidding. This dream couldn't have been more blatant in it's message. I mean, it was in all-caps. Here I was, struggling to forgive myself, despite knowing that how I saw myself was not how my Creator viewed me. I knew if He could hear my thoughts he would shout His epic love for me and tell me how wrong my thoughts were. Well, He saw my internal battle and He spoke. Just one word—the one word I needed to hear from the One I wanted more than anyone not to disappoint. And He did so through someone ELSE'S dreams!

After I shared this dream with my friends on the phone, Donna dropped this bomb on me: *"Jen, sometimes there can be things that* are literally like suspenders strapping us down...when we were meant to rise." She shared Isaiah 61 with me:

"The Spirit of the Sovereign Lord is on me, because the Lord has anointed me to proclaim good news to the poor. He has sent me to bind up the brokenhearted, to proclaim freedom for the captives and release from darkness for the prisoners, to proclaim the year of the Lord's favor and the day of vengeance of our God, to comfort all who mourn, and provide for those who grieve in Zion—to bestow on them a crown of beauty instead of ashes, the oil of joy instead of mourning, and a garment of praise instead of a spirit of despair. They will be called oaks of righteousness, a planting of the Lord for the display of his splendor." (Isaiah 61:1-3 ISR)

"Jen!! This is you!" she shouted, as she figuratively threw my suspenders off for me. I knew she was right; that thing had been strapping me down, when I was meant to be free. It had been strapping me down when I literally had Isaiah 61 tattooed on my arm (and she had no idea when she said it).

My Creator had literally given His son's life so that I could be free. *"God showed His great love for us by sending Christ to die for us while we were STILL sinners!"* (John 3:16) STILL sinners.

Stop beating yourself up for that thing, friend. You were meant to be free, too. Don't let that thing strap you down from what you were designed to be.

I had no idea the significance of my new freedom, or how important it was that month to pay attention to words spoken over my life. Spoken words have spiritual power, and it was critical that I not just pay attention to them, but to take a stand for my inheritance

Finding His Timing

in Him, and who He created me to be!

Another war was about to be won. As I headed into 2022, I chose to get a refresher course of my coaching training. While there, a major shift happened—major victory.

Have you ever had one of those moments where you knew you were supposed to do something—maybe even put on this earth to do it—but you were completely terrified? You had a passion inside of you burning to be authentic, to be crazy transparent, simply because you really wanted to help people like you. That was me at the end of 2019, before I wrote my first book. Putting myself out there with that much transparency and authenticity was one of the hardest things I've ever done. But now, on the other side, I would do it again in a heartbeat, because it has been the best thing I have ever done for myself and for others.

The stories.

The lives.

I wish I could tell you them all. If anyone's down for a four-year coffee date, let me know. I'll gladly tell them.

I believe my courageous friend, Jacqueline, was placed beside me during this coaching refresher to help me get my heart where it needed to be. She helped me to feel safe and to process further, in order to keep running forward, leaping over the obstacles that were placed in my path. She inspired me, loved me, prayed for me, and continued to call out the deep desires of my heart. She saw what He had placed inside of me to do and helped me bring it forth.

Authenticity is our greatest asset. It's not easy, but it's simple. In sharing the pain, the ugly, the mess-ups, and the imperfections in our lives, we truly help people. We have to be vulnerable with the embarrassing things or the things we're ashamed of in order to give people the freedom we want them to experience. I want to give you my authenticity (well, authenticity and joy) so that you can enjoy the freedom I long for you to have. Or maybe by this point you just think I'm weird, but we can't win them all. I can't change your life for you, but if I give you my authentic self, maybe some portion of it will inspire you that you, too, can overcome hard things.

I went deeper, bringing my authentic self further out into the public eye. At the time, I was 38 years old and single. There were many reasons that were a part of my journey, but one of them was because of my internal struggles. I hated labels, so my purpose for sharing my struggles was not to put any label on myself, but to be transparent with my struggle. Because we all struggle, and I didn't want that person who is struggling to think they are alone, or that it will never get better, or that it will not ever become clear.

I took the plunge, and for the first time shared publicly on social media about my struggle with same-sex attraction. What was my label? My label was that I had battled it out with my God, and that journey was one of the most beautiful journeys I had been on. But I had kept a mask on through that journey, and with my first book, it came off.

I knew there were people out there who were hurting, feeling alone, and I cared more about them than I did about what anyone might think of me. I knew who I was. Falling more in love with my Creator was the only reason I got to where I'm at today—a place of

Finding His Timing

peace. A place I never though I would ever get to.

If you're struggling, I get it. If you don't know the answers, or you're confused or feeling trapped, I understand how you feel. Lay it at your Creator's feet. You don't have to know the answers. Let Him lead you. He will light the path!

A coach doesn't lead a team to a win without knowing His players. Your Coach (your heavenly Father) knows you, friend. He knows you better than you know yourself. Lay it at His feet. You will win; and you will get to a place of total peace. I wouldn't trade the peace I have now for anything, and I would never want to go back to where I used to be—feeling absolutely stuck, afraid I would be confused forever. There is nothing I want more than more of Him. Take your mask off before your Creator! Live fearlessly.

Jacqueline gifted me with an incredibly thoughtful gift at the start of the coaching refresher week. It perfectly matched her and her husband's entrance into my life, because His timing in bringing them to me had been perfect. I knew my Creator was up to something big; it was a t-shirt in celebration of who she saw in me, a "Beautiful Badass." That's right. Sexy Jen receives that! I felt so seen and celebrated for who I was. For who I was designed to be. I was also ready to go beat up all the "bad guys" and put on my Elektra costume...that I don't have. YouTube-ing how to spin two Sai's (three-pronged swords) simultaneously however was a must.

Later that same week, Jacqueline shared why she bought the shirt —and specifically a white one—saying she'd normally buy black but felt like it represented where I was at right then, coming into more light. I was finding my answers. I was finding my peace. I was finding more of Him.

Finding His Timing

As I was sitting in one session of the coaching training, I got a buzz on my phone, it was the verse of the day from the Bible app, and to my shock, it read, *"Therefore Yeshua spoke to them again, saying, "I am the LIGHT of the world. He who follows me shall by no means walk in darkness but posses the light of life."* (John 8:12) I immediately thought of my new white "Beautiful Baddass" shirt, and I sat there, stunned.

Over the next few days, I battled the desire to be even more authentic. It was as if my Creator were taking Thor's hammer, swinging it around and launching it right into that spot I needed to feel it, hear it, and use it to smash what needed to be smashed in my life, because He knew that's what I wanted to do more than anything. Be smashed. No, no, I mean, continue to be authentic with you!

Another friend, Trina reminded me of the context of John 8:12, and the story of the woman at the well. There was much opposition for that chapter of the Bible to even be in there when it was written. Biblical scholars questioned it's authenticity.

Think about how many people can relate to this woman's imperfect journey and all that she was carrying! How alone she felt, what happened in that space, and how Yahaveh spoke to her. He knew the moment in her journey when and where to engage with her. He didn't rush her to that moment; He knew when she was ready. What grace in love! How tragic it would be if this woman's story weren't in there. What an INJUSTICE that would be for all the people who have been able to relate to her and relate to their God because of her story!

It would be an INJUSTICE if we removed the unpleasant parts of our own stories or kept them hidden!

It would be an INJUSTICE to the people that need us as well as to ourselves!

Be bold, friend! Be fearless! Be you! Be that beautiful badass inside of you, and allow grace for yourself in the process. When you're ready to take another step toward more authenticity, I am ready to cheer you on! I believe in you! And I believe you can do hard things!

There are things that move us out of God's timing or strap us down, but what if we were designed to leap away from those things. Leaping from such things was part of the tribe of Dan's calling. In *A Time To Advance*, Chuck Pierce explains:

> *"Dan's territory was the place where Jeroboam set up one of the golden calves, leading Israel into idolatry. Part of Dan's redemptive call was to "leap" from idolatry, which he did not do."*

The tribe is associated with the 10th month, which is the month when these stories were unfolding. I had the chance to leap, too. I had not only leapt from labels of my former identity, but I had leapt from the fear of what others would think of me. Looking back, I truly believe the light from the invisible map was setting things in order for what He was about to do next.

A friend who was reading my first book messaged me, *"JEN! Did you see what number is stamped on the bottom of chapter 8 in your first book?!"* We both were stunned. It was page 111. What's the significance of 111 you ask? Well, as I had been diving deeper into His timing and His order of things, I had also been reading the book, *"Numbers That Preach,"* by Troy Brewer, which said:

> *"It's all about the awareness of the presence of God. It's like*

He's saying 'I'm here with you, and I'm going to bless you'. He is speaking about deep revelation going on in the ordinary parts of your life. The number 111 is all about that, an indicator that God's presence is here if you're willing to humble yourself and seek after Him. That He wants to increase you and bless you in amazing ways!"

I was flabbergasted, as that's exactly what I start talking about in the beginning of that chapter; how I saw Him do incredible things in so many lives around me as I was hopping from gig to gig in the entertainment industry. But my book was published back in 2019!? I certainly didn't plan for that to be on page 111!

As I shared that story with another friend, she exclaimed, *"Jen! That's not all! It's also on chapter 8...which is the number of new beginnings!"* She asked me if I knew what Mark 1:11 said. I didn't. She shared that it's all about the Father declaring how He is well pleased with Yeshua, and that Yeshua is going to do great things. She said, if 111 is being brought to your attention, He's saying the same thing to you: that He is well pleased and is going to do great things in you and through you.

STOP! Are we for real right now? Can His timing be THIS specific!?

It was certainly getting trippy. What a message to receive right then! When life feels slow or we feel like we're in the in-between as we wait for what's next, it can be so easy to get down or defeated. It was a great reminder, just when I needed it, from a great Creator. I felt Him showing me quite vividly that He was going before me and how He had been behind me in my first book—more than I ever realized.

Finding His Timing

He goes before you too, friend. There's so much going on that we don't see. I had no idea the significance of how the numbers 8 and 111 were aligned when I wrote my first book back in 2019, but now I could clearly see He was working on it, down to that very detail. He is in the middle of your life too, friend—working on the details.

This journey became a hunt for the details, noticing those lights as they popped up along the path, leading the way forward toward the grandeur map, a plan all laid out before me, before time.

If I could go back to that day, I would say:

"Keep leaping! You were designed to do it! To rise! He's aligning you for it as you align to Him and to your design! He is so proud of you!

Be bold. Be fearless. Be you! He will protect you. He will renew! He is doing great things inside of you! Let it permeate within you, and let it spill forth around you! It will continue rippling beyond you and ahead of you.

As the rock sends ripples over the waters, embrace His spirit, embrace His flow, embrace His design, and watch where it will go!"

Finding His Timing

Finding His Timing

CHAPTER 11

Embrace the torch of true identity alongside Esther

As we rolled into the eleventh month of the Hebrew calendar, Shevat, that year, Psalm 1 was brought to the forefront:

"Blessed is the man who shall not walk in the counsel of the wrong, and shall not stand in the path of sinners, and shall not sit in the seat of scoffers, but his delight is in the Torah of Yahaveh, and he meditates in His Torah day and night. And he shall be as a tree planted by the rivers of waters, that yields its fruit in its season, and whose leaf does not wither and whatever he does prospers."

As I reflected on those words and those "trees" in my own field (and who was planted there), I saw trees bearing good fruit and trees bearing bad fruit. The day Yeshua (Jesus) met the woman at the well in Samaria (John 4) was in the month of Shevat. That was the day the roots of her spirit connected to the water of life...and yours can, too.

That month, as I paid attention to my own mindset, it was as if my Creator had perfectly timed this month to equip me with everything I needed to continue to overcome. January had always been hard for me because it came right after the emotional highs and lows of the holiday season, my work typically dried up, film production dropped, and people took several weeks off. I was running out of money, as I often did in January, but I felt equipped with the skills and knowledge I needed to handle when I got frustrated or discouraged. I spoke out loud that my help was on the way! I declared truth, often when I didn't see it or know where or when it would be coming.

All month, I made my declarations and battled my thoughts. What's funny is that there was an area where I didn't ask for help or declare that help was coming in, but help came anyway! Be careful what you wish for. Two friends showed up at my house unexpectedly and hijacked my entire day—in a good way. They made me feel like a queen as they ransacked my closet, pulling out all kinds of outfits, and did a full-on photo-shoot with me in the outfits they chose. They helped me bring out more of my femininity and get me back to the roots of who I was (the woman I was designed to be). They helped me to see it and celebrate it. All I had to do was look down.

Here's something crazy to think about: Shevat is the month where the focus is on declaring your help is on the way. But it's also a time for you to look at who is bringing buckets of water to help quench the drought in your fields, to help awaken the roots to new life?! To produce new life? He made it so obvious. He was awakening me, to the femininity He created in me.

Around that same time as I was embracing this new identity, I jumped into a fashion and beauty challenge with a fierce and bold friend, Linda. I joined her amazing online group of women from around the world, where she challenged us all to show up boldly for life. Valentine's Day came and I shared that a lot was hitting my spirit.

I decided to get dressed up all fancy, even though I had nowhere to go that day other than my own mirror. Why? Well, because it was Valentine's Day and I could feel something new and exciting brewing inside me. I declared, "*I LOVE MY HEART! And I love the overcoming journey it has been on. I love the whole thing–all of it.*" Tears filled my eyes as I said it. I was 38 years old, never married, on a journey that, until recently had been filled with confusion, fear, regret, and shame.

I honestly thought I would always be stuck there. My heart was in such a place of confusion. I cared so much for other people that I didn't want to cause anyone pain, so I stayed single. I associated marriage and deep, committed relationships with potential hurt. I just knew, if anyone could ruin a good relationship and break someone's heart, it would be me.

I used to be so disappointed in myself for the road I had let myself go on, but as I shouted, "*I LOVE MY JOURNEY and I LOVE MY HEART!*" it felt so different.

In February, I caught up with a friend I hadn't seen in many years; only occasional Facebook messages. Not only had her husband left her and her children, but he did because he was gay. My heart wanted to weep for her, not because he was gay, but simply for the pain the whole family was enduring because his choices had broken up their family. That could have been me. I could have been the one that hurt so many hearts, because I struggled for so long with same-sex attraction.

If that is you, friend, if you've been a part of breaking up a family for any reason, the same God who has forgiven me for all the things I've done that caused me regret and shame, has already forgiven you!

In that moment, for the first time ever, I looked to the sky and said, *"Thank you! Thank you my journey has been what it IS! Thank you for every part!! And thank you for walking with me in every season. Thank you for never leaving or forsaking me!"*

No two journeys are the same; my journey is not yours, (that would be highly odd: Hey, other me!). But I do hope that you hear hope in my story. I want you to experience freedom in the hope that if you do carry anything like I did, I believe you can get to a place of peace and freedom.

That Valentines' Day, I shared with my online group that for the first time ever my heart was ready for marriage.

Whoah! Calm down, Jen! Don't get all crazy! My heart was just finally ready to be open and honest about everything that I had been through. It was no longer in a place of confusion and shame and I was finally starting to feel alive in who I really am. But now, I couldn't wait to give that gift to my future spouse. I had figured out who I was and who I was ready for. Please, let it be Superman...or Batman...OK, fine. I'll settle for James Bond. He doesn't have to be in costume. At least, not all the time.

One important part of Linda's 28-day challenge was to declare love over different parts of ourselves. What started as an *"I love my body"* challenge became, for me, a month of declaring love and acceptance over who God designed me to be.

He knows what we need to heal. That month, He brought more healing by speaking love over His design.

All this happened during Linda's challenge, which occurred in the twelfth month of the Hebrew calendar, Adar, a month where your true identity should be reflected, a month to remove the mask and enter joy. This month aligns with the Biblical story of Esther.

Clearly, I had taken a mask off and was letting my true identity be seen. I was finding joys in the most epic ways, but perhaps what was most epic was seeing the appearance of yet another light flickering on along that parallel path. Could our lives be this directly in alignment with His timing that all the stories in the Bible suddenly correspond with our own? It sure seems that way. Could I be superhuman? No, but He is! I'm pretty sure a superhuman wouldn't hit so many curbs. Unless I'm Curb-Woman.

It wasn't just my new physical identity that was coming forth. on the second day of this new month, I had a call with a friend, Chris, that was supposed to be about his need for a logo design, but ended up being about words he had for me and my spiritual identity.

Without hesitation, he spoke about how he saw me on stages: *"You are a torchbearer. There is one who will take this message and be in front of people, and that is YOU. You will be in front of people. It's the one to many; multiplying what you've been taught. I believe your artistic ability to create in the natural will be used to create in the place which is unseen in the hearts of those you run with. You will have the divine insight to remove the rot, the things that are actually opposing the heart of the Father. Your place of overcoming is going to be the authority you have to help do it with others."* He went on for another thirty minutes, and spoke a blessing over me.

A torchbearer. Such an interesting word since I envisioned this entire journey from confusion to clarity as walking into the light, but also a flame leading the way. I knew my Creator was making sure I heard who I was, but He also wanted me to know that He was with me where I was, He was walking alongside me, but He was also waiting for me on the other side of the challenges I was about to face.

There is a scene in the Biblical story of Esther where she takes off a metaphorical mask, revealing her true identity before the King. When she did, her enemy, Haman, and his sinister plan were revealed, as well. He was working in secret (behind a mask) to annihilate Esther's people (the Jews) but his wicked scheme was exposed. When you remove a mask you've been hiding behind, you can end destructive patterns and enter into the true joy of who you really are. A mask always hides destruction and stops joy. It was time to get into celebration mode and end particular seasons of my life, just like Esther.

It's so crazy that all this coincided with Linda's womens' group challenge. The month started with declaring love over ourselves as we got dressed up everyday, and became a month of declaring love and acceptance over the gender He designed me to be. I saw more of my real self—a feminine self—come out in each picture I posted. I saw a woman! As the month rolled on, I shared raw truth, stories of my journey, and stories from inside that group. I took more of the mask off. In doing so, I entered joy.

After carrying so much regret, shame, and confusion for so long, it was so refreshing to leave those weights behind. But as the month went along and I looked at the photos of myself I had posted, I didn't just see greater freedom, I saw a whole new face transforming right before me. She was coming out—His design for me was moving to the surface, and it was beautiful. I couldn't believe I could actually see it!

But I had several masks to remove, and the last one was the most terrifying to remove. Counselor Bill, and his wife, Jacqueline, had become like second parents to me. In Adar, I spent some time with them in their home in Pennsylvania. I was carrying a cloak of heaviness that I knew my Creator wanted to exchange for a garment of praise, but it was only going to happen if I had the courage to let the light in. I had to expose what was in darkness inside me.

One courageous morning, while taking a walk with Jacqueline, there was a giant tree branch laying across the sidewalk. I shouted, *"Don't trip over that branch!"* but she did. She tripped right over it two seconds later, and I chuckled. It's not like I can't relate. Once, a friend told me to be careful backing up my car, so I wouldn't hit her car, which was parked right behind me. A second later, I backed right into it.

As we walked, I released things I had been afraid to expose to anyone—the things I had actually done with the female in that relationship I ended. As we returned back to the spot where the giant branch had been, it was gone! The obstacle was gone and our path was clear. *"WOW,"* I thought. *"What a visual for what just happened inside me! He wanted to make sure I remembered that secret had been tripping me up and when I released it to a friend, it was removed, and could no longer trip me up."*

I allowed light to penetrate that darkness on that visit, and so many broken areas of my heart made giant leaps toward healing, simply because there was a safe space for me to talk about them. Chains came off my soul and I was set free from things that entangled me. Ecclesiastes 3:11 came rushing back to my mind: *"He has made everything beautiful in ITS time."* I couldn't have missed it, it had been staring at me on the coffee mug on their kitchen counter.

Could it be that simple? In His perfect timing, if we simply let the light into whatever darkness we might be carrying, we become free? It sure seemed so. These lights flickering on along my path were for freedom—my freedom! These lights are for you and your freedom, too! I think I need more of them.

They were getting stronger and brighter around me. Things that had seemed like accidents were now revealing intentionality and planning, even in the smallest of details. One night, I did a Mikvah in my bathtub and completed all seven steps. As I was praying to my Creator I started a second set and didn't realize it until the third dip. I Mikvah'd twice in the second month of Adar, the only month in the Hebrew calendar that has two months of itself. The only month with two moons in its cycle. Could my body innately know what it's designed to align to without my cognitive awareness of it?

The question piqued my curiosity. Just like the story of Esther we had exposed and removed an enemy and his plan, and we had overturned oppression. I had been very susceptible to manipulation through my emotions, especially because of my not wanting to treat people poorly. I could be loyal to a fault, and to my own detriment.

I was struggling with feelings about being a bad friend, like I was abandoning a former friend (the female) because I needed to set strict boundaries with her. At times, my emotions almost gave in to her pleas for help right when I was about to call or contact her after being totally silent. One friend messaged me to ask how it was going and we talked for over an hour. I knew my Creator had intervened. Then my roommate messaged me asking to go on bike ride (2nd intervention). I knew I had my answer: it wasn't time to contact her and He made sure I didn't.

They both expressed how I was being set apart from this person. I saw the Haman in my life trying to oppress my emotions, trying to take me out—the incessant text messages that blew up my phone in the middle of the night (500 of them in one night at the worst of it), the verbal abuse, blatant hate, and daggers from the enemy were so easy to identify.

Being Biblically set apart is for a purpose, and I knew any lie that I was being a bad friend was being negated with His truth of what He was up to. He was setting me up for the next season. It was time to celebrate the end of this season of my life, which included my overwhelming sense of loyalty.

No more interruptions from the enemy. I wasn't going to fall for his diversionary tactics anymore. I was convicted to stay in alignment with my Creator and keep moving forward into the next season He had for me, to move through my circumstances and into His blessing.

If I could go back to that day, I would say:

"You've got it! Keep your eyes on Him! He is protecting you. He is leading you! Keep moving forward!

You are not a bad friend! You are loyal, giving, and full of acceptance and love! Don't let lies seep in. Take every thought captive and align it with truth—who He says you are and Who He is! Align with Him and His design! He is equipping you. Not only for now, but for what's to come!"

Finding His Timing

CHAPTER 12

Marked from birth for the journey

As new lights appeared along my path, it felt as if I was being given a pile of keys to open every door I encountered. It was up to me to grab hold of them and unlock the right doors. That was a totally different approach to scripture than I had experienced most of my life.

Growing up in church, I heard some verses over and over again, but never quite understood them. I often felt like there was more to be mined from them, but didn't know how. My understanding has gone to a whole new level, thanks to my mentor and diving into so many Hebrew things. During my visits to Israel, so many passages that had confused me before made so much more sense as I saw the context right in front of me. What if it were all meant to be that way? What if we've been invited into an experience with the Father where He shows us exactly what He wants us to see? What would happen if we stopped asking, *"how does this verse apply to my life today?"* ...and instead asked, *"What did He want to show us about this verse back then?!"*

What do I mean? Well, here's one example:

A friend texted me a photo of a gate in Jerusalem called, *"The eye of the needle."* Yeshua (Jesus) talks about it in Matthew 19:24: *"And again I say to you, it is easier for a camel to go through the eye of the needle than for a rich man to enter into the reign of the Elohim!"*

I had heard that verse quoted umpteen times growing up, but it was always one of those verses that drifted aimlessly around in my brain, but didn't connect to anything...until I saw the photo! What once felt so mysterious and hard to grasp became so clear! As if I was being invited INTO the photo itself, to understand it personally. The many times I heard it my brain would break: *"Huh?!? A camel can't go through an eye of a needle. That doesn't make sense."* Why even use such an analogy? It's so odd. Why that animal? Why a needle? When is a needle ever used to describe an entrance to anything?! So many questions. This must be Sci-Fi, Sci-Fi doesn't have to makes sense.

"WAIT! The eye of the needle is an actual place?!" I was flabbergasted.

In Yeshua's time, the "eye of the needle" was where a camel got into gated cities at night after the main gates were locked. In order for the camel to go through the gate, it had to take everything off and kneel down. It's so small you couldn't get a full grown camel through it with all your luggage and parcels! But if the camel knelt down and released what it was carrying, it could get through.

Finding His Timing

As I stared at the photo, I felt a wave of understanding wash over me: *"That's the position of surrender!"*

The body position of surrender is on your knees in total humility! The load you are carrying falls off!

I realized that the biggest shifts in my own journey—the long-awaited changes that brought peace and opened doors for me—every single time, came right after I surrendered something I was battling to my Creator:

When I surrendered my fears of what others would think of me.

When I surrendered my mistakes from the past.

When I surrendered the need to have it all figured out.

When I surrendered my limiting beliefs about how to do it!

When I surrendered the things I treasured most!

When I surrendered my desires for what I thought I wanted.

When I surrendered whatever I was currently carrying!

When I surrendered myself, and realized it had nothing to do with me at all, I just wanted more of Him.

It's all about surrender. Not a camel. Not a needle. But the disposition of my heart! It's not an easy place to get to, but when we arrive, every single time we do it, we enter into the next space and place He has for us! But surrendering your load is the key. That's the only way to get to where you truly want to be. Are you willing to let it all fall off?

I wasn't the only one enjoying this breakthrough. One of my coaching clients was experiencing lies about her own identity being broken off. Lies that she was alone and isolated, that no one cared whether she stayed or disappeared. I knew I was put here to help silence that lie in every instance I could.

The more I stepped into this new identity as a coach, the more urgently I sensed the importance of working on myself. Old beliefs and lies kept popping up to test whether I really believed in the changes and growth I had experienced, but my Creator perfectly walked me right through each test to freedom.

Then came the test I wasn't ready for. I couldn't study, I couldn't cram. I didn't see it coming at all, even though I had heard about it my whole life.

I went speed dating when I was 24, and they didn't put an age limit on it. What would you do when one of the men sitting across from you has zero teeth?! You might stare. You might enter shock. At least, that's what I did. I mean, it wasn't like I could have offered him some of mine. Please don't smile, I'm scared now.

But the worst part was when the host almost didn't let me in because she thought I was 13! She had to verify my age by asking my friend. I was out of college!! Ughhhh. I NEVER LOOKED MY AGE!

At another First Steps to Success seminar, I had to confront another false belief that had hindered me my whole life. After five years of consistently plugging into personal development events, you'd think the growth, learning, or breakthroughs would have stopped, but they didn't. At this conference, we got the added bonus experience of getting to do a service day with Kings Ransom Foundation. While sitting with two friends afterward, it occurred to me why I had always struggled with words like "pretty" or "cute."

I shared how, my whole life I never felt like I had a voice. Not just because I was so deathly shy, but because I also had been viewed as this tiny little girl for so long. I always looked younger than I actually was. People who guessed my age were usually wrong, sometimes by decades. Sure, it's great when you're at a theme park and you can win a prize at a game you're too old to play, but not when you want to be taken seriously, or to be seen as someone worth listening to. Add on being someone who was slow to speak (if I spoke at all) and you can see why I felt unseen. Who would want to wait that long for someone to formulate their thoughts and finally build up the courage to utter even a sound. I felt stuck in that place for so long. It wasn't until I was established in my career that I even started to find my voice and the confidence to use it.

Words like "pretty" and "cute" were leftovers from my childhood, when I felt invisible. Tragedy struck my life, and part of me died. The invisible girl stayed unseen, right up to the present. But wait, Jen, what was the breakthrough? I'm getting there. Hold your horses. Yours, not mine. I don't have any. I hate horses.

Recently, an incredible human named Diane messaged me out of the blue, saying, *"Jen! Have you ever had anyone tell you to look up your Hebrew birthday?"* I hadn't even thought to look, even through I had been leading a group of people through studying the Hebrew calendar. She said she sensed that the Creator was telling her to tell me to look it up, so I did. I looked up all the passages that were tied to

Finding His Timing

that day in Biblical history.

Verse after verse talked about HIS VOICE! I had chills everywhere. Aye, Captain! Me whole body! On the very day I was born he marked me and my identity with "HIS VOICE!" For so long I had believed I had no voice, so He made sure His voice was the key to my first book. I titled my first book *Finding His Voice* without knowing the significance of His voice in my birth. Yes, I cried. I felt so seen by my Creator! I was blown away!

No wonder He brought those memories back to mind while I was chatting with friends: He was inviting me to break through that belief next. He was inviting me to break through feeling and believing the lie that I was just a "little girl" my whole life!

Full-grown circus elephant are massive. Circus workers train them as babies by chaining them to a spike in the ground. The baby learns that it isn't strong enough to break free from the chain and the spike. That mindset continues through the elephant's life, even into adulthood. As a result, this massive elephant that could easily pull the spike out of the ground doesn't, because the mindset it learned as a child tells it it can't.

My wrong belief was my chain! During one exercise, I was challenged to ask myself, what needed to change in me. I sensed that I needed to step out in faith in something someone had told me to do several months prior, and stop believing that I'm just that "little girl" who doesn't have a voice! It was time to embrace that His voice is inside of me...and He wants to speak!

One of the most impactful moments of the event was possibly the easiest to skate past: I knew I needed to dig down into my heart and find and forgive anyone who had been in those moments where I had chosen to feel like I didn't have a voice. But who did I most need to forgive? ME. I had chosen to believe a lie about myself and let it hold me back, I had to forgive myself for that.

I whispered, "*I forgive you, Jen, for believing you didn't have a voice. I chose to feel invisible, not seen, and that I was just a little girl. I chose to believe it. I release you, Jen. You owe yourself nothing; I bless you with a VOICE—His voice that will reverberate through you to those who feel like they don't have one!*"

In that moment, this baby elephant felt released to step out into a brand new future! What future is that? In that moment of breakthrough, I birthed a new vision for the kind of coaching I do today: I help people identify what's keeping them stuck, break free from it's influence, discover who they truly are, and what they really want to do, and then package what it looks like! The truth is, my life today shocks me;

...I shouldn't have escaped confusion.

...I shouldn't have escaped feeling like I don't have a dad.

...I shouldn't have escaped a mediocre life.

...I shouldn't have escaped being that little girl that didn't have a voice.

But guess what, my friend, your past does not dictate your future, just like mine didn't. Let's go, Dumbos. We've got a whole new world outside just ready for us to fly into! Use those big ears to receive these words and go! Wait! Use your real name in that sentence, not

"Dumbo." That's dumb. We're leaving those old identities behind.

Business coach Carmen O'Quinn once said, "*Yahaveh (God) has designed you with ALL you need, to do whatever your DESIRE is. Ever felt like you lack something? Friend, you were designed with everything you need to succeed. It starts with you believing it, even if you are the underdog. How dare you doubt it? The desire was put in you for such a time as this…your destiny is to succeed! Your desire reveals your destiny! If you're not doing something you're afraid of, you haven't stepped out in faith in a little while! What have you traded it for? It's still in there!*"

Are you ready to break free?

Who are you? What is your identity? The Creator met me with my identity hidden in my birth-date, and He revealed it to me with perfect timing. He will meet you, too, in His perfect timing, with secret treasures He has hidden in your identity. He is just waiting for you to come looking for Him.

If I could go back to that day, I would say:

"Yes, Jen!! That is how special you are—how special we all are—to your Creator! He gave you unique identity on the very day you were born!

You are His creation! You are highly valuable! Continue the hunt! There is so much more He wants to show you! So much more for you to discover and it's not just for you; it's for all those you care about! It's for redemption! It's for the Kingdom! Fly, baby, fly! You were designed to be free!"

Finding His Timing

Finding His Timing

CHAPTER 13

A light that leads others out— transition with the Israelites in the wilderness

It became obvious that, the more I surrendered and walked in even greater authenticity, the brighter the lights of this invisible map became.

On a visit to my hometown of Grand Rapids, Michigan, I went to dinner with my friend, Laura. She mentioned the verse John 15:13 which says, *"No greater love than this, that one should lay down his life for his friends."*

She said, *"we often tend to think that verse is about someone actually dying. But what if it's more about someone laying down what others think of them? Like their actual reputation? Laying down what everyone in their lives even strangers might think of them. For the sole purpose of helping other people? That's what YOU do, by being so vulnerable, by sharing all the stuff that's been so hard to share...you really love people.*" Tears flowed as that verse hit me in a whole new light.

A few weeks later, we celebrated Memorial Day, remembering so many who gave their lives in combat. I shared that passage on social media, but this conversation was in the background of that post, infusing the quote with more depth and meaning.

So many people lost their spouse, their father, their mother, their son or daughter. What a disservice it would have been to them all if we stayed stuck in fear, afraid to give up our fear of what someone else might think of us in order to help our fellow man!

Our military veterans were willing to sacrifice their lives for our country and our freedom. What about you and me? What are we willing to sacrifice in kindness for those around us? A cup of sugar? I think we're capable of more than what we've settled for.

You have overcome so much in your journey! What if it's those places of vulnerability, in sharing the hard stories of what we've been through and how we got through it, that could actually help our fellow man where they need it most?

I took a crazy spontaneous trip to Pensacola, Florida with my friend April. It was crazy because we actually didn't know why we were going. Both April and I had just been studying the Hebrew calendar and felt like our Creator was telling us to go. We had no idea what we'd be doing, we just went!

Wait, what?!

What makes it even crazier is that it was the Hebrew month called Iyyar. Nissan, the month before, was when the Israelites were leaving captivity in Egypt. Iyyar was the month was when they arrived at Mt. Sinai. So Iyyar was the transition of the journey. As Chuck Pierce says in the book, *A Time to Advance*:

> "The Israelites were transitioning to a new place in their relationship with the Father because they didn't know much about God other than the stories passed down from generations. They had lived as slaves in Egypt and knew about the Egyptian gods but they didn't know much about the One who had rescued them from captivity. In the wilderness, in transition, they learned His nature through the life and death realities of the wilderness."

In the wilderness, they learned that He is our healer, our provider, and our banner of victory!

One night during our visit to Pensacola, I told April, *"I wish I had training in how to do more spiritual things"* but the more I thought about it, it occurred to me, *"maybe this is exactly why I hadn't; it's something you have to experience with Him! He wants to develop that relationship—more specifically, that journey—with us! He doesn't want someone else taking you on that journey; He wants to lead you in it Himself!"*

During that trip to Pensacola, He showed us, step by step, what to do. Then we did it!

I had never in my life anointed anything while praying over it or circled a building seven times while praying over it. I had never anointed four corners of a church or put my hand on someone's forehead as people were praying over them. Giant No. My internal dialog screamed, *"Whoah!! What am I doing?! Lol! I don't know, but He distinctly told me to do it! OMG, my hand is on his head!"*

It was such an honor to be lead to do that alongside the pastor and our friends, who are members of that church. We all did it together!

Whatever He puts in your heart to do, you don't have to have any of it figured out. He's just asking you to trust Him, to ask Him to show you! That's the beauty of it all: you're better together, you and Him! That's where it all starts. What if that is how we get to that place of being able to be vulnerable and share the things that are so hard to share? What if He is wanting us to simply ask Him, so He can show us how? Meaningful connection with the people in your life comes through true, brave authenticity with the Father first!

At the start of this trip to Pensacola I prayed, *"We're here because you showed us to come here, so what do you want us to see? Show us what you want us to do!"* And look what happened! I laid my hands on a man's head in prayer, and many other things.

There's no doubt in my mind that I could not have been as vulnerable and authentic as I have been these last five years had it not been for finding this personal development company. Every single conference, I find that much more healing and breakthrough that accelerates all the things I know I was put on this earth to do.

I was so excited to head back to the next First Steps to Success conference, because that's how we help each other. We're better together; our heroes knew that. They gave their lives so that we could enjoy freedom. Let's honor our heroes, and fight for freedom for each other! Freedom from things that would oppress us on every level, spiritually, emotionally, and relationally! Freedom for me and you! It's time to honor those who died by meeting your neighbors needs with the very thing the Father has equipped you with! I believe in you!

Life was sure lighting up. I was sure lighting up. I was my own little lightening bug. In fact, in my neon coral wetsuit you could have mistaken me for one. Thank goodness I wasn't actually that bug, or I would be lit in the wrong places and they'd be looking at the wrong things.

I was on the Gulf Coast, walking along the shoreline in that neon wetsuit as I looked at the most colorful and translucent creature upon the shore *"What is this?!"* I gasped. I thought it was a jellyfish. First mistake. I should not be identifying sea creatures. It looked magical. It just seemed to draw me in. I couldn't stop looking at it. I took several pictures, as I noticed how the light caught it at different angles but was completely oblivious to all it's dangers.

It was my first in-person experience with a deadly Portuguese Man of War. The real sea creature, not the figurative one I wrote about earlier.

After surfing on the beach I had felt the nudge to just plop down in the shallows and take in the ocean waves and the scenery. A young mom had the same reaction when she saw me sitting in the shallows in my bright neon coral wetsuit. Thankfully, she just said, *"I love your wetsuit!"* not, *"What is this?!"* I know I look odd.

This young mom had been combing the sand nearby, looking for seashells for her son. After a brief chat in the shallow waves, we exchanged goodbyes and she turned to continue her search further down the beach.

I suddenly remembered the "jellyfish" and yelled back to her, "Hey! There's a cool-looking jellyfish back there your son might like!" She went to check it out and then ran to grab her family so they could admire it. They all stared at it with the same wide, curious eyes.

I returned to my solitary thoughts, quietly considering each wave. After a few minutes, she returned, this time with her young son. She asked, *"Is it okay if we keep talking to you?"* *"Absolutely,"* I beamed.

We chatted for a good while as the waves crashed over us all. Suddenly, she asked me *"What are you doing tonight? Want to go out with my husband and I?"*

"Actually, I'm here with my roommate," I chuckled, *"but I bet we'd love to!"*

As we exchanged numbers, she hesitated, as if she felt she needed to explain: *"I don't normally do this by the way,"* she said. *"I never go out with strangers and definitely not ones I just met on the beach that very day. But I don't know how to explain it, I just feel drawn to you."*

That night, the four of us met up for the most enjoyable dinner conversation. We closed the place down. We couldn't stop chatting. It was kismet.

A week later, she texted me, *"Jen! I'm almost done with your book! I just read 8 hours straight!"* Not only had she ordered my book, she had finished it and was already following me on YouTube, encouraging me every time she communicated.

I don't know what you believe about what you see on social media

Finding His Timing

—or anywhere else, for that matter—but, maybe, you know how easy it can be to feel discouraged when you're hoping to make an impact within it. I was going through a discouraging time.

If you've ever poured your heart into a passion project, working endless hours to create something for the world, something you believe in that won't release your soul, that keeps you up at night, I see you. I know how it can feel at times like you're in the baby stage of growing it, feeling so much passion, and it's barely moving forward. If you're an online content creator, you watch the likes, shares, and subscribers religiously for some kind of validation, and it doesn't seem to come. For a long time, I sat at 200 subscribers on my YouTube channel.

I would get discouraged so easily. That might sound silly, but when it's the one thing you are working so hard on because you just want to help people and connecting them to resources, thoughts enter your head: *"What is it going to take to get this thing to move?! There is so much here that could help so many desperate people. This is taking forever! It's moving like a snail."*

Your God sees you, too, friend. In fact, He sees you so much, I think this next part is for you just as much as it was for me.

I was spending my Friday night editing an incredible interview, and tears were filling my eyes as my friend, Jacqueline shared her story of what God had done in her life. She had such a heart to see others be set free of the same things she had been through. As I listened to her story, a thought washed over me: it doesn't matter if The Overcomers Movement went big. What mattered was "the one." What mattered was that individuals were experiencing breakthrough, and we got to be a part of it.

I didn't need to reach masses of people; I just needed to reach one—the one who feels stuck and alone in silence, who needs to feel seen and heard in a safe space, who is desperate to be set free from the burden she's carrying. I was gripped, watching my own interview with Jacqueline.

Talking later that night with Jacqueline she reminded me of a shepherd who leaves his flock of ninety-nine sheep to go after the one who had wandered off and was probably feeling super lonely, afraid, hurting, and maybe even injured.

She said it to me then, and I'm saying it to you now: *"You are making an impact. It only takes one person to start a revolution. The enemy wants you to feel insignificant, but he's a freaking liar! Don't let him take one more moment of your life from you—you have mighty work to do."*

Would you leave the crowds to go after the one? I would. I see that hurting heart in the corner of the room and that image grips me. It's why we do every single thing that we're doing at The Overcomers: to go after that one. That's His heart!

Friend, don't let anyone else's success make you feel insignificant! If you are helping just one, you have the heart of the Father!

You know deep inside what you were designed to do, and why. I believe in you. If you are being courageous with what you believe in, do it for the one. In time, you will be connected to the exact people who need your message. Be real. There's no way they won't find you. It might not be in the way you're expecting. It could be a woman walking down the beach when you're in a bright orange wetsuit, staring into the waves, looking like the odd one, and thinking that a

Finding His Timing

Portuguese Man of War is just a cute little jellyfish.

Be open to how He chooses to show His light through you. The right ones will be drawn to you–the ones who need your light.

If I could go back to that day, I would say:

"Yes!! Keep following those lights. Keep being that light. The more you connect with Him, the brighter it will become— the brighter you will become! They need you! They need Him through you.

It's that light that will lead others to the same map! His design from the very beginning meant for them to find! It's all in His time!

Do it for the one! He's only just begun!"

CHAPTER 14

Focus forward—on the coming victories

Some victories were more emotional than others. My precious mom was flying down from Michigan to spend some time with me in Texas, when she texted me a photo. In the photo was a perfectly-timed devotional, printed and sitting on top of her luggage, which said, *"God has not given us a spirit of fear, but of power and of love and of sound mind."*

Victories like this made me weep. And if you know my story with my mom, you'll know why. When you've been through horrible tragedy—especially the kind that can take decades, if not more, to heal—it can be so easy to look backwards and stay paralyzed in fear, not realizing that you are. The feelings are so real: the fears, the loss. You've already fought through so much, and trauma can cause you to build walls with the ones closest to you. People grow apart as their healing journeys stall or move in different directions. I'm very grateful that, even though mom and I had gone through very different journeys since dad died, we had maintained so close through the years. As a result, I was there to see her have a major breakthrough.

Mom used to hate to travel—it filled her with dread and panic—but my incredible mom chose to walk forward to take authority over her own spirit and speak peace to her mind as she prepared to travel. She knows, that on the other side of that decision is something she really wants—in this case, to be with me! I was so freaking proud of her, knowing the journey we have had and all that she has had to overcome to get here. She mastered her mindset and took authority over it!

Have you ever noticed themes or patterns in your days or weeks? During my mom's visit, I detected a theme of walking forward.

That week, I was on a call with another friend, diving in, exploring her vision for her business. As if on cue, the story of Lot in the Bible hit both of us. Lot and his family were fleeing the destruction of Sodom and when Lot's wife literally looked backwards to see what was happening, even though they had been warned not to look back at the death. She turned into a pillar of salt!

We're meant to walk forward and not even look backward. Looking backward doesn't bring life, it brings death. Walking forward in what you can't yet see takes faith, but brings life! Forward is life and backward is death. It sounds easy, but what happens when you look back at things that hurt you? What happens when you look back at things that you wrestle or struggle with? What happens when you remember how you felt, alone, heart-broken, abused, taken advantage of, abandoned...the list goes on!

Looking backward at those things keeps us STUCK!

Where is your mind focused?

Where are your thoughts focused?

Where are your words focused?

Walking forward takes focus and action, but is it worth it?

Let's be real, were we designed to walk backwards? Try it. Like me, you probably look ridiculous. Your body wasn't designed to do it well naturally. Unless you're Micheal Jackson. If you are, just beat it. I'm not talking to you.

Back to the story.

My incredible friend, Jacqueline messaged me out of the blue one day, *"He is not letting you stay in the old, Jen...He has so much more in store for Jen 2.0!"*

I replied, *"It's funny that you say that because I can just feel it. I can feel that I'm entering into an entirely new season and I can tell that my new season is so done with the old and the old me. There's no part of me left that has any desire to go back to the previous seasons. Which is a huge thing to be able to say. Because in any season prior I still had that desire. So it's cool to be at a place where you know all you want is what the next season holds. You don't want what use to be things that were a desire before. It's cool to feel it and be so ready for it, but for someone else to see it and say it, it's an extra dose of confidence that's where we're headed."*

Talk about an extra dose of confidence! When His Voice hits you, it's a done deal. I asked the Creator, *"How do I really know which voice is You?"* He answered, *"If you're ever confused if it IS Me...then it's not Me. I am not the author of confusion. You will know when it is Me, as you always have."*

In that moment, I knew it was Him. Done deal. He was confirming a passage I had read months before which had been pivotal to my confidence.

"For Elohim is not Elohim of disorder but of peace, as in all the assemblies of the set-apart ones." (1 Corinthians 14:33)

Around the time I had been hearing it, I felt it, and I was seeing it. I was browsing Instagram when I "happened" to see a new account set up by the stranger I had just recently met on the beach, the one who had been impacted by my book and everything that The Overcomers messaging is all about—finding the gold within us, and how He (the Father) not only heals the brokenness in our lives, but that He fills it with gold!

She was courageously posting a picture of herself everyday (something she had never felt comfortable doing) letting Him tell her how beautiful she is. As I scrolled through her photos and read her posts, I saw it: she was letting Him heal what she felt on the inside. She was receiving His words about what He saw in her: her identity and her beauty. That she's absolutely beautiful.

I was so moved. There are no adequate words when you get to see the Father helping a new friend heal, especially when you know your words and your passion were part of the healing process.

That's what is out there, waiting for you to walk forward, friend:

stories from the souls who cross your path, that take you behind the scenes to reveal what He is doing to impact them. Those are the stories that keep me choosing to walk forward.

Where do you want your life to go? Set your course and walk forward. Take authority over your mind and tell it where it's allowed to look and where you will allow yourself to focus.

Every morning, my mom chooses what she's going to believe, no matter what thoughts might try to get her attention. She tells me, *"Jen, I learned this from you!"*

(Let's grab the tissues, for all those who are teary-eyed like me. Just make sure they are 2-ply. We're not going to mention what happened when I used 1-ply tissues to dab my eyes as I listened to another friend, Brookelynn, pour out her story. Okay, maybe we are. I had tissues stuck to my eyes the whole time she told it. But hey, hearing people's stories of how they've overcome so much in their journey with their Creator always gets me.)

Never doubt the impact you are making by choosing to walk forward, friend. You never know when or how it might be helping even those you care for most!

He has not given you a spirit of fear, but of power and of love and of a sound mind! (2 Timothy 1:7)

He has so much more in store for you!

My roommate invited me to tag along on a short trip to Sedona, Arizona. As I stood in line to board my flight, an elderly couple caught my eye. Well, to be truthful, I caught their eyes. Have you seen what I looked like?

The gentleman reacted enthusiastically to my hair, which was spiky and magenta. I quickly learned that they were traveling to Sedona for a life-saving medical procedure. Before I could ask more, we were directed to board, which interrupted our sweet conversation. Just then, it hit my spirit that I wished I had a moment to pray for them, whatever their needs were. I shot up a quick prayer as I waited in line for my turn to board, *"Father, if I AM supposed to pray with them, make it obvious. Let there be a seat open next to them."*

As I made my way down the aisle, I spotted my two new elderly friends, and, sure enough, there it was...an open aisle seat right next to them. Not only that, they waved to me when they saw me coming. I stopped in front of them, *"would it be okay if I sat with you?"* They giddily replied, *"oh absolutely!"* Yay! My hair hadn't frightened them.

As I settled into my seat, we continued our conversation about the medical procedure they were anticipating. They didn't mind sharing details with a stranger with pink, spiky hair. He was a father of seven grown children and he had real concerns about the procedure. I leaned in gently and said, *"Well, let me be honest, the reason I wanted to sit next to you was because I hoped to be able to pray over you both as you head to do this, if that would be something you would be okay with?"* Their smiles said it all, with tears in their eyes.

As the plane took off, heads bowed in reverence, we went boldly before the throne of our Creator, the great Healer, who had obviously brought us together that day. I brought their requests before Him, and took the opportunity to declare who our God is!

The rest of the flight, we continued getting to know one another, and I learned about more dynamics in their family that needed prayer. It was such a powerful and beautiful time. I saw so much evidence of my Creator in that appointment. He kept my eyes focused forward on what He had for me; it was the thing I cared most for: people.

In Sedona, April and I made our way around the boutiques downtown. It wasn't long before it happened again, one boutique had a few garment racks out on the sidewalk, and as we browsed the owner struck up a conversation with us. Within minutes, she was spilling her heart out about her daughter and the weight of concern that was on this momma's heart. I asked her if it would be alright if we prayed for her and her daughter right then and there. Her face lit up and she eagerly agreed. So there we stood, outside a little boutique, praying over a total stranger. I laid my hand on her shoulder and brought her and her daughter before our Creator.

Victories were happening all over the place, as I continued walking forward. Not just for me, but for the Kingdom. I could see them happening in the spiritual realm, as divine appointments were popping up around me.

If I could go back to that day, I would say:

"He has so many more appointments for you! For others! To carry His light! Keep walking forward. Keep walking in faith. Focus forward! He goes before you! Pay attention to those nudges! I bless you with eyes to see, ears to hear, a heart that has compassion, and hands that know how to reach out and touch all those He puts before you! He has not given you a spirit of fear, but of power and of love and a sound mind! Be strong and courageous with all that He is walking you into. It is for you!!"

CHAPTER 15

Believe in the unseen and gifts from the other side

As we entered the fifth Hebrew month of that Biblical year, Av, the invisible map's lights continued to flicker on, each new glow a gift that brought healing as their warmth wrapped around me. It was as if they were designed to envelope me with their presence as they switched on.

According to Chuck Pierce in *A Time to Advance*, the fifth month, Av was "*intended to be the month Israel entered into the promised land. God's plan had been that every year, Av would be a month to celebrate His goodness. It was when the two spies came back with the report that 'He would give the land into our hands' and they were the voice of faith amidst unbelief.*"

After a year of virtual events, we were attending a First Steps to Success event in Pensacola, Florida. This event was not held in a hotel ballroom, but a church—the same church I had visited a few months prior. At one point the pastor directed us to say to the person next to us, *"He will do it again!"* I turned, not knowing who had just walked up to me. We locked eyes right as the words flew from our mouths. It was the new co-owner of that very personal development company, the very person I had gone and *"spied out the land with"* prior to us being there in Pensacola. He had made sure the two of us made eye contact right as we delivered that message to each other! We couldn't have orchestrated that moment, but I knew the Almighty had...with perfect precision.

The conference—in fact, that whole month of Av—stands out in my mind for another reason. I would've given anything to hear from my dad after he passed from suicide back in 2004. At this conference, I fully believed that happened.

WAIT. WHAAAAT?! Crazy, right? Even as I write about it, tears are about to burst out all over again. But first, I need to back up. I have to tell you some things that, until recently, I was not ready to talk about publicly. But with what happened at this conference, how could I not?

Remember Bill, the professional counselor (and total stranger) who pulled my book off a shelf and started reading it? CRAZY! Remember how he stepped into my life as kind of a father-figure along with his wife, Jacqueline, who became such a close friend and encourager? Their appearance in my life was such an important catalyst that allowed me to get free enough to get here.

They have been such incredible friends, and great listeners who have seen me cry the deepest of tears. They held space in the battles in my spirit as I worked through my crap and pursued authenticity, and they spoke so much life into me to continue the fight.

Finding His Timing

We were together again at this conference in Pensacola, and I spent the week after processing and celebrating with their family in Pennsylvania.

I experienced two major moments of healing: one required massive vulnerability, so I needed a safe space to get there. Jacqueline and I traveled to Jersey shore and found that safe space as we walked the beach together.

The first moment of healing came as we were working through wounds at the conference in Pensacola. The speaker instructed the audience to stand if they had been hurt by a woman. Then other women came and stood in front of each one standing, in proxy for the one who had hurt them. They asked for forgiveness on behalf of that person. As Mr. O'Quinn said, *"It's about making you right for what they did wrong."*

I stood and like a magnet, Diane, flew right in front of me. We had been friends for as long as I had been attending these events, and she had intimately known my journey.

How did she know? Because she, too, had been a safe space for me. She had been the very first person who I opened up to back in year one of these conferences, way before I even came close to being ready to write my first book revealing it all. Back in those first years, I had been going through so much intense, messy, and painful healing that after every event I sent emails to the company, thanking them and sharing what my God had done through their efforts.

She had watched it all. I knew she had prayed through it all. And she loved and accepted me as she continued to watch me painfully walk it all out.

Finding His Timing

As she stood in front of me for this exercise, she said, *"It was like a magnet, Yahaveh drew me right to you!"* She asked for forgiveness on behalf of any woman who had, *"abused me, touched me, and taken advantage of my heart that had opened up to them."* She saw right through me and said everything I needed to hear. As she spoke, I saw the faces I knew might never voice it. I sobbed as my friend looked me in the eyes, and I was set free. There was no hiding from the truth of her words.

That Sunday, the last day of the conference, something huge happened, which led me into the hardest part of this story but set in motion the second major healing. The speaker laid bare raw how he felt like a hypocrite and why. It was raw authenticity in front of everyone. He shared about his health battles with food. I wanted to weep. I saw in him the leader I knew was there—the one who was willing to 'go there,' those deep places where the real-life lessons and moments of true growth are found.

Watching him courageously share his journey as vulnerably as he did that day led me to my next breakthrough. Leaping into the unknown can be terrifying. Some battles require a profound sacrifice of self. It's like jumping right out of your own skin. Yuck!

But man! The more I let go of me, the more He put into my path more than my heart could have imagined.

After I released my first book in 2020, I went through a season where I felt like an absolute hypocrite, too. As you've already read, right after I wrote a book revealing my struggle with same-sex attraction, I fell right back into it. Ok, let's take the gloves off—you and I both know I didn't fall into it; I chose it. Surrendering was one of the hardest things I've ever done.

But why did I surrender? Because of all the things He had been showing me as I studied the Hebrew calendar. Not the answer you expected, right? It sounds crazy to me every time I share what happened, but it's true!

This is what can happen when you simply give Him the opportunity to show you more—not out of judgment or condemnation, but simply out of the love of a Father who wants more than anything to take a walk with you, to lead you by the hand, not going any faster than you're able.

I was tormented with the guilt and the shame for the choices I made in that season right after my first book released. The feelings completely overwhelmed me, as I expressed through sobs that *"I had disappointed the One I love more than anything in this life—Him!"*

But that same One whom I thought I had disappointed so deeply answered back through a friend's dream. She had no idea I was struggling to the depths that I was when she shared that she saw me and my future husband walking on the sand. One word was written in the sand: FORGIVEN.

I wept that day. I wept as I felt His love wash over me. He knew what I needed to hear and in one word delivered the message through someone who didn't even know I was struggling.

Sometimes the hardest person to forgive is yourself. We beat ourselves up day after day while the One who created us isn't doing that…He's whispering freedom through the voice of another.

Maybe you need to hear that you're FORGIVEN, in all capital letters.

Maybe you need to hear that when you take the leap to be authentic with your Creator (and with yourself), it's worth letting go of it all. It's worth leaving your skin behind.

What happens when you let go of it all? It's not as much of a bloody mess as you might expect. You've already read about several people He brought along my path as I continued to surrender.

But then, my dad arrived. Seriously. During the forgiveness exercise (yes, a lot happens to me everytime I go through it) more came out about my dad. I realized I still needed to forgive him for not being here.

In my journal, I wrote, "*I need to forgive you, Dad, for not being here. Not being here now to tell me how proud of me you are. To hug me and just hold me for a second. I chose to feel like there was always something missing, that I was waiting for a voice that I would never hear. I chose to feel like I wasn't worth staying for, to be able to tell that to. When I've had a Father ever since Who's taken my hand in every moment and told me not only how much He loved me but showed me that I was on the right track. That He WAS with me and He was enamored with me. I release you, dad, for not being here to tell me that, too.*"

What happened next still shocks me. I wrote all that in private, in silence, in my journal. No one could have known what I wrote down.

Next, they instructed us to stand if we had been hurt by a man. Several men stood in front of those standing, in proxy for the one who hurt them. They asked for forgiveness on behalf of that person.

A man approached me to stand in proxy for my dad. As he spoke,

Finding His Timing

a few tears fell, but then, as he hugged me he softly said in my ear, *"I'LL SEE YOU ON THE OTHER SIDE, Jen!"* The floodgates opened. I completely lost it. What did he just say?!

That voice wasn't this man in front of me. I knew that voice was my dad!

What a gift! A voice from the other side; a moment I'll never forget.

There had been many moments like this I'll never forget with so much healing.

Is it hard? Yes.

Is it messy? Oh my gosh, yes!

Is it painful? Unbelievably so!

But is it worth it? I would do it all again in a heartbeat, knowing what came on the other side of embracing and leaning into it all.

You are worth it, friend. Surrender it all, and watch Him surround you with those who will be champions for your success. Let Him envelope you with so much more, as you continue to walk toward your own freedom and those lights I've been telling you about. If you feel anxious about it, ask yourself...what if it is so much better than you think it will be?

As that conference ended, a large group of us decided to meet up at a local bar for dinner. We were seated around a large table, and I found myself next to another woman who had been in the community of those attending those same conferences for over a decade. We had not yet had the pleasure of really getting to know one another.

As the dinner progressed, it was not long before I realized how divine this gift was. She asked deep questions, like why I was so excited to be a coach, what my heart bled for, and how the weekend had just been for me. As I answered, I watched her eyes fill with tears. Everything I was sharing was hitting sensitive spots within her. She responded to my passion, cheering enthusiastically for me to step into being a voice in this arena, reaching the ones who struggle with their identity.

Within minutes, I was sobbing at the table, paying no attention to the crowd sitting around us. She placed her hand on my shoulder, saying, *"Jen, you HAVE to do this, there's people out there that need this message so badly—including one of my own—and I haven't known how to help him!"*

Listening to this mom's heart, weighted down with the cares of one she deeply loved, and seeing a glimmer of hope as I described my journey, I couldn't help myself. Here, this entire time, there was someone right in this community who was desperate for answers. Someone needed my help, and she was right in front of me.

Those lights along the path weren't just for my warmth and healing; they were designed to heal others, too. And I needed to help turn them on.

If I could go back to that day, I would say:

> *"Yes, Jen! Those lights are needed all around you. He is leading you to so much more. Not just for you, but for them! Let Him continue the work.*

Finding His Timing

These glimpses from the other side are only the beginning. There is so much more in store! Let Him envelope you! Let Him envelope them! The work is far from done! He is far from done!"

Finding His Timing

CHAPTER 16

Moses, Mt. Sinai and Pipeline Beach Oahu—a God who bee-lines to you

That next month, the lights from that map were so bright there was no chance I would miss them. It was the sixth month of the Hebrew calendar, Elul, the month in Biblical history where our Creator revealed Himself to Moses and the Hebrew people at Mt. Sinai. Could He possibly want to reveal Himself to me? To surprise me with powerful moments of His presence? Well, that's precisely what I believe happened.

But I can't start the stories from that month without taking you to Pipeline Beach, Oahu, one of the most famous surfing beaches in the world. People line up on the shore to watch the professionals catch a wave. What did I do? I biffed so hard just coming out of the water when I stopped tumbling feet over head, I had no idea if I was still connected to my board, if my hoo-ha was exposed to everyone as I re-gathered myself on the sand, or if anything was bleeding. Pretty certain I looked like a sea zombie.

As I stumbled onto the shore, the first man I walked by in the crowd had a concerned look on his face, *"Are you okay?"* He asked. I had zero clue. Zero clue if I was exposed, if I was bleeding anywhere, or what the heck just happened. But man, I wished I had taken more seriously the words of a surfer a guide; *"Whatever you do, don't ride a wave into the beach."*

Whoops. There are so many things in life we miss, like the time a friend yelled out to me from the AirBnB bathroom, *"Jen! Come look at this!"* Imagine my hesitation. I walked in and saw her face in total shock as she pointed to her vape that had just dropped in the toilet. She had just asked the Creator whether she needed to stop vaping, and to make His answer clear. Seemed pretty clear in that moment. Meanwhile, not noticing at all that her underwear was still at her knees.

What if there's something more we should be seeing? Something more that's right there in front of us? What do I mean? Back to Pipeline Beach. I was out in the waves when an older gentleman came up right beside me. We chatted between waves, and as each wave approached, he seemed more concerned with me catching one than him. He'd give instructions between each, subtle tweaks I could make, and even helped lift my board in the back at times to catch it, cheering me on with each one. He'd catch one, then paddle right back to me and we continued like this for what felt like several hours. He was so patient, kind, and humble, a gentle soul that I guessed was in his 70's.

As dusk set in, we shook hands and I paddled to shore. I didn't

Finding His Timing

learn until after I hit the sand (horrifically) and rejoined my friends that this man had entered the water earlier and bee-lined immediately over to me! My friends shared that it was such a bizarre sight, because he seemed to see me and know he wanted to come to me! Wow, I thought. Why was I so special?

Later, as we were packing the Jeep, a car pulled up behind ours... my new friend! The man who had bee-lined for me in the waves. We all stood in a circle continuing to chat with this sweet man, when we discovered that he was none other than Jock Sutherland, the infamous surfer well-known in the 1970's! Inside, my jaw dropped. Obviously not wanting to cause a scene.

This was who I had just spent the whole afternoon with in the waves?! This was who was guiding and teaching me? This was who had bee-lined for me? Unreal. What a gift! What blew me away the most was how kind and patient this older man had been all day!

But that's how our Creator is. He sees us and bee-lines to us and, like a good Father, wants instruct us, guide us, and even give us a lift to get going and ride that next wave that comes in life. He is quietly whispering words of belief into our souls that we can do it, that we are designed for this. Never rushing us, or even asking to be beside us, but patiently waiting for us to soak in His companionship. Does He have to? Surely not—He created the universe—Yet He does. We are that special to Him. He loves us with the gentle patience of a father. And that is where the story gets crazier.

I should have guessed this was going to be a spiritually powerful trip, especially when Jenn—the one who exclaimed, *"Jen, come look a this!"* from the toilet arrived.

On day one, she wept as I shared the updates to my journey and how I had been able to forgive myself. She needed to hear that.

Then, late one night, she was sharing about a healing event in her own journey. She asked her father what he really wanted to do and watched him cry as he shared the dreams and visions he had kept to himself for so long. His brother had committed suicide and the burden of that had hung on him for many years. She had given her father a safe space to be real with his pain, and release it. It may have been a life-or-death situation and she was able to lead him to life.

Tears came quickly as I thought of how angry I had been over the previous five years, that I couldn't give this freedom to my dad like she had given to hers. She and I had these conferences and this healing, but I couldn't go back and put this into my dad's hands.

She saw my tears and encouraged me to let them out. The floodgates opened as I shared my deep frustrations about it all. But I also appreciated how beautiful it was that her dad had hugged her when she had found healing at these conferences, because he was sitting next to her. That's what my dad would do anytime I cried tears like this...he'd just walk up to me, say nothing, and hug me so tight until the tears stopped.

She said, *"I'll hug you."* As she was hugging me, she quietly asked a bombshell question:

"Jen, have you ever forgiven yourself for not getting to help him?"

I cried so hard I couldn't see.

She kept repeating the words that I needed to forgive myself as I cried some of the deepest tears I've ever cried. I was crying so hard I couldn't speak. I knew how to walk through the steps of forgiveness; I knew what I needed to say right then. But I was crying such deep tears I literally couldn't speak.

This friend picked up on that and softly said, *"repeat after me."* It came out. One. Word. At. A. Time. A root so deep I couldn't even say the sentence without help. One. Word. At. A. Time.

"I. Forgive. You. Jen. For. Not. Being. Able. To. Help. Your. Dad. In. That. Moment."

Processing that moment of healing the next day, I was overwhelmed by the image of my Creator as a patient Father. He's right beside us and wants to guide us to freedom. My friend Jenn waited with each word until I could say it. And with that, a giant root inside me finally released.

A month prior some anonymous friends had gifted seven tickets to these First Steps to Success conferences to veterans in memory of my dad. I couldn't help my dad, but these seven veterans were going to get this life-changing message put into their hands. This moment, as this root was released, put words to the feelings I hadn't yet known how to express. This gift hit so deeply it was beyond my ability to make the words come out.

The tickets. The trip to Hawaii. The deep conversations with someone who understood so intimately. The stories about her dad. The gift from some friends. It all worked together to dig up a deep spiritual root. The root of failure.

That month in Oahu was a major turning point in my life. I was completely engulfed in the presence of the patient Father. I felt His joy, His pleasure, and His acceptance. I felt it the first day Jenn arrived; as she brought His presence to a level that had me on the verge of weeping just while riding down the road in our open-air Jeep, blasting worship music and singing as loudly as she could as we went, not realizing she had never done that before. I felt it the night we watched *The Shack*. I had blocked out that movie, in my brain not wanting to watch it since I lost my dad. But I didn't remember that I had blocked it until we started watching it.

As the movie started, I suddenly remembered all the things I had said about this film and why I didn't want to watch it, and the friend, Don, who had told me to watch it eighteen years ago. What if I was supposed to watch it with this friend now? It felt like a divine appointment, because this friend related to my struggle of same-sex attraction.

One night, the two of us noticed we were both sunburned, but only on our hands, faces, and feet. It reminded us of the Biblical account of Shadrack, Meshack and Abednego (Daniel 3), who were thrown into a blazing furnace but didn't die because of the presence of the Father.

Interestingly, we decided to stay up and watch this film because of our sunburns. So there I was, finally watching this movie, sunburned, next to someone who could relate to the second half of my journey, which might not have happened if I had seen it years ago.

He was showing me His presence through my whole journey—in the flames and out. But it goes so much further than that: He also gave me a glimpse of His love through the documentary, *The Heart Of Man*.

Finding His Timing

As someone in the documentary shared their story, something new about my dad's story bubbled up and broke me; when you're so broken you're thinking about ending it all, it's not Him. It's not His Voice. Your identity is under attack by lies.

Hearing that shattered the belief I had been dragging around that my dad's identity was rock solid. Don't hear me wrong, there is no doubt in my mind that he loved the Father with everything he had– more than most people I know. But this was showing me something specific: he needed help with his identity in that moment.

Suddenly I saw how the two halves of my story are linked: the story of tragic loss and suicide, and the story of struggles with identity. Until this moment, I had thought they were unrelated. The suicide was an action by someone else, while the struggle with identity was internal to me. One was outside my control, the other was my choice.

But they were related, and powerfully. I'm called to help people with their identity because I have struggled with my own and have overcome, but until this moment I had zero idea that this struggle was directly linked to the trauma of losing my dad.

Those who struggle with suicidal thoughts are really struggling with their identity.

My Creator had waited until He could speak into both halves of my journey before I watched *The Shack*, and that's how I knew it was the right time to watch it. It was time to accept watching it, and that is why it was appointed for that night with Jenn. Two friends who had been burned in the fire but had not died. Because of Him!

The night we watched it, I had set my alarm for 1:00 a.m., saying that I could start it, but I needed to go to bed at one so that I could be diligent to get up to work remotely in the morning. The alarm went off and Jenn asked me what I thought so far. I sat in stunned silence until I could squeeze out one word: *"overwhelmed."* Then the tears poured out of me.

I felt curtains falling all around me, putting me into a holy place. I wasn't afraid. I knew exactly what it was. I knew that feeling. It was His presence.

As I sat there physically feeling my Creator's presence completely surrounding me, I cried harder. It was so beautiful. *"Yes, Jen...and it's been My presence that has healed you these last 18 years."* I cried harder as Jenn comforted me, encouraging me to let it out.

After I regathered myself, she turned to me incredulously and asked me, *"Are you really going to say no to finishing the movie to the God who has physically engulfed you right now because you think you need to be diligent? He knows you're diligent!"* She was right. We stayed up and finished the film. Way to go, Diligent Jen.

There were many more moments of healing on that trip; so many profound messages of what happens to our grief when we cry. How life is birthed inside us. How He uses that soil to redeem. We become a garden of His presence, giving life to others and it goes with us wherever we go! I didn't need to go to Hawaii to feel more of Him; I take that garden with me everywhere.

John 1:14 says, *"the word became flesh and made His dwelling among us."* The word translated *"dwelling"* is actually the word for *"tent"* or *"tabernacle."* That's what it felt like when His presence engulfed me, like I was inside a sacred space.

Finding His Timing

Thank goodness this friend had challenged me that night not to go to bed, but instead to get lost in His embrace and receive all He wanted me to do in me that night. He speaks to us in so many ways and in so many places, some sacred, some still.

I guess I shouldn't be surprised that, early on this trip I awoke from a bizarre dream where everything was on fire. We were all driving down a road in Oahu in the Jeep, when we looked out the window and saw flames engulfing everything. The next morning Jenn asked me how it made me feel. I answered, *"I was in awe!"* The Holy Spirit is sometimes described as a fire, and the Bible uses fire as a symbol for cleansing. The fact that a month of healing started with a vision like that seems significant. We spent that month running to Him, and He made Himself known. You could say He fell like a fire–a cleansing, engulfing fire that blazed a trail. Fire that engulfed. Fire that set for freedom, and ignited a passion for others that could engulf the world in awe, as it had done for us.

While my Creator is a patient, faithful, kind, and good Father, He is also an all-encompassing fire-healing, cleansing, purifying fire. He is a Father that wants to give us experiences with Him that leave us saying, *"what the heck just happened?"* Like the day I biffed on the beach.

He is also a fire that wants to engulf us so totally that it takes days, if not weeks, or even years, to process through the beauty of what He's showing us.

He loves and values us so much, He desperately wants to bee-line it just for us. His eyes are on you!

CHAPTER 17

Shift into an enormous fruitful future

The following month was the seventh Hebrew month, Tishrei. I knew things were shifting. Biblically we were in the month of completion, with things ending so that new things could begin. Think of the story of Joshua at the walls of Jericho—how many times did they have to circle the city before the walls fell? Seven. The people didn't fall, thankfully; the walls did.

Right at the start of that month, I had a vivid dream about the moon. My friend, April and I were lassoing the moon together with two very long ropes and because we were, we were so secure. There was safety and assurance in it. Reflecting back on the dream and the significance of when it came, I realized that light phases of the moon dictated the cycles of Rosh Kodesh. The Hebrew months follow the cycles of the moon, and each new month begins on Rosh Kodesh. We were lassoing the moon by following it's cycles—His timing. We were stabilizing our lives by anchoring to that cycle. It was vision! In his book, *A Time To Advance* Chuck Pierce said,

> "*Tishrei is the month of reflected light, which is different than what we see in April when we have the light of the sun. This is the light of the moon, which changes our environment, the way we process time, the way we work, the way crops grow, and the way we harvest.*"

I knew I was on to something. Not that I hadn't felt that with all the stories prior. But the dream was so powerful, and I was preparing to step into a new season that month of completion and fullness. As I moved out of my apartment in San Antonio and into a new apartment in a nearby town, I felt the completion of a season of my life. I was stepping into the fullness of a new season, including a new location.

There was no way I could miss it, because the apartment I was leaving in San Antonio was literally falling apart. There were gaping holes in the walls that continued to get worse. I'm sure we had a leak in one of our pipes somewhere, the wall behind the toilet was so damp it crumbled when you touched it. I'm also pretty sure I heard creatures scuffing about in the walls, so I was haunted at night by the thought of what might crawl out through that big hole. Fix-it Jen to the rescue! No creatures coming after me! I duct-taped a giant plastic tub to the wall as a barrier from whatever lived beneath it. Unless, of course, it was a Rhinoceros. He could've gotten through my tub.

When the complex's actual maintenance man finally arrived, he had a bucket of paint. Paint? I have a hole. He didn't speak English, so I shrugged and let him do his thing. Thirty minutes later he said he was all done (with a thumbs up), and left. What could he possibly have done with paint in 30 minutes? He had nailed a piece of plywood to the wall and painted over it. Perfect.

I guess it could have been far worse. My neighbor had their ceiling cave in on them just one month prior, so at least I'm not in that situation. Yet. I stared at our second floor ceiling where the damp wall was. Please hold, I thought. Time to go.

Leaving the old apartment with the gaping holes seemed like a fitting metaphor to the old season I was leaving. Little creatures inside, ceilings that might cave in at any moment. The new place was immaculate and felt whole and clean, like it represented my spirit and how it had shifted. I was no longer living in fear that my upstairs neighbor's sofa may suddenly fall on top of me. Or an entire cupboard of dishes.

In *A Time to Advance,* Chuck Pierce said, *"divine providence creates a new beginning. God will release certain revelation that will start your beginning in a new way."*

That felt crazy to me because it seemed to be a departure from what I had been doing up to that point. Soon after, I was invited to attend a prayer meeting with a group of business leaders who were praying over a new chapter in the life of their business. This wasn't the kind of thing I was used to being a part of, but the Father made it clear that He had a purpose for me being there.

The book continued,

> *"It's the month you need to ask the Lord how you are to get to the place where you are sure you are flowing in what He is doing."*

Tishrei is the head of the Hebrew year, a time of new beginnings. That felt crazy to me, too, because that business meeting was literally about new beginnings in that business. I had a contract increase greatly that month, which felt like a new beginning. But then, Tishrei is associated with the Hebrew tribe of Ephraim, whose name literally means "double fruit." Guess how much the contract increased? It doubled.

Even more interesting, the Prophet Samuel was from the Hebrew tribe of Ephraim. Would you believe that my women's Bible study group had just started the books that feature Samuel?

Chuck Pierce said about the tribe of Ephraim:

"Over 20,000 warriors from Ephraim came to David at Hebron. They were described as being mighty men of valor, famous in their father's households. Many from Ephraim defected from Israel to Judah during the reign of Asa when he turned the nation back to God."

I also happened to be reading a book about King David. Any guesses what the book focused on? Identity.

I imagine mighty men of valor like that will someday help our nation find our national identity and God. I began to see how powerful and important all these intertwining stories were for today... for right now.

"The men of Ephraim contributed to the restoration of the temple! Ephraim is mentioned in almost every chapter of the book of Hosea, which describes Israel as an unfaithful wife. Hosea lists the idolatry, unfaithfulness, and iniquity of Ephraim and describes

him as a silly dove going from place to place for help and as a wild donkey intent on pursuing his passions."

Those who struggle with identity often have this fruit of their life. I knew this to be true, because that used to be me! This is the first time I have ever referred to myself as a "wild donkey," and I think I want it to be the last. I like the "silly dove" better.

Look at what can happen when you are secure in your identity:

Honor...

The perception of a King (David)...

The restoration of the temple (the tribe of Ephraim).

These are all the fruit of a restored identity.

Too often, we look down on those who struggle with identity. Imagine what would happen if we started speaking into them who they really are!?

The lights of that illuminated map—and the path running parallel to our lives—wasn't just flickering on this time; it was beckoning with a mission!

Another terrific book about King David, is *And David Perceived He Was King* by Dale Mast. A passage on page 69 jumped out at me because it mentions his connection to Chuck Pierce, the author of *A Time to Advance*. "WAIT" I gasped. *"These two authors know each other?!"* I knew it was confirmation that my Creator was connecting me to another powerful resource. I was figuring out what resources and details I would need to go into a new, seven-month coaching program about identity and alignment for The Overcomers and was using both books. I guess I shouldn't have been surprised that the two authors KNEW EACH OTHER! What a koinkidink!

As old things were ending, so much new was beginning. We came back around to Chesvan, the month in Biblical history when the flood started (it ended a year later in the same month). It felt different to me that year; we don't often think about the flood from the perspective of those on the ark. They had to leave everything they knew behind. It was a new beginning for them. How scary! Or terrifying, rather. Can you imagine stepping out of the ark and seeing absolutely NOTHING? Nothing at all, on the entire earth. Talk about a dystopian nightmare you might see in a SciFi flick. What planet are we on? That would have been my question. But they stepped out courageously into the unknown, and look at all the new that birthed in that first year.

I left things behind as I settled into a new season and new surroundings in Boerne, Texas. My new identity was one of the most prominent changes. That month, I was gifted a mixture of anointing oil from my friend, April. The aroma washed over my senses, but it was the color that shocked me the most—it was green, a color I associated with the identity I had rejected almost my entire life. The Creator had designed me with a good identity, but it wasn't until recently that I accepted it and forgave myself for rejecting it for so long. What's more, April didn't intend for it to appear green; it had started out blue as she mixed it. Blue represented the identity I had embraced, before I knew the truth, and green represented the truth about my identity I had rejected, thinking I wasn't good enough.

There was so much symbolism for me in this gift, and April

hadn't intended it at all. When I aligned my identity with truth, it turned green, just like this oil had. I love how my Creator shows His fingerprint in little things. He will keep a flood moving until He has dealt with whatever root He is trying to dig out so He can heal us!

The oil that symbolized my identity shift was just the first message from my Creator that month.

As I was preparing for the next First Steps to Success event in San Antonio, I knew I was supposed to pack my shofar and prayer shawl. I had brought them home from my first trip to Israel with Dani Johnson in 2019, where she showed me how and why she used them. The Creator made it clear in my spirit to bring them along. I was glad I did, because I was invited to help prepare the ballroom spiritually before the conference started. April and I prayed over the room, circling it seven times, anointing the corners, blowing the shofar, and inviting His JOY in.

He gave me a nudge that there would be a time during the weekend I would need to pray for the "Armor of God" for the speaker. That time came Friday evening. Her son and I prayed over her as she prepared to teach the spiritual equipping season.

I received so much new revelation about identity that weekend, sometimes in odd ways. A friend told me she had seen me in a bizarre dream, "...*you were 300 lbs, had electric yellow pants and blue hair.*"

Say WHAT?! Insert me, shocked face, blank stare, not knowing how to process such a thought. Initially, I rejected the thought. No way would I ever be that enormous...or yellow. But here and there it circled back into my thoughts. I finally asked my Creator, *"What is this?! Is there more to this that you want me to see?"*

That's precisely what happened. Had I dismissed it, thinking it was silly and had no meaning, I would have missed the richness of what He wanted me to see. Before I share what He revealed about that dream, there's another story to tell.

It reminded me of something my Creator had shown me years before, in an exercise I had done several times. We were instructed to take a look at our current mindset about different areas of our lives. I noticed a pattern in my answers:

What had I been programmed to believe about...

Myself? ...I am HARD on me.

Money? ...HARD to come by.

Marriage? ....HARD to hold on to or find a good one.

People? ...HARD to talk to.

Success? ...HARD to come by.

Education? ...HARD to learn.

Politics? ...HARD to change.

Business? ...HARD to grow or learn.

People who don't perform? ...HARD to change.

Self-image/beauty? ...HARD to see.

Failure? ...HARD to believe otherwise.

Love? ...HARD to find.

Religion? ...HARD to trust.

Men? ...HARD to trust.

Women? ...HARD to keep.

Normally, I would have picked one mindset to focus on changing, but the pattern was like a blowhorn in my face. My hair would have been everywhere, if I had any. Got it, but WHY IS THIS HERE?! What is it about this one word?! What happened next I'll never forget:

Michael Jackson's song, "Man In The Mirror" played, and the words *"If you wanna make the world a better place, then take a look at yourself and make a change!"*

It was like He dropped a golden shovel right into my hands and we were about to dig into what He intended for me to find in my soul. Just then, figurative shovel in hand, our trainer said, *"This is the deciding moment, looking at the man in the mirror and saying THIS is where it changes!"*

With tears in my eyes I flashed back to right after my dad died, and the feelings that overwhelmed me as I made a life-altering choice.

I chose to say, *"THIS DOES NOT DEFINE US!"*

Suddenly I realized, I had claimed my identity at that moment when the flames around me could not have been hotter!

Have you ever been in a moment, and you don't know where it comes from, but you can just feel something big welling inside of you?

No, not the gaseous kind; the kind that's speaking the truth of who you are. You don't know what it is, but you can feel something lit deep inside your soul? Is it Him?!

I felt it back then, when I uttered that phrase so passionately, without even knowing why. But man, did it burn furiously inside me that day. Who I was couldn't help but explode out of me. Good thing it wasn't that other kind. Those are deadly.

What if He was helping me fight back then, knowing in that moment how important claiming identity would be for me?! Twenty years later, seeing what that phrase stirred up deep inside my soul, I could weep.

Confronted with this repeating word, hard, I needed to know what He was showing me. As we sat there, silently processing to ourselves, I felt stuck, as if there were a wall in front of my eyes. I couldn't see it but I knew it was there. It was the first time going through this exercise that I couldn't see how to dig deeper. I had zero idea why I felt so many parts of my life were hard?

What do you do next? I felt helpless for a moment. It had always been easy to dig around a broken mindset in the past. Then I remembered who my Helper was. I engaged with my Creator, *"Father, show me the way to the root if it's a root YOU want to remove!"*

Creator: *"Do you want to remove it?"*

Me: *"YES!"*

Creator: *"Why?"*

Finding His Timing

Me: *"Because it keeps cycling and I feel stuck!"*

Creator: *"Why?"*

Me: *"Because it's too hard."*

Creator: *"Why?"*

Me: *"Because there's so much to do, I'm doing it on my own, and I just can't get past a certain point."*

Creator: *"WHY?"*

Me: *"Because I don't know the way."*

Creator: *"WHY?"*

Me: *"Because it feels bigger than me."*

- LIGHTBULB -

...It's BIGGER than me. Hmmm,

...it goes beyond ME!

Suddenly, He revealed the need to go further. Before me. Who came before me? Who came before them? Who came before them?! As I traced it from generation to generation, new light came on, and He led the way.

Up until then, here had been a wall, but He was gently taking me through it. (I knew it! I'm a superhero! We can now go through walls.) "Why" was a key word that took us through.

Me: "Mom did her best. She only knew what had been given to her."

Creator: "What was given to her?"

Me: "That life was hard. Her dad grew up in the Great Depression!"

Creator: "Do you think that maybe there's a belief that was passed from generation to generation that life is hard?!"

I knew the next answer....... "YES."

I knew the next step; to identify all those in my lineage who had ever believed that life was hard. As I did, He lit it up like a pathway, lights turning on with every step I took. It was part of every generation, all the way back to my grandpa's great-aunts who had lived on so little. I remembered the stories that had been passed. Not only was he raised by his two aunts, but there was one story he made sure none of us ever forgot.

The story of the ORANGE.

Every Christmas, grandpa gave each of his children (and later grandchildren) a single orange. Why? He had grown up so poor that a single, solitary orange was a gift that brought them joy once a year! That's how hard life had been for them. The belief carried on, generation to generation: life was hard and you never know when it will become hard again.

For the first time in five years of attending these events, I was being shown a root that went deeper than me, back through my family

Finding His Timing

lineage, all the way back to the Great Depression!

Even though we were walking through walls, I was flabbergasted by this. Fortunately, I knew the steps of forgiveness, so I walked myself back through every generation that carried the belief that life was hard, until I got to me. Why? Because, friend, my family is not responsible for my freedom—I AM! And you are responsible for yours, no matter what came before you.

I closed my eyes and whispered, *"I forgive you, Jen, for adopting that IDENTITY that life is hard, when that's NOT who you are! I release you; you owe yourself nothing. I bless you with removing the LIES. I bless your burdens and the weights you feel with feeling LIGHT, and with being EASY. I bless you with knowing that your identity is tied to the One who says His burden is easy and light! I bless your identity with being NEW ground filled with JOY and not despair. I bless you with an abundance of new JOY."*

Friend, did you catch the journey you just went on in reading this? If you haven't yet, here it is. Here is the depth I would have missed had I not engaged with my Creator to understand the bizarre dream of me—300 pounds, electric yellow pants and blue hair—and the wall I couldn't see past.

I had a block in both stories, so what was my next step? I asked Him, *"What is this?!? Is there something more YOU want to show me?"* and *"Show me! If there's a root you want me to see, help me trace to it!"*

He had already revealed the bizarre dream as we dug into that generational root and released it. It was in the blessing. What do I mean?

Finding His Timing

I saw her as the blessing of joy was spoken over me more times than I could count that weekend. How poetic, that Joy, the animated character in Disney's *"Inside-Out"* is drawn with electric yellow clothing that's just glowing and short blue pixie cut hair. She's not 300 pounds, but what IS that enormous? ...her JOY. She's so full of joy she bounces around from room to room, spreading it on everyone, everywhere she goes. She literally carries light everywhere with her. Mannnnnnn, what a gift, to have that dream spoken over me, and my future! To think I could be that enormous with joy. I asked Him to show me the way to release it and receive the blessing of speaking it over my life, after releasing so much despair!

If I could go back to that day, I would say:

"Yes, Jen! Those lights are needed all around you. That is a part of your identity! Receive it! Walk in it! It's what He does in the place of despair—He replaces it with Joy!

Your future is enormous! Because His love is enormous! Continue letting Him show you who you truly are! Who He is! The hunt is far from over! There is so much more to find!"

Friend, why do I share all this? Being real and transparent with you is not for me. I've already gone through it. That part was for me. Sharing this is for you! Don't get me wrong, it is not easy. But is it worth it? Yes. 10,000% yes. You are worth it! I care about your freedom just as much as I do mine.

Have you ever felt stuck, like there's a wall in front of you and you just can't see past it? You have an enemy attacking your soul, and the battleground is your mind. If you choose to believe you can't walk through it, you will stay stuck there, just like I was. Business coach

Carmen O'Quinn once said, *"What are YOU a prisoner of? You are a prisoner of your thoughts. 'As a man thinks so He will be!' Because whatever it is that you believe about your life, is what your future will be!"*

If you're ready to get to the other side of that stuck, friend, it's time for a new experience!

Man, I sure want my future to be full of enormous joy! I want to see what other superpowers I might have!

What life do YOU want? Are you ready to dive this deep? Are you ready to engage with your Creator in ways you haven't before? Are you ready to do the work to identify who you are, and what you were designed to do, and then launch it to the world?

I'm looking for you.

I want to give you the same golden shovel the Creator dropped into my hands! Why do I continue to go to these conferences? Why am I sharing all that I share? Why am I passionate about connecting those who need help with those who have overcome? Because I don't just go for me and my own continued journey of healing. I go for you.

If you're ready for life to look different, I want to partner with you to help you walk into it. Please connect with me and let me know. If you're not ready yet, it's ok. I'll still be cheering you on. Go light up the world with your story! I believe in you!

CHAPTER 18

The gift of timing in your birthday, His design, and who's behind you

The downloads continued and my confidence for stepping into spiritual warfare grew, for myself and for others. It might have helped that I began to view myself as 300 pounds of joy.

But then I got sick—really sick (must have been all the added-on pounds). I didn't know what to do about it, so the first night I was sick, I talked to the Creator and prayed deliverance over every ailment because I was so miserable. I had never done that for an illness before. I declared that His healing power and perfect blood were flowing through my veins, according to Colossians 2:39, which says:

"They're completely out of touch with the source of life, Christ, who puts us together in one piece, whose very breath and blood flow through us. He is the Head and we are the body. We

can grow up healthy in God only as he nourishes us." (MSG)

The physical battle was one thing, but God was showing me the warfare for my identity was at a whole new level. That Thanksgiving, I had a major revelation about our actual identity and how it connects to the day we are born.

What I'm going to say next might be pretty unpopular, but it's one of those things that, once you know, you can't not share that you've found it. With the entire world, of course. I'm feeling generous.

Have you ever had a birthday feel unfulfilling? No I'm not talking about the insatiableness often associated with the day—like getting that gift you really wanted—or having expectations around dear friends or family doing this or that–but that deep-down feeling that something about the day just doesn't feel right? You've wanted more out of the day, but not for you, for our world?

You're not alone. Frankly, I have a hunch there's boatloads of people out there who are going to identify with what I'm about to say. But I will caution you, if you're not ready to have a day you hold really dear to you turned upside-down, I would stop reading now. Here is your out for this chapter.

But for the curious—for the one who wants to join me on this treasure hunt—boy, do I have something to show you. Something which answered that feeling in my spirit that something just felt off with birthdays, every year that passed.

But before I share the gold, I gotta back up a bit to what He revealed just prior. We were heading into 2023, and as I pondered the coming year and the expectations that went with it, a big one for me

Finding His Timing

was that I would be turning 40 right smack dab in the middle of it.

Oof. Forty, a birthday in our culture that is viewed as such a bad number to hit! All the dark jokes of being "over the hill," every store carries black decor for this important occasion.

So many of us try to hide the fact that we are 40. Why? Because, *"it's all over now—the best part of my life is behind me."* Do you hear what I hear? SO MUCH DEATH spoken over the day, and this time in our lives!

But then a different thought rose up: so many Bible stories where the number 40 was significant!:

The story of Noah and the ark in Genesis.

The Israelites' exodus from Egypt.

Yeshua's (Jesus) days spent in the wilderness.

Moses' time with God on Mt Sinai.

Goliath coming out to the field looking for someone to fight.

Each place 40 was important, there was a transition that came with leaving behind all they knew! In fact, the entire world they knew. But what came next?

A NEW BEGINNING.

A PROMISE.

A BLESSING.

But that's not all that hit me.

In all those accounts, can you also hear how important the heart position was of those present? What would have happened with the account of Noah if they had not chosen to listen to or trust the Voice of their Creator about what to do, and what He was doing? That He was going to be cleansing the earth?

What happened to the Israelites after they left Egypt? They chose not to believe that a new land and a major blessing were given to them, as their inheritance and they first had to wander...for 40 years!

You tell me, how important is it that we listen to the Voice of belief and fully believe in our inheritance? I think something has been stolen from us.

Instead of being reminded that 40 is a time of great transition, new beginning, promise, and blessing, what are we told? What are we given? So much DEATH.

It's time we reclaim our rights to the new! It's time we reclaim our rights to His truth! It's time we realign with His design for 40! O.K., Jen...how do we do that?

Here's where it gets crazy. I told you I found something that could be unpopular. The next holiday we came to will always be special to me, because I was welcomed into another family's celebration. We were enjoying a lively conversation, when this question came up in my spirit and out through my mouth: "*Why DO we have birthday cakes and blow out candles? Where did that come from?*"

We did some digging and found that the first use of a birthday cake and candles originated in the Middle Ages. The Germans made cakes to celebrate Kinder-fest, and candles on cakes started with the Ancient Greeks to honor Artemis, the goddess of the moon. The lit candles on the cake represented the glow of the moon, and the smoke carried their wishes to the gods who lived in the skies. The candles were placed on the cake to represent the "light of life."

Enter my fury (with exclamations not appropriate to insert here) to learn of such an origin and intent! What the flip-flop?! Wait...you mean, birthday cakes and candles originate from worshiping a foreign god, and they literally would blow out their lights?! AHHHHH! Oh, and we stand in circles clapping as the birthday person blows their lights out?! Aren't we designed by the Creator to be a light and to let our light shine?! Yet here we are, year after year, literally blowing our lights out on the day of our birth—the day associated to our identity—and coming into agreement with the opposite?!

Jen is fuming. Holy crap, is the enemy crafty! But I'm on to him! I've think we've got some contracts to cancel. No wonder, every year on our birthday we can feel so unfulfilled! Our spirit knows something is not right! Something is wrong with this design!

Maybe now you're wondering (like I was), what would leave us feeling fulfilled on such an occasion? Is there more to that cycle that we should be seeing...or doing? As it turns out, there is!

If you're anything like me, I want to go back to the earliest design, the earliest intent of such an occasion. What do I mean? I mean the design and intent of our Creator, not man! We all know man will fail us.

As I dug deeper into history, I found so much richness, so

much blessing, and so much new. Did you know that the Hebrews would celebrate every birthday by speaking a blessing? It's called the shehechiyanu: *"Blessed are you, Adonai, source of all life, who has sustained us, and kept us alive, and brought us to this time!"*

That's just the beginning; there's so much more to celebrating your birthday. The day also weaves in;

- Psalm 118

- Gratitude and thanks

- Giving back and making the world a better place

- Cleansing with Mikvah practices

Reminders of our inheritance and where we came from. We speak this important blessing over the birthday person, and it is woven into our very identity, intentionally, on a yearly cycle of renewal!

Wow! We have replaced light with darkness, all that richness meant for us to remind us of our identity from generation to generation all the way back to creation. We could have all that, or a cake and candles…literally blowing out the light we were meant to shine into a dark world.

I don't know about you, but I want to reclaim my inheritance! I want to come into alignment with my Creator's original design! I could not wait to turn 40 in 2023, and reclaim all the significance and meaning in 40. I didn't see death; I saw excitement in that transition.

I SAW NEW LAND!

I SAW BLESSING!

I SAW PROMISE!

I saw fulfillment, on a day, on a life, and on a design that we speak so much death over.

As you look at your identity, your birthday, and even this year, what do you want? More importantly, are you willing to ask the hard questions, like why do we do "X" over and over again…where did this tradition come from?!

I mentioned that we're on a treasure hunt. The Creator has been taking me on this hunt. Look what was found! Want to go on a hunt like that with your Creator? I invite you to join me in the hunt for more gold! There's an adventure just waiting for you to join in the hunt. It can and will leave you much more fulfilled!

If that's you, by the time this book is in your hands, I know we'll still be in the hunt. We'd love to have you with us. At the back of the book is information about our monthly zoom calls.

The Creator's perfect timing was behind this revelation, as it always is. Another light of the invisible map made itself known, along with this revelation in the Hebrew month of Tevet. Tevet is the month when things that are out of order manifest. It is associated with the tribe of Dan, who had a redemptive call to leap from idolatry but failed to leap. Wait, what? The month where I got so much revelation about pagan idols associated with our identity through our birthday celebrations is the same month there's a call for leaping from idolatry?! Unreal.

Things that are not His design and are out of order are idolatry. I read that idolatry moved the tribe of Dan out of God's timing, and it occurred to me that idolatry—whether conscious or unconscious as an act in our modern culture—is the very reason we shifted out of our awareness of the Creator's timing? Of the grandeur illuminated invisible map running parallel to our own?

Identity became so simple, distinguishing the truth from the lie. But to discover truth, you have to hunt, and I was on a hunt. I was hunting for His truth and His timing. I believe identity is found within His timing. Could that be what we were meant to find? Did the Creator intend for us to finally, fully know ourselves when we discover His timing?

Speaking of knowing who we are, I re-watched one of my favorite childhood movies, *The Lion King*, with a friend during the month of Tevet. It is packed with revelations about identity.

Don't hate me, but *"Hakuna Makata"*...is a horrible phrase.

Wait. Stop! Don't hear what I'm not saying, I LOVE *The Lion King*! It was one of my favorite films growing up as a kid, and still is, but before I get into the things He revealed, I've gotta back up to another story. At the start of January 2023, that question that had been hitting my spirit was back: *"where did this even come from? When did we start celebrating the New Year in the way that we do?"*

We began our hunt for answers by looking up the definition of the word "new." Again, we were shocked. Maybe like me, you just assumed you knew what the word "new" meant! But our jaws dropped as we read out loud one definition of it: *"the beginning as the resumption or repetition of a PREVIOUS act or thing!"*

Wait a minute, that definition literally reveals that our entire thoughts around New Year (a "New Me!", "Starting Over!") are off!! I shouted, *"No wonder it's so common for new year's goals to fail! Our entire thought processes around the expectation of what the word 'new' means is wrong! We literally set ourselves up to fail!"*

Why? Because, by definition, in order for something truly to be new, it has to be based upon a previous act or thing! There has to be a foundation of something first! It's not a starting over, but a building upon what has already been done! Oh. My. Golly.

But the hunt didn't stop there. We looked up *"where did celebrating NEW Year's even come from, and the giant lighted ball that falls to earth even start?"* Imagine what we found. A quick Google search showed us:

> *"...the first known record of New Year's celebrations began about 2000 B.C. in Mesopotamia. This occurred at the time of the vernal equinox, which is toward the end of March. Babylonians would have a religious festival named Akitu taken from the Sumerian term for barley. They'd perform various rituals, which would last for 11 days. Besides celebrating the New Year, Atiku also marked the time that Marduk, Babylonian's sky god, defeated Tiamat, the evil sea goddess. The origin of January 1 marking the New Year specifically dates back to 46 B.C., when Julius Caesar developed the solar-based Julian calendar. This was after the old lunar-based Roman calendar became ineffective. Another reason behind making January 1 the start of the New Year was to honor Janus — the Roman god of beginnings who had two faces. To celebrate the occasion, ancient people would offer sacrifices to the god of beginnings, add laurel branches to their homes as*

decorations, and exchange gifts."

Can I puke now? So the entire celebration of the New Years has been aligned to worshiping a foreign god, too?! Enter me fuming again.

As I was fuming at the deception and all the programming I had unknowingly aligned myself to for years, I continued my hunt: *"okay, if that's NOT my God's design....what IS His design for the new year?"*

I was already reeling from learning the definition and root of the word "new" that we had found, but then we learned that He didn't design for us to celebrate a new beginning once or twice a year, but four times a year! He planned four "beginnings"...every year!

SIGN ME UP! But what am I signing up for? That's what takes us back to *The Lion King*. In that same conversation that led us to dig into the definition of the word "new", the hunt also led us into what at the time felt like a bunny trail, but wasn't.

I've always wondered why He (God) so often refers to Himself as the lion of the tribe of Judah? What is it about the lion that is so important, why a lion?

April shared, *"Priscilla Shirer talks about a scene in The Lion King where Simba is still a cub and is surrounded by the hyenas. He lets out a squeaky childish roar and they all laugh at him...but then, a loud ferocious roar follows. And they all tremble and shake at the sound! Mufasa, his Father, was behind him!"*

"THAT'S IT!" I shouted. *"There's so much identity in that image!*

No wonder it's a LION! We all struggle with identity, even when we know who we are! Even when we know we're the heart, the muscles, the brain, or the voice. But when we know where our identity comes from—and Who is behind us—we have;

The heart of a LION!

The muscles of a LION!

The brain of a LION!

And the voice of a LION!

He is a LION, and when we align with Him, we become so much more than who we are! Our identity is not just us. He is behind us! A LION is behind us. So if you're a strong personality, you don't just have strength as your part of the body, you have the strength of a LION, inside you because He is behind you!"

How interesting is that when you think about the definition of the word "new" as the repetition of a previous act or thing? What have you been given since birth, friend? What identity? It's not about starting over. It's about embracing who you are (and who He is) not just once a year, but multiple times.

Did you know that lions have the ability to see in the dark? This revelation was shared in that same conversation. They have white patches under their eyes that absorb the light of the moon, which allows them to see in the dark and hunt their enemies!

When you align with the Father and look at His design, what is it all aligned to? The cycles of the moon! His light! That's what the entire history of the Bible based it's timelines off of! Whoah. Now we're really getting somewhere.

When we align with Him, we align our identity with His—and His identity is a lion! His identity gives light and sight into our darkness! It equips us with the ability to fight our enemies! To fight for our identity!

In the movie *The Lion King*, Simba's identity (king) was anointed when Rafiki schmeared his head! Scar, the enemy, wanted to steal Simba's identity!

We lose our identity when we complain. As Simba in the Lion King said, *"I never get to go anywhere!"*

When we chase false expectations and self-gratification we end up in bad, dangerous places. Young Simba found himself surrounded by hyenas! But even the hyenas knew how powerful his father's identity was: *"Mufasa! I even just hear his name and I shudder!"*

Simba spent years in the jungle eating bugs (which was not what he was designed to eat), running away from his real identity! He embraced a *"Hakuna Matata"* lifestyle of avoidance! Yes, I said it. And the crazy thing is, when we sing along we're embracing the same lifestyle of avoidance.

It wasn't until Rafiki got ahold of him that he began to recognize and embrace the truth. Listen to the wisdom that Rafiki used to bring him back around: *"I know your Father; He's alive! Do you know who you are? You are Mufasa's son!! Look harder! You see He lives in you! You can either run from your past or you can learn from it."*

Finding His Timing

Rafiki spoke identity. This wasn't a new identity that he didn't know already. Rafiki opened his eyes to the identity he had since the beginning. As Simba reflected back, he heard the voice of his father: *"Remember who you are! You are my son!"* Simba remembered who he was, who was behind him, whose son he was, and in that identity he returned to FIGHT his enemy. He found his voice and confronted Scar: *"Everything you ever told me was a lie!"* When he embraced his true identity he began to differentiate the truth from the lie.

Friend, the enemy comes to manipulate you with flattery when you do not posses your true identity, but the Creator comes to you to edify your identity!

Now more than ever, it is critical that we know who we are and where our identity comes from. We need to know Who is behind us, whose design we will follow and why we participate in certain occasions. If we don't, we might by default be aligning with the manipulation of the enemy, who wants nothing more than for our lights to go out!

How interesting is it that for so long we've celebrated New Years cheering at a giant ball of lights fall.

Our Creator has so much more prepared for us, and for the lights He has placed in our lives. It's time to hunt diligently for their purpose in our lives.

Finding His Timing

CHAPTER 19

Your blessings are on the way, stay in line—the month of the new year of trees

The eleventh month of the Hebrew calendar is said to contain "the month of the new year of trees." It sounds weird, but trees and their fruit have a lot of significance throughout the Bible. You often see trees used as a metaphor for spiritual growth. After all I had learned from the previous Hebrew months, I kind of expected trees to make an appearance in my life that month, but I never thought it would be so literal.

About six months before my 40th birthday, I made a surprise trip to Kissimee, Florida with two friends. As we were preparing for our trip, we talked about the other trip we were planning, to visit Israel in the spring. As we counted down the days to our departure to Israel, something caught my attention, with all the revelations He had been showing me about His design for the number 40 and how often in scripture the number 40 was associated with transition, blessing, and promise.

Counting backward 40 days from our departure to Israel my finger landed on the date of that Monday of our trip to Florida. April pointed out that we were scheduled to visit an orange grove that day! I gasped. Remember when my grandpa gave us oranges for Christmas to remind us of where we had come from? Forty days before my fortieth birthday in the month of trees, my friends were planning to take me to an orange grove to set vision for my next forty years!

But that's when it got crazier. My friend who had planned the trip didn't even know this next part. I looked down on my Hebrew calendar and I saw a literal tree icon printed on that very day the calendar. I looked up and said, *"Look there's a tree on here, and it says 'the month of the new year of trees' on that very day!"* We both were instantly overcome with chills and so much expectation of what He wanted to show us that day.

He did not disappoint.

He poured out insights at the grove. It was a terrific day. We ate lunch by a lake, we blew a shofar, and April spoke a blessing over my next forty years. We found out later that even that moment had a deeper significance. She read Psalm 1 over me, which is an important Psalm in Shevat. It reads:

"Blessed is the man who shall not walk in the counsel of the wrong, and shall not stand in the path of sinners, and shall not sit in the seat of scoffers, but his delight is in the Torah of Yahaveh, and he mediates in His Torah day and night. For he shall be as a tree planted

Finding His Timing

by the rivers of water, that yields fruit in it's season, and whose leaf does not wither, and whatever he does prospers. The wrong are not so, but are like the chaff which the wind blows away. Therefore the wrong shall not rise in the judgment, nor sinners in the congregation of the righteous. For Yahaveh knows the way of the righteous, but the way of the wrong comes to naught."

As we toured the orange grove, I wondered why there were oak trees in the field with the orange trees. They weren't just scattered here and there, they were planted in the same visual root line as the orange trees. When I asked the guide why they were planted that way, he had no answer, but I could feel there was more to it, so I dug for answers. I was shocked by what I found. Oak leaves have healing oils that heal any illness or disease in the fruit trees, but only when they are planted in the same line as the orange trees. If the fruit tree is out of line, it doesn't benefit from the oak trees. How crazy is that?

It's not so crazy when you think about the spiritual correlations. All creation speaks of Who our Creator is, because it's His design. Psalm 1 says a healthy tree yields fruit, does not wither, and whatever it does prospers when it's in line with the Healer. It's not expected to be perfect, but simply in line with the One who is. That's the truth that was spoken over me that day.

Shevat is also associated with the Hebrew tribe of Asher, who are described as "the happy tribe." Their inheritance was the most fertile land of the promised land, and they were blessed with numbers. Reading that description, I had to laugh because of all that He had shown me about finding joy recently, the parallel to the Pixar character, Joy, and the dream from a friend about me looking like a 300-pound Joy. Finally my friends surprised me with a delightful hunt

Finding His Timing

to find "Joy" with a visit to Walt Disney World's Epcot park.

I felt joy in my spirit as I declared, *"My blessings are on the way!"* The intentional meditation and consumption of joy would produce more of it. And I saw it in full bloom as I stared out at that orange grove. It wasn't just one orange; it was a massive grove filled with trees filled with oranges. It made me think of a whole grove full of joy. I saw my legacy: the blossoms of the orange trees, with seeds full of life, seeping into the orange trees because they are in line with the oak. In line with righteousness. The tree knows its foundation and digs in with its roots, and therefore its fruit will be bountiful and nourish generations.

The story of the orange was becoming so much bigger, and going so much deeper. I felt like I was on a new hunt. After we arrived at Epcot I spotted a painting of the Disney character "Orange Bird." I had never heard of that character before. My curiosity was piqued even further when I learned that it wasn't just any character, it was the character associated with the beginnings of Walt Disney World and its original identity itself.

I saw the Creator aligning so many details during our hunt. On the way home we were looking through our photos and saw the ones that the Disney team takes and enhances—you've seen them; they add a character into a photo that they take of you at the park afterwards. We had no idea what character it would be, but sure enough... there was "Orange Bird" in our photo. Only the Creator could have orchestrated all this. I knew He was up to something—leading me to something, revealing something. When we align with Him and with His design, He shows us who we are. What a fun hunt it is!

If I could go back to that day, I would say:

"Yes, Jen!! All creation speaks of who He is! He is talking to you, revealing things to you! Continue looking, asking, and letting Him reveal all that He has to show you! It's so much bigger than you think it is!

The vision He has for you goes beyond you! It will nourish generations. It will heal generations. That's who He is! Stay in line with Him! Align to Him! Watch what He does. Watch what He grows! The future will be bountiful!"

CHAPTER 20

Your blessing is on the other side of the transaction

In the month Adar, I was off to Israel. It was my second trip and I should have guessed how perfectly-timed and specific the Creator's messages to me would be. What I didn't anticipate was the amount of surrender I would experience this time, leading up to it. If I hadn't worked through this surrender in my heart, this would be the end of the book.

I had fully paid for this trip back in 2020, to go with the mentor my Creator had used to change my life so dramatically. Here we were in 2023, finally getting word that trip, which had been postponed indefinitely due to the pandemic, was finally going to happen. What we didn't know back in 2020 was that my mentor would retire. I too was happy for this season change for her, because she had spent 30 years giving everything that she had to thousands of people. As the trip rebuilt steam to embark, I was told I had been put on a different trip—without my mentor.

I had been anticipating this time with my mentor for three years, but the company had sold and she had dropped out of this trip. This level of surrender was one of the hardest, and I know I wouldn't have handled it as well if it hadn't been for her teaching. That's not to say it was easy by any means; I struggled and battled through so many intense emotions for months. But each time, I took those feelings and brought them before my Creator, often with tears cascading from my eyes.

I knew my feelings were my responsibility and no one else's. Had I not dealt with them in each wave that tried to overtake me, I would have drowned. But each time they surfaced, I sat in my bathtub, releasing every bit of them. I felt cheated, manipulated, and that I had no choice. It felt unfair, and I felt left behind. Not by my mentor of course—don't hear what I didn't say. I knew her incredible heart and who she was, I knew the circumstances had caused something different to happen. I released it all, working through forgiveness of things I didn't understand—things I felt I couldn't even pursue understanding in. Why? Because I heard my mentors words ringing in my ears through the entire thing: *"Do the right thing, no matter what!"*

Deep down, I knew what that right thing was. It was to take myself out of the equation, to take out what I wanted, and instead do what no one else was doing. I saw the two new leaders needing people who believed in them, too. People who show up even when it's not perfect. So to question why this was happening, or even relay the feelings I was struggling through wasn't to be voiced at the time. It was my job to love them too, to choose to have incredible trust that my Creator had me, and that He was doing something far greater than

Finding His Timing

I could understand, even if I never knew why. I had to trust that He would redeem it all. Traveling back to the Holy Land, I had no doubt He'd be there waiting for me once again, it just wasn't in the way I had been anticipating. I had to let it ALL go. If I hadn't, I would have missed out on everything He did with me on that trip. And boy, was He specific with what He revealed this time around.

I saw His timing at work before we even left. One of the new leaders, April, asked to meet with me to take a look at any Biblical parallels with the timing of this next trip. As we looked through the agenda, we noticed we'd be entering through the gates of Jerusalem on Rosh Kodesh, but not just any Rosh Kodesh; the first day of the entire Hebrew year, called Nisan. The new month is also described as though you are *"standing at your promised land and preparing to enter a new season of inheritance."* We were entering the Hebraic month of Nisan or Abib/Aviv. According to Chuck Pierce's book, *"A Time to Advance"*:

> *"Abib is a Hebraic term for the stage of growth of grain when the seeds have reached full size. The harvest was waived before the Lord this month (Leviticus 23:4-11).*
>
> *As the first of the months of the Hebrew year and our Passover month when we fully cross into the new season, we are standing at our Promised Land and preparing to enter a new season of inheritance. Allow the Lord to deliver you from every hindrance that would keep you from entering your place of fulfillment.*
>
> *Every month is linked with an understanding of the 12 tribes. This is the month linked with the tribe of Judah - the apostolic leadership, warring tribe, who knew how to operate with sound.*

Finding His Timing

This is a key time to praise!"

You can imagine my delight in reading this timing! When at last we stood on a promenade overlooking the city of Jerusalem (King David's Kingdom) we declared that the fullness of our harvest was being secured and that every seed that was sown would prosper in new ways! We blew our shofars, releasing sound! But He didn't just present me with any seed in that moment—it was so intentional, so specific. I saw that we'd be at King's David Kingdom that day, and it was his son, Solomon who constructed the first temple–King David's seed! I declared that every identity seed, every seed of knowing who we are, would prosper in new ways.

Our tour guide was from the Hebrew tribe of Judah. He had traced his lineage back and knew he was in the very line of King David and Yeshua! My shofar sat on a table while we were at the promenade, and he asked whose shofar it was. I replied that it was mine, that I bought back in 2019 on my first trip with our mentor, and I had brought it back to the holy land with me. He asked if I knew how to blow it properly. He picked it up, and showed me how to do it so that a strong sound comes out. As he did, it dawned on me that a descendant of the literal tribe of Judah—who can actually trace his lineage back to King David and Yeshua—just blew my shofar! I was floored at the significance of the legacy, and that we were literally in the month associated with the tribe of Judah and releasing sound.

Only the Creator could have lit up that light from the parallel path so epically in that moment! He was making sure I saw as clearly as possible that I was following His design!

The name, Judah, is a Hebrew word meaning "give praise." It is also associated with the hand, as Chuck Pierce explains in His book

Finding His Timing

"A Time to Advance":

> *"the HAND is a symbol of strength and power. That when we lift up our hands to the Lord we are presenting Him all our strengths and abilities. This is a way of saying that we are putting ourselves totally in His hands."*

When I was out on the promenade in Jerusalem, making declarations in the first month of the year, I lifted my shofar with my hand high into the air. I just knew I needed to do that, but not because I had remembered this about the tribe of Judah; He dropped it in my spirit!

When your spirit, your identity, and your Creator are aligned, He shows us what to do! I had obeyed it, even if I didn't know what I was doing at the time.

That identity message was woven into my whole trip, even across the transition from the month of Adar to the month of Nisan that happened while we were there. Adar is associated with the story of Queen Esther; how she had to take off the mask of who she was to enter into joy. There's much more to that story (as I mentioned earlier) but as I reflected on how it coincided with our journey, it all tied back to identity.

We have to stop looking through someone else's eyes (or visions) of who we are, what they are programmed to see about us. Take off that lens and look through His eyes. Align with Him and His design for you. I mean, why would you try to through someone else's glasses, anyways? If you've ever tried it, you know what I mean. Right, "Four Eyes"? It's literally painful. It can make you go cross-eyed.

When we look at the world through the lens of His design, we are able to see so much more from His perspective. Take trees, for example; He designed them to show us so many things. But when we turn away from His perspective of the tree, and make it an object of worship, we get out of alignment with Him and move into idolatry. Many religions around the world worship trees, including many Christians (that's a story for another day, but if you're open to having your traditions challenged, I encourage you to do some digging for yourself and look up the origins of Christmas trees. Don't hate me. Hate the enemy.)

Back to Israel.

We visited Abraham's well, described in Genesis. Our guides shared how Abraham was elevated in society because of his success. He sensed people were putting him on a pedestal and chose to remove himself. Maybe that was what my mentor had done, whether by conscious decision or not, when she retired. I saw a possible parallel. As we watched a reenactment of the time Abraham went to sacrifice his most-beloved son in obedience to the Father's voice, it all became so clear to me: we all made sacrifices in obedience. Abraham, Dani, and even me. I had surrendered my hope of sharing my trip to Israel with Dani. Dani had taken herself off a pedestal. Abraham laid his future on an altar. We all yielded something in obedience to His voice, no matter the cost, with the hope of inheritance flickering in the future. I had no idea what mine would look like, but hope remained that one day, it would appear. That thought kept me walking forward.

But it wasn't long before I got a glimpse of what that inheritance might look like, and this is where my sacrifice came into play. You see, had I not been on this specific trip with this specific group of people, I

Finding His Timing

would not have received a key revelation.

One morning, I was standing on a porch of our accommodations overlooking the fields in the distance. My friend, Dallas was standing nearby and we struck up a conversation that ended up on dreams. I was telling her about a dream I had on my first trip to Israel about ham. Yes. In my dream, I passed Dani a plate of food and it tipped over, spilling all the food. She reached down and picked up a piece of ham and threw it at me, hitting me in the forehead, and we both started laughing. You might be chuckling at the image, too. But four years later, Dallas' response wasn't laughter. She looked very seriously at me.

"Jen," she said, *"you do know that Paul had a dream about HAM, don't you?"* I didn't. She continued, *"Oh yea, he had a dream about HAM specifically, and it meant that he was called to the nations!"* Instantly, chills ran through my entire body. Whether her interpretation was correct or not, inside something resonated with her words. I felt it. What I was feeling I didn't know, but whatever it was, I knew it was Him. Nations, here I come! Hah! OK, Jen, where you going? I didn't know. But in that moment I knew He did.

At the Cave of Macpelach, which Abraham purchased to bury his wife, Sarah, when she died, I took away three significant insights about the transaction needed in identity.

1) As Abraham went to purchase the land, he declared, *"I'm here to bury my dead."* In Genesis 23:4 *"I'm a sojourner and a settler among you, give me property for a burial site among you so that I bury my dead from my presence."* It made me ask myself what dead things I need to bury and leave behind me?

2) Our guide explained that Abraham paid a shekel for the gravesite, even though the seller wanted to give him the land for free, as an exchange between friends. Yet Abraham insisted, and paid multiple shekels for the land. That the word, "shekel," actually means, "weight." How interesting is that? He was there to bury his dead. What is a weight in that story, in that instance, or in that transaction? In that transaction it was a release, a letting go, a payment. It was a release of a burden and a weight he had been carrying.

3) Abraham knew that it was important for money to be exchanged because he wanted to own it. Why? Because he knew that if he didn't own it, someone could come in and say, *"Oh, you didn't really do this. This didn't really happen. You didn't really go from not owning it to owning it. You didn't really make a transaction. You didn't really make a change. Nothing happened. Nothing changed."* He knew the importance of going through the transaction process. Once he had that purchase completed, he knew that inheritance of that land was possible. That land that had been promised to him and his people was now within reach. The promise was on the other side of the transaction. The inheritance was on the other side. He knew that owning it was the first step to fulfillment, knowing it could not be argued against in the future.

In the cave, I asked myself, *"What dead things inside of me do I need to bury? What am I going to choose to release and lay down in that exchange? What weights am I going to choose to bury here today?"* Then I knew I had to own it—own what used to be, acknowledge that it happened, and declare that I was burying it there that day. On the other side of that exchange stood my inheritance, my promise, and His full blessing of my life. Friend, what dead things inside of you do you need to bury?

Finding His Timing

The Hebrew month of Adar marks the very end of the Hebrew calendar year, celebrating the ending of things. It's not coincidental at all. Our Creator is a God of order and great design. He was working in my life there, and in your life now. He designed a process and a calendar for you to experience the exact same kind of transition in your life that I did in the Holy Land.

What dead things will you bury, knowing that on the other side you're going to step into your next season of blessing, inheritance, and promise in your life? It's time to go to the graveyard.

It's interesting how insights started to piggyback on one another during that trip. For example, the importance of burying dead things took on even more life as we journeyed to the Sea of Galilee and the Dead Sea. The Dead Sea is overwhelmingly salty and no life grows there. Why? The Sea of Galilee isn't salty. It blew my mind that it's due to the fact that the Dead Sea does NOT give life to the bodies of water around it, whereas the Sea of Galilee does. So easy to see the difference when you're standing amidst the abundance of foliage and flowers that surround the Sea of Galilee and the complete absence of life around the Dead Sea. You can't help but notice the vast difference.

It brought to mind the verses in Matthew 5 about being the salt of the earth. *"You are the salt of the earth, but if the salt becomes tasteless, how shall it be seasoned? For it is no longer of any use but to be thrown out and to be trodden down by men. You are the light of the world. It is impossible for a city to be hidden on a mountain. Nor do they light a lamp and put it under a basket, but on a lampstand, and it shines to all those in the house. Let your light so shine before men, so that they see your good works and praise your Father who is in the heavens."*

The next day, as we stood at the Mount of Beatitudes where Yeshua (Jesus) delivered His famous sermon on the mount, someone asked me to read it out loud for the whole group.

I was interested to find that only about 20 people were in the town at the time Yeshua gave this message. So how were there over 5,000 people in attendance that day? How did they all know to be there in time to hear it when He gave it? In marketing, there is no medium more effective than word-of-mouth testimonies. Word had been spreading. People had been following Yeshua because of the miracles he had been performing throughout Galilee:

1) He healed Peter's mother-in-law.

2) When He cast out demons in Capernaum.

3) He walked on the Sea of Galilee.

People were starting to gather to hear him speak because of the miracles and healings. At that gathering, He performed another miracle, turning the two fish and five loaves of bread into enough food for the whole crowd, and then some! So why did they gather? Because He was giving life!

So, you tell me how important it is to bury the dead things inside us. How important is it for the impact we want to have on those around us? How impactful will we be to the bodies (of water) around us if we're full of dead things, things that are not giving life?

The city of Capernaum is where all the miracles started. It's also where Yeshua said to the fisherman on the Sea of Galilee, **"Come with me."** He later commanded them to declare that, **"the Kingdom** *of Elohim has come near."* I think He knew other kings and other kingdoms would try to take or claim authority over people's lives.

Genesis 22:2 says, *"And He said 'take your son now, your only son Isaac, whom you love and go to the land of Moriah. And offer him there as an ascending offering on one of the mountains on which I command you.' Abraham rose early in the morning and saddled his donkey and took two of his young men with him and Isaac his son and he split the wood for the ascending offering and rose and went to the place where Elohim had commanded him. And on the third day Abraham lifted his eyes and saw the place from a distance. So Abraham said to his young men, 'stay here with the donkey while the boy and I go over there and worship, and come back to you.' And Abraham took the wood of the ascending offering and laid it on Yitshaq, his son. And he took the fire in his hand, and a knife, and the two of them went together. And Yitsaq spoke to Abraham his father and said, "My father!" and he said, "Here I am, my son," and he said, "See, the fire and the wood, But where is the lamb for an ascending offering?"*

Abraham gets to the top of the mountain, prepares his son for sacrifice, and as he's raising the knife to obey the Father to the very point of sacrificing his son, a messenger stops him and says, *"Abraham, do not lay your hand on the boy nor touch him for now I know that you fear Elohim seeing as you have not withheld your only son from me."*

As our guide was sharing this story, as he asked us, *"how old do you think Isaac was when this happened?"*

My entire life I had thought Isaac was a young child. Picturing him as a young child it was so hard for me to process this story because I thought, why didn't Isaac react? Why did he not squirm and struggle? Or throw things at him? Why was it not more of a battle to tie up his son? You'd think a child would scream and run away.

But Isaac was NOT a child; he was, in fact, in his late 30's. What?! No wonder this story was so hard to process before. Not only was Abraham willing to obey the Father's voice—up to the point of being willing to sacrifice his own son; to surrender everything that he loved—but so was Isaac. Isaac was so willing to obey the Creator and have faith in his father that he was willing to accept what was going on was supposed to happen. He was willing to obey and surrender to death. This entire time I had thought Isaac was a child. Not only was he not a child, but he, too, had to surrender.

As I processed this revelation, I saw the parallel to Yeshua: being willing to follow and obey his Father's voice, even unto death. Fortunately for Abraham, after the messenger stopped him from sacrificing his son, the messenger declared the blessing that would be upon Abraham and his legacy. This is what happens when we obey the Father's voice. What's on the other side? A blessing.

Another passage that had been playing on repeat in my brain the entire time was Proverbs 3:5-6 : *"Lean not on your own understanding, but acknowledge me in all your ways."*

How many times do we go through circumstances thinking we're hearing the Creator's voice, but then our own thinking gets in the way? We question the Creator's words to us, thinking this doesn't make sense; *"why would I do that? I don't understand. I need to understand before I obey."* But that's not what this story shows. It doesn't say obey once it all makes sense to you. It says, obey before you understand, and *trust who I say I am. Trust who I have been to*

Finding His Timing

your forefathers and what I have shown through their example. Am I not trustworthy? Will I not bless you because of your obedience?

I don't know about you, but I sure want to be in a place where I choose to trust the Father with my whole heart, even when I don't understand. I don't want to lean on my own understanding, but to simply obey when I hear Him and to have faith in who He says He is.

As the trip went on, more lights came on, revealing the Creator's perfect timing throughout history. Maybe you're like me, wondering as you've read all these stories, how did we ever lose sight of this? If they were aware of their own identity and tribe in Biblical history, where did we go wrong? Why did this get lost?

The answer was right in front of me as we stood outside the city of David, the walls of Jerusalem that once held the tabernacle. The walkway and arch were broken to smithereens, laying in rubble on the ground, thanks to the Romans. No wonder we lost connection to the roots of who we are. The connection was broken and left in rubble. No wonder we're all trying to put the pieces back and figure out who we are. There are reasons identity was lost.

But not everyone has lost it. We were at a promenade overlooking the city of King David, gaining new insights about the story when Abraham was being obedient to the Father's voice, where he was even willing to sacrifice his son, Issac. It's one thing to read about the stories; it's a whole other thing to be in the very places where these historical events took place (not to mention hearing them from our tour guide who literally came from the Hebrew tribe and lineage of King David himself!) He blew my shofar. Oh wait...I think I already mentioned that. Sorry, it's just too cool. But like I said, not everyone lost their identity. Some have held on to it and can trace it all the way back to the beginning!

The revelations of the lights from the illuminated map continued to make appearances as the trip continued. Did you know the seventh day of the Hebrew month of Nisan was the day the Israelites entered the promised land? We realized that we would be returning home from Israel on the day after. Did you know that, according to Jewish law, mourning was supposed to happen for at least seven days, (sometimes 30). We were simultaneously mourning our mentor and her absence on this trip just as they had mourned Moses and his death before they entered the Promised Land.

At the banquet the last night of the trip, we were all sharing our biggest takeaway from the trip. I shared how, for me, it had all been about identity. From the Romans to the Greeks, the Catholics to the Germans—so much stolen Kingship. So much stolen identity when He is the King, our Creator! It is His authority and desire to connect us to His original design and all the ego from generation to generation that has tried to insert itself and say "their way" was best. So much ego instead of humility.

Why was King David chosen? Because of his humility. He was reminding me that Kingship is all about humility. He raised the humble, and here we were, getting a second tour of the Holy Lands and reconnecting to our roots with our guide who was literally from the lineage of that very King himself. He blew my shofar. You remember.

What a gift! What a gift it is to get reconnected to your roots. Imagine having never lost sight of who you are.

If I could go back to that day, I would say:

Finding His Timing

"Yes! He is reconnecting you to your roots! The roots of your design! The roots of His timing! The roots of His Kingship! He's untangling all the mess from centuries past to show you the truth of who He is and the truth of who you are!

It is time! Time to redeem. Time to unearth it all! Time to reclaim all that was lost! I bless you in reclaiming truth! I bless you in mending what was broken! I bless you with Him answering that call to the nations through you! He is the healer! He is restoring! He is redeeming it all! You will overcome. They will overcome. He has overcome! And He is not done!"

Finding His Timing

Finding His Timing

CHAPTER 21

Hold up truth and embrace the waves with humility

After I got back home from my trip to the Holy Land, I took an adventure to the Gulf Coast to visit one of the oldest oak trees in Rockport, Texas. I knew I had valid reasons to be full of expectation. To see a tree?! Crazy, right? Anyone who knew me as a kid is thinking, "Jen, you took a road trip to look at trees? What's happened to you? You didn't grow up with any appreciation for nature or the outdoors...it was dirty and there were bugs." Don't worry, I'm smirking at this, too. Of course, if you're a new friend, you might believe I'm obsessed with trees. I'm okay with that. We do hug.

But it doesn't seem as crazy as when I think back on all the adventures I had that year, journeys I took simply because I knew I was in pursuit of stories about the grandeur parallel map. The map that revealed more of His design. More of Him.

But not just any stories; stories from the past that have been held up for generations!

But come on, Jen. Come back to reality. You just went to the beach...right?! Wrong. I'm time-traveling, remember? You have to time-travel to go back to the past. And it just so happened to be the very first time April and I had planned an adventure specifically during the Feast of Pentecost (known in Hebrew as Shavou't) one of the many feasts we're told to remember in scripture. Don't worry, I didn't realize this, either, until I started studying the Hebrew calendar.

Shavou't was the time in Biblical history when Moses received the Torah (The 10 Commandments) on Mt Sinai. Being new to the feast, April and I were on another hunt. We were hunting for all the things our Creator might have to show us! As we dug in and did our research, He showed up and showed off.

Walking up to this old oak tree in Rockport, we were struck by how enormous it was. Branches stretched farther to the left and right than I had ever seen a tree reach. As I took in the sight, I said, *"Look at the beams!! There's just two. One on either side of its arms, helping hold it up because it's so massive and there's so much weight to it! Who does that remind you of!?"*

"Moses!" we both exclaimed. There is a story in Exodus of Moses overseeing a battle against the Amalakites. As long as he held his hands up before the Lord, the Israelites were winning. But he got tired, and as he lowered his arms, they began to lose. So Aaron and Hur held up his arms on either side.

But why did that vision come back to mind (beyond the obvious fact that there were beams on either side of this oak, and Moses had two arms that were important to hold up to win the battle)? Everyone has two arms. Well, most everyone.

First, it brought back to mind the passage in Isaiah 61:3:

"The Spirit of the Master Yahaveh is upon Me, because Yahaveh has anointed Me to bring good news to the meek. He has sent Me to bind up the broken-hearted, to proclaim release to the captives, and the opening of the prison to those who are bound, to proclaim the acceptable year of Yahaveh, and the day of vengeance of our Elohim, to comfort all who mourn, to appoint unto those who mourn in Tsiyon: to give them embellishment for ashes, the oil of joy for mourning, the garment of praise for the spirit of heaviness. And they shall be called trees of righteousness, a planting of Yahaveh, to be adorned. And they shall rebuild the old ruins, raise up the former wastes. And they shall restore the ruined cities, the wastes of many generations." (TS2009)

The Oak of Righteousness. Moses has been remembered for generations. He received the Torah at Pentecost. What holds up righteousness? ...TORAH! Torah is the Oak of Righteousness.

It all came full circle right in front of me. Torah holds up righteousness. It was given to Moses on Pentecost. When his arms were held up, they were winning! When his arms were lowered, they started losing.

Friends, what if that's it?! If you're losing, and you don't know why, mabye you're forgetting to hold up the righteousness of our Elohim! What do I mean?

Have you ever been to the ocean or the beach and just felt

immediately welcomed into the serene? It's like your soul just knows... here I find rest. You take in a deep breath. Outside of the water, obviously, not in it. It's almost as if you haven't really breathed a deep breath in weeks. You exhale. What is that?

Could it be that we're simply engaging in a design, an invitation from our Creator who knows we need such moments? There, in those moments, we win. We win on levels we can't even begin to explain. What if, as I said before, it's in our very design? His design. A design to win.

Psalm 29 says His voice is on the waters. I've been on a hunt my whole life to find it. What if at the water, we're simply home and we can feel it. We can feel it every time it calls. I've learned His voice does call—we see it all over scripture: *"Come to me...all you who are weary and I will give you rest."* What if He knows our design will find rest when we come to the water?!

What else are we forgetting that's in our very design? Our spirits know when we're not in His design; we feel confused, in chaos, filled with worry, and not at rest. What if He just wants to sit with us, to begin (or continue) our journey with Him? I think the answer is in 1 Samuel 12: *"they forgot their Elohim!"* How does this happen?! How has it happened over centuries?

I might lose some of you here as I share this next discovery, and that is OK. This is for those who want to hear it and are willing to stay open.

Recently, I watched a video about the origins of the modern education system. People behind it weren't interested in developing people of high intelligence, but a system that output a workforce.

Finding His Timing

Intelligence. Did you hear that? Their goal was NOT intelligence.

Have you ever wondered what would happen if we operated life in the way they did in Biblical times? They placed so much more value on sacred things. They valued set-apart time with the Father, His creation, cultivating the innate intelligence He gave them to navigate life according to His design, His cycles (calendar), and His creation? He uses His creation to teach us every day: not for us to become 'gods,' but for us to know who we are and who He is!

What does the modern American education system teach? How dumb we are. Come on, who actually remembers how to use letters inside of an equation? A + B = xzy. I'm pretty sure that's wrong. But what the flip-flop? No, modern education programs you to believe that, with enough education you can become an elite part of society. Maybe even a master. Or, dare I say it, a mini-god in our own minds? They'll even give you a certification of it. Congratulations, you're not dumb.

Please hear me when I say I am not knocking education. I'm absolutely knocking our focus. Could our focus simply be on the wrong thing? What are we forgetting in our pursuit of education?

I want to share something raw, ugly, and private with you and it is never easy to do. So why do I share these stories? I believe this is why we're here. I want to continue to show up authentic with you and my Creator, and the more I lean into doing so, the more freedom I find. It's all about freedom.

Anytime I've ever tried to lean on my own understanding...holy crap, did I derail! If you've read my first book, you already know much of the story, but there's more, because I'm human and I make mistakes. Because I listen to the wrong voice at times (mostly my own voice.)

It's in those moments when I think I have to understand something that I get stuck. So stuck that I couldn't even see my stuck, until someone else shared a personal story, and the Creator smacked me with my stuck right in my stuckiness with the words, *"if we're not careful, we become what we judge."*

Trainer Carmen O'Quinn was sharing how she had always held a judgment against people who behaved a certain way. Until one day she realized she had been behaving that way, too. She could "never understand" people like that until she became one. How many times had I heard Dani Johnson say, *"we judge what we don't understand."* Gasp! It hit so much deeper. How many times have I sat in the seat of judgment simply because I didn't understand someone else's actions or decisions?!

But when I don't understand, if I don't let it go…I'm in judgment?! Ahhhhhhh! I was absolutely mortified, gut-punched, and appalled at that realization about myself. If you can feel my shock, and recognize this same tendency in yourself, don't worry, we're all hunched over, ready to hurl together.

It was never my intent to judge anyone! But my lack of letting those feelings go–of not releasing the need to understand why they did what they did–had put me in a seat I never thought I would be in: a seat of judgment. UGHHHHHH. YUCK! I told you it was ugly. But when I saw myself sitting there, about to hurl, I knew I had to own it. Why? Because I did not want to become that thing I didn't understand. It was too important, and so were those people, even if I didn't understand their motives.

Finding His Timing

It was time to let it all go, to release it! I had to forgive those I didn't understand. I didn't need to know their why. I had to forgive those I felt abandoned by when we needed them. Was it easy? No, it never is. Was it worth it? Holy crap, yes!

I had to remember who my Creator is, the One who said, *"trust in the Lord with all your heart and lean not on your own understanding."* That night in my bathtub, alone with my Creator, that's exactly what I did. So grateful He has a design to wash it all off. There was a lot of stuckiness to wash off.

How does this happen? How do I get here? Well, friend, you're not alone if you're asking that. In fact, even King David, the one described as the most beloved of the Father, got off track. He defeated Goliath, in 1 Samuel 17, shouting; *"You come against me with sword and spear and javelin, but I come against you in the name of the Lord Almighty!"* But it wasn't long after that that David found himself on the run, hunted by King Saul. In 1 Samuel 21, someone offered him Goliath's spear to defend himself and he replied, *"There is none like it, give it to me!"* He defeated Goliath with only five stones and his faith, and yet in fear for his life, he took Goliath's sword (and ironically the five loaves of showbread). Yahaveh's (God's) word, is symbolically shown in the Old Testament as showbread, and in the New Testament referred to as the "Sword of the Spirit." He forgot how he fought Goliath with only simple faith in who His Yahaveh was! He forgot His Elohim!

Yet the Father was right there this whole time, ready to meet with him as he took the showbread, calling out to him, *"Remember me, remember who you are, remember who I am!"*

Everything we need to live a life of victory is available to us at any

Finding His Timing

time: the answers, how to win, what to hold up (His truth). Just like those two beams held up the mighty oak's arms! Just like King David knew how to defeat Goliath.

We start to lose when we forget to hold up the Torah (His voice). When we forget to focus on who we are and who He is. Hold that high! If we're not intentional, it can sneak up on us without us even realizing it happened, and it can be ugly, just like anytime anyone jumps out at me. Don't try it. You don't want to see it.

But there's hope and there's a design. You were designed to live a set-apart life! To remember the Elohim. To live in the sacred and not the mundane. Which do you want, friend?

Finding His Timing

Finding His Timing

CHAPTER 22

A date with Him for your identity

I knew what I wanted. I could see the Creator's timing at work as we rolled into the Hebrew month of Tammuz again. In Biblical history, Tammuz is when the spies were sent to scout out the Promised Land and report to the people. Of course, to enter the new land, they first had to believe the land was their inheritance.

Like clockwork, I started seeing so much correlation to this story and this timing. I was coming up on my own transition–my 40th birthday. We've talked about the importance of the number 40 in Scripture: The Israelites were slaves for 400 years in Egypt, then they wandered the desert for 40 years. Forty days after Moses died, the Israelites entered the Promised Land. Forty days before my birthday I was given 40 gold and black balloons, each with a note inside speaking identity into to me each day until the transition. Unbeknownst to the giver, the notes correlated directly to the story of Moses and the 40 days right before the Israelites entered their Promised Land.

Later that week, it was my turn to lead the devotional at my Crossfit gym. The topic was heroes of the faith. I knew Yahaveh had been talking to me about sharing about King David and why he was my hero. Little did I know that nudge led me to finding yet another piece of gold in my own journey. Apparently, the Israelites' transition into the Promised Land had some similarities to my own journey into promise.

I shared how in the hours after I heard the news of my dad's death, I also heard a subtle whisper say, *"I will never leave you or forsake you."* Those words appear in Hebrews 13:5 and in Deuteronomy 31. Moses was encouraging the Israelites to take possession of the Promised Land: *"Be strong and courageous, do not fear nor be afraid of them, For it is Yahaveh your Elohim who is going with you. He does not leave you or forsake you."* Later he tells Joshua (his successor) the same thing, but adds *'And it is Yahaveh who is going before you, He himself is with you. Do not fear or be discouraged!"* Joshua had massive, daunting shoes to fill, especially with the challenge of leading them into the Promised Land.

For years, I've clung to Hebrews 13:5 because of the *"I will never leave you"* part. It wasn't until decades later when I realized the depth of the *"or never forsake you"* part. I shared about all the inner healing I had experienced the previous years with Dani Johnson. How I got free from shame, regret, and all the times I messed up, and how I got

Finding His Timing

to share with the whole world all those stories I thought I would take to my grave. As I head into my own "Promised Land" of identity. Having found my answers and becoming free, the second part of that verse brings me even greater comfort! No matter who might forsake me, He hasn't and He won't! I declared it and now I am walking into the Promised Land.

Of course, most people know what happened after Moses declared that blessing over the Israelites. The people of Israel chose to receive the negative report of the spies who checked out the Promised Land and refused to enter. I knew I was entering into dangerous territory. I almost missed out on the significance of the following month, Av, which was all about celebrating His goodness, entering the land, and entering promise. I almost listened to the voice of unbelief!

The whole year had been one big object lesson about identity, and He capped the whole thing by asking for a date with me! About my identity. He was showing me that my birthday was a date with Him to celebrate my identity! I have a date with Him every year now! That's my birthday plan, my birthday promise! Had any other plan actually happened I might have missed that appointment.

But before I tell what actually happened, let me first go back a moment to our trip to Israel. On our way to Israel we got stuck in London, Heathrow airport for 12 hours. We missed our connecting flight, having already spent the previous night traveling across the Atlantic, groggy and ready for real sleep. We just wanted to reach our destination and it was stolen. Insert all the feels, frustrations, and exhaustion.

Thanks to my amazing travel companions, we were able to spend those 12 hours inside a club lounge, despite the frustrating situation.

Finding His Timing

Joy entered with Sapphire Sally (the silly character I created for the little moments of life) enjoying some tea time with her friend, and some tiny tea cups.

As the tea took over and the fatigue wore off, we began pondering the place we were in. What could He be showing us right now? He obviously knows we're here. He obviously knows we're on our way to His land, could He have wanted us to take a pit stop here first?! That's where the story gets interesting.

I believe wholeheartedly His answer was "yes". Why? Because on that layover, He showed us so much about kingship. How could we not see it? England is ruled by a throne. It's everywhere. But wait, what about the King (the Creator)? Isn't He on the throne? How must He feel? The concept of humility hit so much deeper. You don't often see humility in any earthly Kingdom. Could He have been showing us at the start of this journey that it's all about humility?

That's precisely what He did, at least for me. It was about sovereignty, because He is sovereign. But what does that even mean? What is His kingdom? It's all His. How many times throughout history has His throne been stolen, chased after by the enemy?

The enemy constantly tries to usurp the throne, yet has NO rights to it! It's easy to see with stories like the Nazi Holocaust, and the story of soon-to-be-King David, as King Saul chased him across the desert. In both stories, the victims had done nothing wrong to be hunted.

At the same time, we had been reading the story of King Saul and David in 1 Samuel 23-25. King Saul chased after David all the way to the caves of En Gedi. Saul was all about himself. David had done nothing wrong, but Saul knew he would someday take "his" throne, even though it really wasn't his to keep. There it is again, the absence of humility. Anytime we put ourself on any throne God has not given us (or for which we've disqualified ourselves, like Saul) we're in the wrong! We're saying we know better than Yahaveh!

He shows us to choose the path of humility–choosing to trust what He chooses to do with His kingdom. Why? Because the throne is already His.

What happens when we embrace humility? Do we really lose? It sometimes feels like we are losing. In 1 Samuel 25, Abigail's humility before King David saved countless lives.

People who pursue a throne or position God has not given them always seem to end up bringing about violence.

But when we choose to humble ourselves, we actually win and we save lives—far more than you could ever imagine. David understood, and was given an Earthly throne because he surrendered to Yahweh's plan by submitting to King Saul, the anointed king.

We become free by embracing His Kingship, aligning to His sovereignty, because He already won. And He won so that we could be free.

What if perfect kingship is freedom? Yeshua redeems all the things that have happened to us (or will happen to us) that grieve us and Him, restores all that was lost, and comforts all those who mourn! He frees us from every thing that entangles, ensnares, or leaves us feeling trapped. What a Kingship! What a King, who knows we simply want to be FREE from ourselves. What a King, who knows that in embracing humility, surrender, and submission, we receive it all.

David is remembered as the greatest king of Israel and a man after God's own heart. What was it about him that afforded him both of these gigantic titles? Humility and authenticity. But most of his life he was pursued by his enemies. Why? Because, in his true identity, he was God's chosen man to be King. Authentic leaders walking in harmony with their true God-given identity are a threat to those who hang onto their power illegitimately. The Creator's enemies will always attack those who walk in authentic identity and intimate relationship with the Creator. Our responsibility is to keep the Creator on the throne of our lives, but that's a real challenge. Selfish desire and the lures of the world work tirelessly to put themselves on that throne. I don't want that to be my story. I want to keep myself in a place where the Creator is on the throne of my life, so I routinely ask myself, *"where have I allowed myself or someone else to take the Creator's throne in my heart?"*

I saw three instances play out before me:

Shortly after becoming debt-free, one of the first things I did to celebrate that huge sprout was to invest in a kayak! It aligned with my vision for the next season of my life: I wanted to be in nature, to hear Him more clearly, and to enjoy every possible day of rest on the water.

When it arrived, it was broken, then it busted more, then I took it to the lake and over 200 cars were there, when just days prior, the place had been empty. I battled thoughts like, *"go home...this isn't worth it...what a nightmare...you're going to have to walk for over 20 minutes from your car carrying your giant kayak...it's going to be hot and you're going to look ridiculous."* On and on they circled. I almost gave up.

Instead I shouted, *"YOU WILL NOT STEAL MY JOY!!!!"* In

that moment, I knew there wasn't anything stopping me from getting in that water. Joy is His throne—His Kingdom.

Reflecting back on it later, I asked myself, *"in what ways am I allowing myself to be hunted?"* The kingdom of darkness is trying to take over the throne in my life, when it has NO right to that position. In the moments when I feel like giving up, when I give in to fatigue and tired thoughts, boom! He wins. He's not supposed to win! I had to stake my claim to the throne of my life. I chose joy. I declared it.

The second story relates to my 40th birthday.

I spent the six months leading up to my 40th birthday speaking life over that transition. Our culture speaks so much death over 40, with expressions like *"over the hill,"* and black balloons. That isn't the Creator's design for us.

After being enslaved for 400 years in Egypt, the Israelites spent 40 years in the desert. From the death of Moses to their entrance into the Promised Land was 40 days. He can redeem so quickly what we think will take a longer when we keep ourselves aligned with Him! Look at that acceleration! Look at how He accelerates your promotion to your identity and promise, as long as you keep yourself aligned with Him and His ways. You could say His design for 40 is acceleration!

I also invested a lot of time and effort working on a plan to spend my birthday someplace tropical. You know how I love being on the water. I did tons of research, called friends I had visited the tropics with before, and let others take the lead. For whatever reason, nothing was locking into place. We tossed around all kinds of locations.... Italian Coast, Greece, Belize, Bermuda, Bahamas, Costa Rica...the list goes on.

In previous years, these trips had come together easily. I couldn't help but wonder why this trip was so difficult to pull together. The deadline to book the trip loomed, inching slowly and menacingly toward me.

About four weeks before the deadline, I thought we settled on a great choice: Costa Rica. Finally! The last last person finally confirmed we were ready to book...only to find our chosen destination had been taken by another group that day! Two more friends dropped out. It seemed settled and done. Now we were back at square one. I was ready to give up, defeated.

I was down to one last friend who was still committed to the trip, Kim. We didn't even have a trip to be committed to: it was all gone and I was wiped out. Just then, she said, *"I think you just need to hold on to hope!"* I let go of it all, rested on those words alone. *"Sure,"* I mumbled, *"I'll hold on, but hope is all I have left right now. I don't even have any urge to try to plan anything anymore."*

It was just the message I needed to hear at that moment. As it turns out, we were in the middle of the month where the two Israelite spies spoke belief over God's promise that they were to enter their new land, while everyone else gave in to fear. *"What if we just went back to Hawaii?"* she asked. I perked up, *"I love Hawaii!"* I said, *"It's always a yes from me!"*

Actually, it all fell into place. We booked our hotel and began getting ready for the trip. That's when I read that the property had a giant banyan tree in the courtyard. A banyan tree! I had a flashback to our adventure in Florida six months prior. Yahaveh took us on an epic treasure hunt so He could reveal what He had to say.

Finding His Timing

We weren't planning to hunt for a banyan tree. Someone just casually asked, *"I wonder where a banyan tree might be??"* It seemed like such a silly random question until we "accidentally" circled the Disney Polynesian Resort on our way to Epcot and learned the construction area we saw was going to hold a massive banyan tree, but it wasn't yet there. We learned so much about Him and His design on that trip through the trees that he showed us. Yet we never found the banyan.

Could this be Him? It had to be! I didn't know there was a giant banyan tree on the property in Oahu we chose to stay at.

Joy flooded back into my soul as I awaited that appointment with Him underneath a tree with deep roots that shoot down from it's very limbs high in the sky, creating more trunks around the core!

Kim had a friend who lives in Oahu, whom I had never met. When she heard we were coming, she said, *"I don't know how you guys feel about surfing, but I have two boards, and I can get a third one if you're interested in that. I would love to take you guys on my day off!"*

What?! A stranger wants to take me surfing...and she didn't even know that we were coming to Hawaii to celebrate my 40th birthday?!

What. Is. Happening?!

But of course it wasn't all just sunshine and unicorn farts. On our way there, we had a layover in Long Beach, just as a hurricane was approaching the California coast. I've never had a layover in Long Beach, and our flight made it out just before they shut the airport down.

A story was brewing. Had all this frustration and re-orchestration not happened, this story would never have happened. I let it all go, surrendered it, a friend told me to hold onto hope, and look what stayed on the throne...joy. The joy I experienced was more than I could have possibly imagined. This was becoming a story even I couldn't have planned.

When you're being intentional and you let go of old identities that are not yours, clarity comes. It should not have surprised me, as I began walking into a new dream, aligned with the Father and His design; that the one who wants to usurp His throne would try to remind me of the past.

On a visit to Destin, Florida, I spent some time on the beach, letting the waves ripple around my feet and talking to my Creator. As the waves grew in intensity, I saw a calm in the water. Calm may look inviting, even peaceful, but experienced beach-goers know that calm water is the sign of a hidden danger: the riptide, which can sweep you out to sea and drown you in seconds.

In a way, the process of overcoming the past has waves that look intimidating and calms that look deceptively peaceful. The Creator allows our past to come back into our lives in waves—it's his process of healing and refining us, showing us who we really are and how far we've come—but it can be terrifying to go through. The enemy tries to make us think that we are going to drown in those waves, and that the comfort of smooth waters will be better, but it's a trap to get us away from the work the Creator is trying to do in our lives. He appeals to our ego, our sense of self, to hang onto comfort, but the only way to get free from the past is to let go of the comfort of self and embrace humility.

Finding His Timing

Friend, what if that's the entire point of it all? To embrace the waves with humility! Humility isn't easy, and neither is taking authority of what we will choose to let reign!

I choose to remember my King! To remember who He is and who I am! To surrender it all, knowing it is His throne.

The enemy does not get to come in and set up his fake kingdom of destruction, chaos, confusion, despair, hopelessness, poverty, fear. Especially not when I'm heading into promise.

Don't let him steal your joy, friend, or put anything in a place of ruler ship in your heart, your mind, or your body that is not the Creator's design!

If I could go back to that day, I would say:

"Yes!! He is the King! It's all His! He is showing you who He is! Let Him reign! Let the things that are of Him reign. And whatever is not of Him, command to leave. You have authority—His authority! It reigns in you!

Remember who He is! Remember who you are!

I bless you with knowing who you are! I bless you with embracing His Kingship! I bless you with walking in His kingdom! I bless you with holding up truth!"

CHAPTER 23

The light that leads you out, the manna amidst Sukkot

So what happened to the third story, Jen? You promised me three stories, and I don't feel like you've told me the one that wouldn't have happened had it not been for all the frustration and re-orchestration around your 40th birthday. You're right. It's time to share that third story. It began in the Hebrew month of Elul, which in Hebrew means, "*I am my beloved's, and my beloved is mine.*" Elul is a time to get ready for the fall Biblical Feasts. Interestingly, I had someone tell me, "*get ready,*" but at the time, I didn't know what to get ready for.

I left for Oahu with great expectation. That giant banyan tree that awaited us on Waikiki Beach felt like an appointment.

In great anticipation of what this encounter might bring, I began digging into anything I could find out about banyan trees and their design. I learned that banyan trees can only sprout and grow with the help of strangler wasps, who pollinate their figs. Figs are mentioned as one of the fruits the Hebrew spies brought back from scouting out the Promised Land. Their inheritance! I also learned that the banyan can grow incredibly broad because of it's root system; it's always growing outward. I felt like He was showing me so much about my journey of identity and giving me a glimpse of what was to come on this trip.

I read that the main trunk of a banyan tree eventually gets choked out by the new trunks that shoot down from it's limbs as it extends and grows outward. The new trunks grow stronger and the old trunk gradually dies and becomes hollow on the inside. The empty trunk is often large enough to serve as a storm shelter for several people. It's the only tree that does that. Banyan trees can also live for hundreds of years.

My identity is like that. The Creator has led me away from my old identity but now I see the hollow shell of that old identity is providing shelter, a safe place for others in their own transition of discovering who they truly are.

The banyan tree had another message for me. The strength and longevity of the mighty banyan tree comes from the roots it shoots down around that old trunk. You could say another "new root" was in the souvenir brought home from Hawaii.

I had a wonderful Mai-Tai on that trip on a visit to Koa Distillers. So wonderful I shipped one home. But that wasn't the only one I brought home. I also brought home a literal Thai. His name is Timothy. I call him Mai-Thai.

I'll explain.

Finding His Timing

First it's critically important to remember the Creator's timing is the key to understanding what happened. The 24 hours leading up to my birthday, I spent a few hours on a layover at the airport in Long Beach and the rest on the airplane. When the sun rose on my 40th birthday, I was in Oahu. I had been on numerous dating apps, and as I was on my way to Oahu, I swiped on the profile for a man named Timothy. We must have matched that evening or in the early morning hours, because the next morning I had a message from him:

Timothy (Mai-Thai): *"Hey Jen!"*

Me: *"Hey Tim - are you on Oahu?!"*

I wasted no time, as I only had ten days on Oahu, and if he was there, I was going to meet this tanned, ripped Asian man with a huge smile, who seemed to love his Creator (according to his bold bio on the app)!

Timothy (Mai-Thai): *"Oahu? No, I'm in Northern California, where are you?"*

Me: *"Oh! Hah, well I'm actually just visiting Oahu. I'm from Texas!"*

Timothy (Mai-Thai): *"Texas? How the heck did we match?!"*

Timothy had set up his profile to only match to others who were within 60 miles of his home in northern California. Even when I was stuck at the Long Beach airport, I was over 600 miles away. So how could this be?

We both knew immediately it must be the Almighty, and that a story was brewing.

Remember the six months I spent consistently speaking life into this transition? My Creator had been showing me the significance of the number 40 about transition, promise, and blessing. I had been eagerly anticipating this transition and everything He had waiting for me in my Promised Land.

The more I talked to Timothy, the safer I felt. Could he be like a banyan? Was he a safe place too? Maybe it was a little early to be asking questions like these, but my spidey-senses were on alert! I knew something significant was happening in my life on my big day of transition.

The banyan tree was showing me something: With it's huge limbs the banyan is the mightiest tree in the world, with the longest longevity, living for hundreds of years and providing shelter for communities of people throughout history. Like the strangler wasps, the figs, the fruit from the Promise Land, and the oranges, this was another message to me from the Creator about the importance of my identity. I had to know my identity, which came from walking into promise. (Maybe Tim and I were also like banyan trees for each other because of knowing our identity).

As we got to know one another those first few weeks, my Creator gently nudged me toward crossing into my inheritance. How do I know? There are countless details I could tell you of the reassurance that He gave as I got to know Timothy, but there's one I can't not share. The day my father passed from suicide, my Creator gently whispered to my heart, *"We got this, Jen—you and Me!"* (as I looked at the terrifying road ahead without my dad). The first time Timothy expressed his affections for me, he didn't say, *"I love you,"* instead he said, "*The words 'I love you' could be replaced with 'I got you' to each other, and then the word 'love' is given back to God, because He is love.*"

Tim didn't know what that particular phrase meant to me. He had no idea the depths of the journey I had been on—not yet. I sat there that day, stunned at his choice of expression, knowing it was another nudge to keep trusting what the Creator had put before me delivered in a way only He could have known. Here was this sweet, kind, Godly, magnificent hunk of Thai man (see why I say I brought home a "My-Thai" now?).

Those nudges kept coming. Soon they were shouting. During those first few weeks, I got my first exposure to Tim's weightlifting competitions. He was at Nationals, and it just so happened to also be Rosh Hashannah, the Hebrew Feast of Trumpets. Between Tim's sets I read about the Feast of Trumpets in *Aligning With God's Appointed Times* by Rabbi Jason Sobel. As I read, I realized that Timothy has a story of surrender and sacrifice with everything in his life—even his own children. Just like Abraham and Isaac, I could see how Timothy was in total alignment with His Creator. Because of his heart to surrender all, I sensed that the Creator would bless him as he had blessed Abraham.

In *"Aligning with God's Appointed Times,"* Rabbi Jason Sobel says:

"Matthew 19:29 says, Anyone who has left everything for my sake, will receive a HUNDRED times as much, and will inherit eternal life". Do you see the connection between the old and the new? All who are willing to leave everything for the Lord and trust in the Lord will ultimately receive great blessing from the Lord like Abraham

and Sarah". He was asking Him to trust the Lord to provide for His future". 'The blessing always exceeds the sacrifice when you are faithful to God and are willing to invest in His Kingdom."

Tim was messaging me during the competition and got excited because they gave him the competitor number 5. *"Jen, this is a Biblical number!"* I knew exactly what he was talking about because of all my dives into my Creator's design for numbers. I knew it was His number for the grace to overcome something. I told him, *"He established his covenant with Abraham with five sacrifices; Israel came out of Egypt ranked in fives; David picked up five smooth stones to fight Goliath; the pool of Bethsada where the lame man was healed had five porches, and the list goes on! I love that you got the number five! YOU are His story of Overcoming!"* Tim replied, *"not only that; look at my lift total! It's 221kg—what does that add up to?! – Five!"*

Tim called me from his car after his sets, and as we chatted I told him, *"I saw God, Grace, and Gratitude, on that stage"* as I was watching him. When he walked on stage and chalked his hands, I noticed that he immediately looked to the sky, acknowledging His Creator. After his lifts, he bowed to the judges and put his hands together, thanking each of them with his movements—God and Gratitude. Then God gave him Grace, stamping him with the number 5 on his singlet. Later he shared that this was the first time he looked to the sky at the start of a competition set. Bowing to the judges with his hands together was part of his Thai upbringing. He could hear his mother in his head, ready to hit him with a frying pan if he didn't show gratitude. Ting!

Later that day I shared how the fifth month is the month of Overcoming, and how I trademarked The Overcomers in the fifth month. It then hit me that the Creator had stamped Tim with the number 5, could we be one?! Weird thought, I know, but it led to so many more revelations. Tim asked, *"Jen, what's 5+5? 10. But what's 1+0 =1. One is unity with the Father. It's why we ARE one!"*

That aspect of "one-ness" became a regular topic of our conversations. As Tim dove more into the roots of the phrase, he said, *"it's not just waiting for sex until marriage, and what happens after."* The modern world looks at the subject with so much ignorance, it's laughable. But what if it's not only about what it means, but what it brings? Could it be about protection of mind, body, and spirit?

What would one-ness SEXUALLY look like?

Have you surrendered your sexuality to your Creator and cleaned house? Have you broken any ties spiritually to other things or persons you've 'one-ness'd' with in the past? There are tools for both surrender and breaking ties to former partners.

What about one-ness PHYSICALLY?

Have you embraced diligence with taking care of your design and your temple with sleep, nutrition, water, and exercise?

What about one-ness MENTALLY?

Have you embraced teach-ability and invested in personal development and never stop, or do you think you already know it all or have arrived?

What about one-ness SPIRITUALLY?

Have you figured out your identity? Do you know who you are

and who He is?

The true heart of the Overcomer is found in the beginning, Genesis 1:27: *"Man was created in His image."* We don't all seem to believe that nowadays, so it's no wonder we don't know who we are and how our identity got lost. We get back to our identity by finding out who we are and who He is! Maybe we all need to be hit with a frying pan.

Tim shared the following insight:

"When God created fish, He spoke to the sea.

When God created trees, and plants, and vegetation, He spoke to the earth.

When God created man, He spoke to himself.

The water is the natural habitation of the fish.

When you remove the fish out of the water, the fish die.

The earth is the natural habitation of the trees.

When you remove the trees from the earth, the trees die.

He is the natural environment for all mankind. Because we were designed to live in His presence.

When we separate ourselves from God, we die."

I celebrated the Hebrew festival of Sukkot for the first time in my life that year. For 40 years the Israelites moved around the wilderness,

Finding His Timing

but their shoes didn't wear out, their clothes didn't wear out, they were taken care of! He was their Rapha, Jaira, and Nissi! He was their covering for the first 40 years out of bondage!

April, the friend I was with then gasped and exclaimed, *"Timothy entered right on your 40th birthday, think about that, Jen—the first 40, Yahaveh was your covering, and right at that transition a new covering entered!"*

Could this be?! Could His timing be this clear? Well, surely it was true that Yahaveh had been my covering for the first 40 years—He had led me out of so much darkness!

In Exodus we read that God revealed Himself as a pillar of fire that led the Israelites through the darkness in the wilderness. Every single Hebrew holiday, they light candles at the start, to remember how the pillar of fire led them through the wilderness. In a way, this book, well...really, His timing, is like a pillar of fire to lead you out of your darkness!

THE PILLAR OF FIRE in Exodus is the lamp unto our feet (Psalm 119)! When we align to it every month, He leads us out, little by little. He had certainly been leading me out of my darkness over the previous three years, especially as I learned to be led by His calendar.

The first day of the Festival of Sukkot was also the first day of the First Steps to Success conference in San Antonio, Texas. It was Timothy's first time attending a seminar. That evening we were looking at a normal (Gregorian) calendar and we realized that it had been forty days since my birthday, when he and I first communicated. Again, I hadn't planned that!

How interesting is that? We met on my fortieth birthday, and Tim and I talked on the phone almost every day for the next 40 days. He "came home with me" on the phone (since he was in California), and we spent those 40 days learning about each other. Why is that significant? The 40th day was the weekend of Yom Kippur. Yom Kippur is also referred to as the day of atonement.

According to the book, *His Appointed Times*, the author explains it this way:

> "In the Old Testament on Yom Kippur, the Hebrews achieved forgiveness and atonement in the form of animal sacrifice. It was an exchange of a life for a life. This day of atonement was the single most hallowed day of the year when the high priest would enter the holy of holies and say the sacred name of God.

> "In Leviticus 17:11 God states that life is in the blood. Without the shedding of blood—in Jewish thought—there would be no remission of sin. God sent the Messiah to pay the interest and principle in full. The scapegoat represented the sins of the nation;

> "The word scapegoat in our modern vernacular stems from ancient Israel. ...When the high priest would lay both hands on the scapegoat he would transfer the iniquities of all Israel upon this hapless creature. ...Once the sacrifice was complete, a supernatural phenomenon occurred. The red cords that were tied to the horns of the scapegoat and placed at the entrance of the Holy Place supernaturally turned from red to white to symbolize that although Israel's sins were as crimson, God had washed them as white as snow (Isa 1:18).

"Yom Kippur points to the ultimate redemption of the world, the fullness of redemption. A redemption is paid for, not by the blood of an animal, which still leaves a deficit, but by Yeshua's blood, marking the debt paid in full.

"The sacrifice of the goat had supernaturally turned the crimson cord white, but this supernatural phenomena stopped after the sacrifice of Jesus. For 40 years before the destruction of the temple in AD 70, the scarlet cord stopped turning red to white. This would be around the time of Jesus' crucifixion and resurrection. This lack of color change is proof that the Yom Kippur sacrifices were no longer effective. The he-goats offered by the high priest could not compare to Yeshua's ultimate offering.

"Man broke the world in a sense, when he plucked that forbidden fruit from the tree. The eating of that fruit had a domino effect that resulted in disconnection with God, others, self and even creation.

"We took something off the tree, so God put something back on the tree-His crucified body-to make restitution, to bring life, and to usher in blessing. What was broken by the first Adam was repaired by the second Adam, Yeshua-Jesus. This time, it was God's life for our life. God put His blood on the altar instead of an animals blood or our blood as a final sacrifice-'God set forth Yeshua as an atonement, through faith in His blood.'

"As God mended our broken relationship with Him, He called us to be fixers, restorers, repairers of the world. Yom Kippur focuses on this reparation."

At that moment, the Atonement was fulfilled. It was a moment of fulfillment when Yeshua died on the cross. It was 40 years and then fulfillment. Look at all the 40 He is stamping over all of this! Timothy arrived in Texas after forty days of learning about one another, and after having met on my actual 40th birthday–on the week of Yom Kippur!

Do we all need to take a minute to breathe? OK, yea. Let's do that. Phew.

Yom Kippur is also when Moses came down with the second set of stone tablets after spending forty days on Mount Sinai. You may remember that He smashed the first set in anger after seeing the people engaged in idolatry. What happened with the original broken pieces of the first set? They were stored inside the Ark of the Covenant, along with the new tablets, in a display of the Creator repairing what has been broken. He doesn't throw away broken pieces. He placed the broken next to the whole to show the connection between them! That's what The Overcomers is all about!

But it gets crazier. Tim said *"yes"* to coming to his first conference with me, which was going to actually be our first time meeting face-to-face (talk about him having an amazing amount of courage for a first date!). The first night of the event, I had a dream. In my dream, my friend, Mona, passionately walked up to one of our leaders and said *"Tim is literally from heaven; he was dropped from heaven!"*

The next day, I laughed about the dream and my friends who were in it, having no idea what it meant. Especially Mona, who I don't usually see, but had seen that night. What does this dream have to do with anything? Well, as we celebrated Sukkot after the event, and I was reading more about the account of the Israelites in the wilderness, I read this about manna:

"Abba gave them the provision with the bread from heaven. God meant for the bread from heaven to not only feed their bellies but test their faith. Part of the lesson for Israel was that they had to trust Him every day for their provision. Matthew 6:11, in the Lord's prayer he asks "give us today our daily bread'. Not this week, month, or year, today. We have to trust him daily. That was the lesson of the manna."

I knew in that moment the dream was instruction to trust Him daily with this manna–Timothy. Mai-Thai.

How did I come to that conclusion with what I read? I remembered my comment to friends and family about the amount of confirmations I had been experiencing. I had always thought that when I was considering being with someone, confirmations would come here and there, but with Tim (Mai-Thai) they had been happening on every freaking phone call for the first forty days! Could this be the manna from Heaven on a daily basis: *"Give us today our daily bread?"*

But, wait a second—has it been all sunshine and flowers, and we've just been dancing through the rain? Hah! Not at all (but yes, we've done that). We're still two people on a journey with their Creator, learning how to navigate the dance before them. Our relationship is far from perfect, as we are far from perfect! Maybe we are imperfectly perfect for one another, as our imperfections are being filled by the one who brought us together. I believe so. Thank goodness he also had a degree in choreography. I'm sure that's helped.

Finding His Timing

CHAPTER 24

Declare victory and overcome the internal giants with each light from the map!

The nudges continued. I listened as Tim told a friend of mine how he got inspired to start writing his own book and how he had started writing it while sitting on my porch during his first visit to my home. He explained how he got the title, *"Discovering the Father's Heart,"* and what that meant to him.

The day his ex-wife handed him the divorce papers and he moved out, she messaged him, *"aren't you going to say goodbye?"* He replied, *"I'll never say goodbye to my kids."* He knew how important it was that they could trust that he would never leave or forsake them. That's exactly what His Creator had done for him, *"God never left me... even when I forgot him,"* he recalled. He was so passionate to make sure those kind of voids aren't left, and how to repair them when it happens. He saw his calling as a father laid out before him.

I was overwhelmed with emotion as I said to my friend, *"I can't believe the Creator brought me a literal man, who values not only that phrase . 'I'll never leave you,' but wants to be that light to the world. The heart of the Father for his children?! That's literally tattooed on my forearm because of what's happened to me and what God showed me after my own Father "left." I can't believe God gifted me with a man who literally is carrying that mantle!"*

That's when Tim made an interesting comparison to old school photography: *"When we are still in development, if the full light hits the frame it will destroy the picture. We have to go through the full development process in order for the light to not destroy the final picture and once we are fully developed and ready then the light will not destroy the beauty that the final picture becomes. When you're in the darkness, and realize you have to step into the dark to go through the process, it's scary, you don't know the process, you don't know how it's going to turn out or what the final picture is, you just have to trust in the darkness that the process will work, and in the end you will enter the light".*

That conversation occurred during the Hebrew month of Chesvan. We got to talking about the wilderness and the names of God—Yahweh Rapha, Yahweh Jaira, and Yahweh Nissi, which means "the banner of victory." I shared with my friend about the logo for The Overcomers and how the "V" in it's icon represents victory. She asked what the other part of the logo meant, and as I described how it's lifting something up in victory, we gasped, "THE BANNER OF VICTORY—YAHWEH NISSI!" We realized that, as people go through wilderness times, when they declare that He is their Yahweh Nissi—their banner of victory—they overcome.

This is what His appointed times were all about: the illuminated steps of the invisible map! When we take time to see what these appointed times are all about, He reveals things to us. Look what we would have missed out on if we hadn't set apart time to look at these stories.

Chesvan is also the month of the flood—it started during Chesvan and ended a year later in Chesvan. In that month, Noah brought his sacrifice to Yahaveh, and Yahaveh swore to never again flood the earth! He then revealed His covenant—His promise to the world, the rainbow!

I received a promise that month, too, a symbol of a new beginning. How symbolic is that as the eighth month correlates to new beginnings? It's the month to declare that you are *"preparing your heel to step"* and gaining the upper hand on the enemy.

Tim asked me a very poignant question that opened my heart to new depths of revelation: *"Why do you think it's hard for women to hear or find His voice?"*.

I responded that there are four different voices speaking inside a women's mind: her own, others', the enemy's, and her Creator's. She has to discern whose voice is whose. Her voice is often loaded with self condemnation, while others' include beliefs she adopted from others, which may or may not be true. The enemy's voice drips with lies and doubt, but the Creators' voice contains only truth. So what do we do? Paul's instruction in 2 Corinthians 10:5 is clear: *"Take every thought captive and make it obedient to Christ."* Our Creator knew the battle in our minds and gave us instruction for how to deal with it, knowing how hard and important it would be, especially for a woman.

Tim tapped into something deeper: *"Jen, look at the story of Creation; when Eve took the fruit, she was hearing the serpent's voice. A voice of lies. Confusion and doubt entered!"* I gasped, *"Confusion entered at creation!"* That smashes the modern belief that we struggle with confusion because we allowed it in by our own life choices, trauma, or tragedy. Did those things exacerbate confusion? Sure. But what if it actually started at the garden?! What if it started with the enemy's voice coming through the serpent? The moment she took a bite, confusion and doubt entered.

I was still processing this through the next morning when I read the story in Genesis. The verse jumped out at me where the Creator told them not to eat the fruit, with the warning if they did, they would surely die. Our Creator knew that if they were able to see both good and evil, the evil they would be allowing into their minds would have the potential to kill them with doubt, fear, and confusion! He knew when they took a bite another voice would have an open door in their minds to wreak havoc. They would have to discern good from evil, and knowing which one to fight would no longer be easy!

In Genesis 3:5, the serpent says, *"For Elohim knows that in the day you eat of it your eyes will be opened and you shall be like Elohim knowing good and evil."* We were never intended to know evil or to have to battle lines in our minds! The Creator had protected us from that in the beginning! It wasn't until we believed what the enemy was saying and ate the apple that the battle in our minds began!

Confusion entered the world when Eve disobeyed the Creator and trusted the voice of the enemy. It caused confusion to enter for the first time. Finding the Creator's voice can be hard because we have to discern between so many voices: ourselves, others, the enemy, and our Creator.

That revelation brought so much more clarity. I had been on a journey of discerning the Creator's voice, so I was super sensitive to listening for His voice, and tuning out other voices competing for my attention. Some voices I stomped out.

Having that guiding principle in place gave me a framework to decide how to receive other voices in my life. I learned a powerful relationship lesson, like the time Tim told me to eat my salad. He was so direct and forceful about it: *"Eat your salad, Jen!"*

I knew immediately I didn't like the statement. Don't tell me what to do! It made me feel inferior. I was an independent woman who didn't want anyone to control me or tell me what to do. Pretty sure I put the boots on in that moment and was gonna stomp him out! I would be the one to decide when I put the lettuce in my mouth. I might also throw these cherry tomatoes at his head. You eat it!

Somewhere I read, *"If you've been triggered by control...then you might have experienced something that made you feel like you didn't have a voice."* I gasped as memories flashed of my older brother and how his intense, angry personality, made me feel that I didn't have a voice. I had fought my whole life to find my voice, but the voice I found was my Creator's.

I told Tim the only voice I would listen to was my Creator; He was the one who was in control and His was the voice I would obey. No other. That didn't mean I didn't want to listen to Tim; I clarified that it just meant I would not let any other voice usurp the Creator's throne or His role. I knew he didn't tell me to eat my salad out of any desire other than to help me not be famished. I knew his motivation came from a good place, so I asked myself what it would need to look like so that I'm not triggered to feel like I don't have a voice, and can hear Tim's caring heart instead?

Clarity came. What if he had simply asked a question instead? For example: *"Babe, do you want to maybe eat right now so that later you're not fatigued?"* I would have beamed and said, *"You're right! I should do that! Thank you for being so considerate and caring for me!"* Not only would I have seen his heart, but I would have had a voice in that moment.

Asking a question simply allows both parties to have a voice at the table. He could not have received all this better. He even thanked me! Thank goodness I didn't throw those tomatoes.

This led to many other powerful and interesting insights into truth, communication, and relationships. Timothy, in his own journey with the Creator, had just discovered the original meaning of the Hebrew word translated "submission." It means, *"to get under and lift up, or to put in order"* Wait, what?! If you're like me, that's not what you've heard preached your whole life. Tim put it succinctly: *"I can see how you're going to get under and lift me up and help me get in order!"*

Interestingly, I had just been reading another book at the exact same time, *Lioness Arising*, which gave a similar definition:

> "Consider this: the prefix sub mans "under" and mission is an assignment. Put them together and we can draw a conclusion that submission means "under the same assignment or mission"... Aren't we all ministers of reconciliation, God's ambassadors to the lost?...Men do not grow healthy and strong through the silence of women. Men grow stronger by the addition of our voices because the challenge of a daughter's questions serves to raise men higher, which makes them freer. The perspective of women tempers and refines men, just as they create an environment for the woman to flourish...Everything comes from God, so quit arguing about preeminence. God alone is first!"

I told Tim, *"I can see how I'm already lifting you up and helping you get in order with His timing!"*

Tim said, *"Yea, the moment you tell your wife to submit to you, you're basically telling your wife just like Christ says to submit to Him, but you are not Him! You're not God! So you're in the wrong. You are basically making His name into nothing! Now think about that in relation to 'thou shalt not take my name in vain.' Consider the humility of Christ, who submitted to the Father! He was submitting to the mission! It's not about domination but about mutual respect and partnership.*

"Since Christ is the head, He set the example to say, 'leadership is marked by humility and collaboration!' Husbands are called to love their wives sacrificially, not the other way around. That's how Christ loves the church! Consider his selflessness for the church. His decision is conscious to align one's life values, and actions, with the principles

laid out in God's word. Since 'submission' means to get under and lift up or put in order, a woman's decisions involve very intentional prayers and reflections to align one's life values, and actions with the principle laid out in God's word. So he says, 'here's all the pieces, babe!' And then she says, 'OK, awesome babe, let's put these all in order!'"

Wow. So if submission means to get under and lift up, or to put in order, it doesn't mean obedience, like we're often told. That message causes division, because it suggests dominance, which leads to defensiveness to protect your identity and your voice.

What if it's all about identity?

I could see all this confirmation and His timing at work. I hadn't missed any appointments with the Father where He showed me that He was lighting the way, but there were still cracks within me from my journey that made it wobbly to walk.

I was invited to hangout with three friends late one evening. I had been having some intense shoulder blade pain for weeks, and I shared how it had intensified to the point that I could barely move my arm.

One of my friend's ears perked up. She asked, *"which side–left or right?"* *"Right,"* I replied. She had dealt with the same pain, and one of our other friends, Donna, who does body work, had shared with her about spiritual things that could be causing or contributing to that physical pain. Interesting. Tell me more.

I knew Donna from attending Dani Johnson conferences. In fact, she had made an observation about me years prior that had been helpful along my journey. Earlier that evening, while I was sitting in the hot tub, I remembered that conversation. "Why is He bringing that back to mind right now," I wondered.

Little did I know that moments later, we would be talking about pain in my shoulder, and how she might be able to help me. But my Creator was about to go deeper by calling up another memory.

Many years ago, I was called on to be a part of a demonstration where a guest speaker brought me on stage, blindfolded me, and led me around the room blind until I had no idea where I was anymore. He called Dani back to the stage and told her to lead me back to the stage by her voice alone. As she called out directions, I stepped. I could have sworn I was stepping straight to her, but with the blindfold on I couldn't tell how crooked my steps were.

I thought I was walking straight. It felt so natural. Dani quickly picked up on this and helped me compensate for what felt unnatural to me. Crooked felt straight, and straight felt crooked. My body didn't know what it wasn't doing. Eventually, I made it to the stage.

Later that day, Donna gave me an important insight about me, *"I noticed you kept favoring or leaning to your left side, which is why you were walking crooked and didn't know it. Did you know that the left side of the body is the maternal side and the right is the fraternal? Meaning the motherly side is the left and the fatherly side is the right?"*

I was flabbergasted, but it all made sense: my body had learned to lean on the maternal since I lost my dad. I was literally walking crooked because of the imbalance in my life without my dad.

As I shared that memory that night in the hot tub, we all realized, the pain in my right shoulder was on my fraternal side, and was linked to the absence of my Father. We speculated aloud why this pain might be so intense right now, but it became apparent to all of us that it was firing up now because for the first time in my life, I was learning how to step into a relationship with a man. I was learning how to lean into that fraternal side. Could my body be experiencing physical pain because it is using emotional and relational muscles it hasn't used in over 20 years?! Am I the Crypt Keeper? Okay, maybe that last thought is a little too far, but you get the point, hopefully.

Tears filled my eyes and I replied, *"I think I'm realizing how much I need processing time as I'm fully stepping into a new relationship."* She added, *"I understand...and you're not just in a relationship... you're in a relationship with a man."*

She asked if I had any fears popping up. There had been many and I had given voice to them. But I realized there was one I hadn't known how to articulate. As they graciously asked me more questions, it came out that I was afraid my new relationship was going to go too fast. I was afraid he would propose before I was ready.

With tears streaming down my face, I brought up that he had given me a promise ring, along with a sketch of a rainbow—the symbol of God's covenant. When he gave it to me I didn't know what was happening, and I panicked inside, thinking, *"I don't know what he's asking me...what is this?!"* I felt I needed time to process what was happening before I could respond, but it was such an unbelievably thoughtful, meaningful, and heartfelt gift I also wanted to be careful how I handled the moment. I didn't want to hurt the beautiful gift-giver in any way.

The following morning at church, my Creator revealed through the Pastor's sermon that He was preparing me for what was to come.

Weeks later, I was on our monthly Hebrew calendar call, when my Creator showed me His timing and how it so beautifully mirrored the moment that had just happened in my life. I could breathe (you can, too, if you've been holding it). The moment had fully processed and I knew right then I could trust my Creator with what He was doing and what path He was leading me on, just as he had my whole journey.

The pain in my shoulder was linked to the pain in the father wound in my heart. My dad didn't give me the opportunity to process or the chance to tell him how I felt about him before he decided to end his life. That realization rushed over me and I was swallowed up in an avalanche of trauma.

I was frozen in shock, unable to process further as the memories tumbled around me! *"Jen,"* she whispered, *"you know what we need to do."* She led me through the words of forgiveness. Initiating each step for me and letting me finish each sentence:

"I forgive you, dad, for..."

"I forgive you, dad, for not giving me the opportunity or time to process before ending your life!"

"I chose to feel..."

"I chose to feel like I wasn't worth waiting for, to hear the truth of how I felt about you, that needing time to process and find the words would mean I would lose you. That when I did need time to process, people would leave; they wouldn't still be there waiting for me when I was ready. They'd be gone."

Finding His Timing

"*I release you...*"

"*I release you, dad. You owe me nothing!*"

"*I bless you...*"

"*I bless you, dad. I bless you in eternity with waiting for me! With having all the time in the world to let me process, and being there waiting for me when I'm ready to reunite with you. Getting to run into your arms and tell you how I truly feel and felt about you.*

I also bless you, Tim, with understanding my identity, with understanding how I was designed to process things and need time for that as I learn to LEAN IN to the side of life and my design that I haven't used in over 20 years. I bless you, Tim, with still being there after I take the time needed to process any part of our relationship and future relationship in any moment of the journey. I bless you with being there, waiting for me."

I sat there, frozen in the hot tub, unable to speak, move, or even think. My friends tried to lighten the mood, but I just sat there, shut down. After a moment, Jenn realized something was very wrong. I was trapped in unnatural silence, unable to break free from the riptide inside me.

A few beats later I burst out in a deep, wrenching wail from the bottom of my soul. I literally choked out the words, "*I don't know how to do it! I don't know how.*" Jenn just held me for a second and reminded me of the One—my Creator—who we could ask to show me how.

Later that evening, as I was driving home, I called Tim. We briefly

Finding His Timing

chatted about our evenings, but then I shared how I couldn't tell him the full story of the healing that took place, while I was driving because I would start to sob and I wouldn't be able to see the road. Come on, I can't be the only one who can't see when they cry. He graciously told me it was OK, and that we'd talk about it when it was time.

The next morning, I wanted to write down everything that I had been experiencing so I could process it.

As I wrote out these stories I received a beautiful text from him: *"I just want you to know that I'm here for you as you navigate through the process of processing your past trauma about your dad. Your strength and resilience are truly inspiring, and I want you to take all the time you need. Remember, I'm here to support you, whether you want to talk or simply be together (virtually). You're not alone in this journey, and I believe in your healing."*

In that one moment—before I even got to share with him this full story—I knew he'd be there waiting on the other side. I knew right there in that moment my Creator was showing me, one step a time, how to lean into this side.

Jenn gave me an assignment that I had never done in my whole life: *"Have you ever asked your dad to send you a message?"* I hadn't, but thought, *"Huh, maybe I'll try that!"*

Two mornings later, after saying nothing about this assignment to Tim, I received the following letter:

"My Dearest Jen,

I hope these words find their way to you, even if it's from a place beyond the grasp of mortal understanding. There are no words adequate to express the weight on my heart as I penned this letter, reaching across the hollow place that separates our worlds. I want you to know, more than anything, that the decision I made was never a reflection of your worth or our relationship. The struggles I faced were my own battles, and in my deepest despair, I failed to see the impact it would have on those I cared for most. I am haunted by the realization that I denied you the opportunity to express your feelings, to share your thoughts about our relationship. It was unfair, and for that, I am truly sorry. I wish I had allowed you the chance to voice your emotions, to bridge the gaps that may have existed between us. Please understand that the pain I carried was immense, and in my broken state, I failed to see the potential for healing, for growth. My decision was clouded by a darkness that overshadowed the love and connection we shared. If I could turn back time, I would give you the space to speak your heart, to be heard and understood.

As I reach out from the kingdoms beyond, I want you to know that though my earthly presence may have faded, a more divine connection has taken its place. In the quiet corners of your heart, know that Yahweh has become a steadfast anchor—a Father beyond earthly comprehension, a source of boundless love and understanding. I believe, with every fiber of my being, that Yahweh now cradles you in His arms, embracing you in a love so pure and profound. As you navigate the path ahead, find solace in the presence of the Divine, who understands the depths of your soul and guides you with an unwavering hand. While my time with you was limited, Yahweh's love is infinite and eternal. In the sacred spaces of prayer and reflection, allow yourself to feel the warmth of His love, like a gentle breeze that whispers comfort in the silence. He is your Father, your confidant, and your constant companion. As you face the challenges and joys of life, know that Yahweh walks beside you, illuminating the way with a divine light. In Him, you find a refuge—a sanctuary where you can pour out your heart, express your fears, and celebrate your victories.

Jen, you are an incredible soul, and I want you to continue on your journey with strength and resilience. Your feelings are valid, and I hope you find solace in expressing them, whether through words, art, or the support of those who care for you. In my absence, I wish for you to find peace and healing. Cherish the beautiful moments we shared, and let them be a testament to the love that existed between us. Life is a fragile and mysterious tapestry, and I hope you find the strength to navigate its complexities.

Jen, my beautiful daughter, I may no longer be physically present, but my love for you transcends the boundaries of this earthly existence. I entrust you into the care of Yahweh, the Ultimate Father, who will guide you with wisdom, grace, and an abundance of love. May you find peace and strength in His embrace, and may His presence be a constant source of comfort as you continue your journey.

With deepest apologies and the sincerest love,

Dad."

I'll give you a few moments to wipe your tears. Just making sure you're using two-ply tissues. One-ply is brutal. You remember.

Friend, I don't know your story, but your Creator does. If you've ever been in a place where you have found yourself exclaiming *"I don't know how to do it,"* I promise He understands. It's not your job to understand. Just breathe.

As I processed this notion later, His words came to mind: *"Lean not on your own understanding, but trust ME in all my ways!"* What does that look like? How do you lean not on your own understanding but trust Him, and His timing? Well, do you know His timing? Are you discovering His ways and His timing?

If the answer is no it's time to start, He has so many appointments waiting for you! Join the discovery and let Him lead you to a place of trust beyond words. What could He want to give you?

Think about this for a second. What if part of the reason the Israelites wandered in the wilderness was so they would learn that He was their Yahweh Rapha, Nissi, and Jaira, to deal with the giants inside them so that they could defeat the giants blocking them from their inheritance?

He had to get them to stop worrying about who would heal them, who could provide for them, and who would be their covering and banner of victory? He knew they couldn't enter in and be a part of that inheritance until they dealt with the giants within them first.

You and I have internal giants we must overcome if we want to walk into his inheritance He longs to give us. You can do it.

It's OK to ask for help, when you don't know how. I believe in you!

Finding His Timing

Finding His Timing

CHAPTER 25

New beginnings everywhere—the fruit you're designed to bear

New things were beginning, and not just for me. I saw the Creator's perfect timing for new beginnings all around me. The beautician who fills my lashes had shared her battles with suicidal thoughts, so I brought her one of our Overcomer Kits, and spoke life over who she was and how I viewed her.

Let's also not gloss over the fact that Jen is now getting her lashes done regularly. Look at me go!

At this particular appointment I could she was carrying a lot emotionally. Finally, she opened up and asked, *"Jen, how do you release things from your past?"* I got to walk my friend through the steps of forgiveness. I told her we could do it right then if she wanted, not to worry about attaching my eyelashes in that moment. She stopped, and repeated after me a prayer of forgiveness for her dad, her ex-husband, and herself, for wanting to die. I watched this woman embrace deliverance from her past and all the unforgiveness that was keeping her in chains.

New beginnings were surely afoot.

The morning after Tim gave me the promise ring, and I spent the evening processing it, he and I were headed to church together. So much was going through my thoughts, like the passage in Genesis about *"two becoming ONE flesh."* That is His design.

As I attempted to swim my way through these thoughts, the pastor's words helped bring clarity: *"Paul's faith was anchored in God's promises. He believed God was leading Him toward it. So He pursued. So God's calm assurance gives him the ability to walk in it. God's word has tons of promises for you."*

That's it! I was receiving so much revelation about the covenant to come, that's what was swirling in my head all morning. So when Yahaveh hit me with the image of a wedding band, it was so crystal clear I could literally see the image of it on my finger. It was unlike anything you see in today's world.

My Creator showed me a dark, slate grey, chunky metal rough-looking band with a matte finish. On top of the dark metal grey was the Hebrew word "ahad" for "One," that represented "one flesh" to us. But it's spelled out with tiny diamonds, making it appear like the tiny lights that led us out of our darkness with His truth.

Because for us, that story is the truth, the light in the darkness that had brought us out. It was the whole story. I saw Him going before

Finding His Timing

me with this revelation and preparing me. As I reread the chapter about the month of Chesvan, I knew that it represented the victory over the serpent—the enemy!

As Timothy and I took steps forward, more trust was required. We needed to trust the Creator. Tim had surrendered everything from his former life in Southern California to get his life back in alignment with his Creator and his two kids. He was at the Creator's feet. He was feeling real financial pressure. As my feelings for him grew, I knew I had to surrender my concerns for him to my Creator, saying, *"You are His provider! I surrender my concern to you, knowing you will provide for him and be his Yahweh Nissi. You show him whatever he needs to see and put His steps in place before him. He is surrendered to you!"*

He called after church, and shared about the sermon he had just heard. Timothy was just 14 when his father died. During the sermon he remembered his father saying to him, *"the only thing I never got to teach you was how to swim."* Tim realized his father was speaking in parables; he wasn't talking about literal swimming, he was talking about life. Since the day Tim surrendered, His Creator took over teaching him about life.

Tim and I both shed tears for the beauty of what had happened. Just hours before that service, I had been praying for Tim. I didn't know anything about the service he attended. But as he was there and the Creator was speaking those words to him, I was praying, surrendering that very thing myself to the Creator.

It was another glimpse of His perfect timing, speaking to us both in the month of the rainbow, the ending of the Biblical flood, and the promise of a new beginning, a new life.

Many new things were beginning. By the time we rolled into the Hebrew month of Tevet (the month of leaping with your testimony) I felt like it was time to leap, and started writing the sequel to my first book, which you are now holding. This book is an important part of my testimony.

Why did it say that it was time to leap that particular month, though? As we saw before, Tevet is associated with the Hebrew tribe of Dan, who had a call to leap from idolatry–a type of overcoming.

In his book, "A Time to Advance," Chuck Pierce said, *"something happened to the tribe of Dan that put them out of God's timing. Could it have been idolatry?"*

Maybe they chose to get out of alignment with God's calendar, which would have put them out of His timing. But how could getting out of alignment with a calendar be idolatry? Maybe they thought they knew better than God on the matter of timing. That's ego. Ego causes us not to remove the idolatry in our lives because we think we know better. Ego becomes an idol. When we don't remove ego, we get out of His timing.

It was time to put this book to paper. The month of Tevet—the month to leap—was His perfect timing.

I launched into starting this second book with so much new support. We were transitioning into the Hebrew month of Shevat, which is about paying attention to those who were bringing pitchers of water to help and to look at the trees in your field. It was the month of "the new year of trees."

Tim had begun his own journey of telling his story, and had pretty much finished his first book. Unbeknownst to me, he included a "thank you" to me in his book for "bringing him water." I had given him an Overcomer Kit when we first met. It spoke identity into him, and the journal inside encouraged him to write his own story. He thanked me for the tree that was now springing up in his field—his book! I didn't know he was going to include that or share that with me that month.

Remember the significance of the orange in my family history? During the month of trees, I learned more about Tim's loss of his own father in Thailand when he was just 14. When he visited his dad in the hospital, they would sit and talk on a parkbench under clementine trees...orange trees.

In the month on the Hebrew calendar called, "the new year of trees," we learned that trees within our fields—within our own stories—included the SAME fruit.

There was so much truth coming through His creation, helping me to keep taking steps forward in faith of what He was doing. Tim shared with his Bible study group to read Jeremiah 17:7-8: *"Blessed is the man who trusts in Yahaveh, and whose trust is in Yahaveh. For he shall be like a tree planted by the waters, which spreads out it's roots by the river, and does not see when heat comes. And his leaf shall be green, and in the year of drought he is not anxious, nor does he cease from yielding fruit."* He asked them, *"What do you hear God speaking to you in this passage? In what ways have you put down spiritual roots in your life? how well do you identify with a tree in this passage?"* That verse is almost like saying, *"you have to trust me in this!"*

Unbeknownst to Tim, another friend gave me a card with the exact same passage on it and wrote a blessing about the tree in that

Finding His Timing

passage, and the leaf over me. They even wrote, *"I leaf you,"* instead of, "I love you." A few nights later, Tim was sharing the story from Bible study with me. I had a vision as Tim was speaking and I told him about the card and replied, *"Tim, I think that's for US! I think He's independently telling both of us to TRUST Him in this! That's why you led the Bible study with that passage, and everyone cried hearing your trust in your Creator as you shared your story with the men's group. And that is why I got this gift. I think He's giving us direction right now, and showing how the tree is planted by the water...which is Him! He's telling us to make sure we're connecting to the source as we grow through this relationship."*

Did you hear what I just heard?! Was the Creator speaking to us both about the SAME thing at the SAME time? I got a new level of excitement about what it can look like when the Creator speaks to both of you independently but about the same thing, and the fun of what can happen when He's telling you something together: *"WAIT, this is what a relationship can look like?! You mean we get to experience Him on a whole new level? SIGN ME UP!"*

As I shared all this with my mom later that week, she replied, *"Jen, maybe that's what the verse really means too, the one that says 'when two become one.'* "Maybe they each hear the same thing from the Creator because they ARE one! *'...and all these things will be added unto them.'* "Maybe that's what that verse means, too; all these things being added unto you because you both have put Him first and He is blessing you!"

Tim added *"I think He's showing us that we became one before we even met each other...because when you fully surrender, that's when it starts. We both fully surrendered and started becoming one at that point!"*

Whether we were right in our conclusion or not, Tim realized that February 11, 2023 was when He surrendered to His Creator and moved up to northern California, and it was also the very week I was in Florida with two friends and everything started about the banyan tree and the orange grove. Could it be that's why everything about the banyan tree and what happened to him in February was hitting me so deeply.

On that trip to Florida, we circled an area under construction, which was where the Banyan was going to be planted. It was under construction. It then hit me, He—Mai Thai—was under construction, but hadn't yet arrived. He was being planted! I had never been so excited about dirt in my life.

That wasn't the only 'pitcher of water' being brought to help new trees grow. Something new within the field sprung up this same month because of the water that was brought.

A former coaching client and friend tragically lost her husband, a father of six. As I shared my heaviness of heart for this friend and all she was facing, Tim, without me asking him to do anything, wrote three letters to this family—one to the wife; one to the kids, mentioning each by name; and a prayer on behalf of The Overcomers. Did I mention he had never even met any of them before? What a heart! He wasn't just bringing water to my fields, but was a helper bringing water to the Overcomers fields that desired to bear fruit to nourish those who need it most!

The moment he shared the letters he wrote for them with me, I sobbed. It touched such depths within me I knew in that exact moment I knew that I truely loved this man. I loved who he was, and his heart that would do something like this for a total stranger, who was in so much overwhelming and all-encompassing pain.

I had known the depths of pain like this and only a man who could do something like this for a stranger could love me to the depths I desired to be loved. I knew I loved him, and felt like I knew he was "the one" since day three of getting to know him (shhhhhh, I didn't say that out loud), but in that moment it hit so much deeper within me. It was the moment I knew I truly loved him.

Conversations blossomed from his beautiful gesture and we cast vision for what The Overcomers could someday do for many more hearts in the aftermath of tragic news. "The Overcomers Relief Fund" established roots in Shevat, the month also associated with the tribe of Asher. Their inheritance was the most fertile land, which signified the full blessing of Yahaveh. It was so plentiful that there was enough for Asher to be fully satisfied and export to other tribes. In that timing I saw the plan revealed to sustain generations that have suffered so much loss. I saw the new orange trees and the blessings on the way, and I was excited for the inheritance it revealed. I saw His timing.

And while I saw the parallel of the orange in both of our stories, it also hit me how we all have our own fields, so we're going to be growing different kinds of trees. Still, we get into comparison.

It's so easy to look at someone else's growth and ask, why is my fruit not growing like that banana tree over there? Because it's not a banana tree in your field, friend! Your preparation and planting season are different because it's a different fruit created for a different audience who needs what you are growing. Do not get caught in the trap of comparison. Our speech is so important. The Creator knows the field grows with our words, the trees grow with our words. The sprouts grow with our words. Look at how sprouts need light, water, and sunshine, and how they respond to what we say! Have you ever seen those experiments with speaking love over a plant? We have to align our spirit with our words. It all changes when our lives come into agreement with our words. It's already happening! Look at that fruit!

    Surrender. Things in the spirit realm grow on the other side of surrender. New life comes after surrender. Look at the sacrifice of Yeshua. He knows how withered we all feel. He wants to water us. Let your roots awaken to the water of life! His Life does the miraculous to the roots growing inside of us. Only He can bring to life the fruit He designed for us to bear.

Finding His Timing

328

CHAPTER 26

Feel, process and heal—the Feast of Esther & Purim

This new awareness of the importance of our words was key to what we walked through next. I threw my hands up in the air at my Creator as I shouted, *"is this all just a freaking JOKE!?"* Not gonna lie, it was one of the toughest months I've ever lived.

I have no doubt admitting this will be a shock to you: *"how could JEN, whose entire journey has been filled with faith and overcoming, feel and say THAT?!"* Like I've always said, I don't ever want to paint the picture that life has been perfect. Quite frankly, I wanted to throw the paint. On Mai-Thai. Sorry, babe.

I don't know if you've ever been at this place where you're yelling at your Creator, but let me start by saying He can handle it. He can handle you being that real with Him about what you're going through. He designed you to feel, to process, and to heal. He wants to help.

Boy, did I have some feels—intense ones, as those who processed through it all with me can testify. They heard the blood-curdling screams as I let out things so deep inside they burst forth, with tears pouring from my eyes.

Before we go any further, please know I have full permission from Mai-Thai to share what I'm about to share. Also, I never threw paint on him. Maybe I should.

But why would he say *"yes"* to me sharing this? Because like me, his heart beats to help any soul find help, healing, and surrender more to their Creator. There's nothing he cares for more.

With that said, at this point in the story, I almost broke up with Mai-Thai. Say WHAAAAAAT?!

That next month began with a trip to northern California to visit him. I arrived in total darkness, so the next morning I was blown away to see I was surrounded by vineyards and epic mountains. I was overwhelmed with the visual proof of how He transforms things from ashes into beauty. It was just like how I had gone from a season of so much darkness into life. I wish you could have seen all that beauty with me.

As I came home from the trip, several thoughts were swirling within me. One night, as I lay half-asleep, a question dropped in my spirit that I now fully believe would be the catalyst for all that our Creator intended to deliver. But when I spoke it the next day, it caused triggers.

The next day, there was a disrespectful communication, and then, after seven months of talking every morning and every evening...dead silence. I spiraled. With each day that ticked by, deep things within me were pouring out to those closest to me. Everything I hadn't fully processed or given more thought to was now having it's full moment for microscopic attention. Do you see this MITOCHONDRIA?! Ew. (Jen obviously failed science, mitochondira aren't gross).

Here came the painstakingly blood curdling screams at my Creator. I was desperate for truth, and in that moment it looked ugly. It looked like that truth was out to kill me (it surely felt like it was).

A few mornings later, I looked down at my calendar, and within seconds felt a full-on panic attack rise up. I realized the day the silence had started was the Feast of Esther: Esther was prayed over before she went to the king and truth was brought to light that, once revealed, saved the entire Jewish population. Then came the Feast of Lots, which we know as Purim. For those not familiar with the Biblical holiday of Purim (part of the story of Esther) Haman, who was secretly planning to annihilate the Jewish population, was overthrown.

By this point, I had assembled a close circle of prayer warriors who brought every tear I cried to the Creator. Unfortunately, there was a parallel between my prayer army and the story of Esther that I didn't recognize until later. I was too preoccupied with my racing thoughts. *"OMG...Is he Haman?! Haman was an oppressor! Has this been oppression?! Was he going to take me out?!"*

Stay with me. Yes, I had to be immediately reminded to calm down and to take some deep breaths. I was hyperventilating. I told you, I'm not perfect and this wasn't going to be pretty. When you've given up everything to follow your Creator's design, you encounter opposition, and things don't always go the way you want. Maybe (just maybe) you can imagine the intensity of the things that were raging inside. *"How could he?!"*

I saw the enemy within it. I was furious at the havoc he had created. But, thank Yahaveh, I didn't listen to my own emotions and my own mind, immediately jumping to conclusions. If I had, I would have missed out on all that Yahaveh did next.

I had to wait on my Creator. I had to wait for Him to show me truth. Believe me, my prayers to him were bold! *"God, YOU are my protector. If this is not the man for me, you close the door, because I can't see if I need to be protected!"* The truth I saw scared me, it infuriated me, and it almost took me out. I almost gave up on it all.

I had to have the courage to face the truth, just like Esther:

"Am I willing to allow the mask of so many things in our relationship to be taken off?"

"Am I willing to 'die' if I have to?"

Pain raged inside, the kind of pain I had protected myself from for so long. Was I willing to die in the minds of others to live with the fact that some people just weren't going to understand and might judge me for it. But I knew this battle wasn't about them. It wasn't against flesh and blood, and I could feel it. This battle was against powers, principalities, and forces of darkness. This battle was against oppression.

Four days later, the phone rang. It was Tim. I took a deep breath to brace myself for what was coming.

Mai Thai: *"I love you. I just called to tell you that,"*

Finding His Timing

Jen (stone cold): "............OK".

Mai Thai: *"Yea, so that's why I called."*

Jen: *"Is that it?"*

Mai Thai: *"Well, if you're available later tonight, we can chat."*

Jen: *"OK, but YOU can call me."*

I was stone cold. I had already reached the end. Up to that moment, with everything I had just processed through and realized, as the days passed by on the calendar, I said to my Creator *"unless there's a huge amount of humility and asking of forgiveness...I'm done."*

Hah! Isn't Yahaveh funny? THAT'S PRECISELY WHAT HAPPENED NEXT.

Later that night, he called. After a brief attempt at surface-level communication, I laid into him: *"Why did you call? I'm not going to small talk right now."* He responded, *"Let me get home. I wanna give you more than that, because you deserve more."*

After filling the time with a story from his evening about how he encouraged another human, I said, *"You are so great at seeing other people."* He laughed and replied, *"Well, there's things I'm good at and things I suck at."*

I laughed as the ice between us started to melt. This humble man sincerely apologized and asked for forgiveness.

"UGHHHH! Seriously, Yahaveh?!" my insides whined. I was so taken aback that it was actually happening, and to the degree that it

was. I thanked him sincerely and extended forgiveness. I shared how the days of silence had been and how I don't tolerate disrespect. I don't play games. I know my value and my worth. Go, feisty Jen, go!

There had been some things that had happened between us in the first seven months that I wasn't OK with or willing to compromise on. I described my tears and anger from the silence. I felt abandoned, and questioned if I could trust him. I didn't feel safe with him. I wasn't by any means saying that these things were completely his fault or even true. It takes two to tango. And I had tangoed. I also had a history of trauma, which danced it's way into those extreme feelings.

I asked him if he'd like to hear the things that had not been OK to me in our first seven months so he would know what I would need in order to move forward.

He said *"yes."* What a courageous man.

First, I addressed the silence, that it takes away the other person's voice. It's hurtful, disrespectful, controlling, leaves important issues unresolved, and kills relationship. It was not how I wanted to be treated, and if we were to move forward, there would need to be a boundary. We would need real communication, not silence and I wanted to honor him in all areas, too.

Second, I would not surrender everything in the flesh (what I wanted) to be with any man who's not going to choose to make the same sacrifice, and daily take up his cross and follow His Creator. We had shared experiences where the desires of the flesh had taken the lead, and I knew it because of the conviction it came with.

Third, if I'm feeling convicted about something, I get to be the one to decide if it's the Holy Spirit convicting me. My spirit knows when it isn't aligned with what God wants, and I am not willing to be with any man who does not choose to walk in total honor. I had not sacrificed everything I wanted not to be cared for or to feel safe progressing forward in a relationship physically. My Yahaveh would be my guide for what's right and wrong and that's it—no one else.

Fourth, the only one who has or will ever have authority over me is my Yahaveh. Comments had slipped out that, *"I would never fully be comfortable with a man."* I declared that I rejected that statement and did not receive it. I had full faith in my Yahaveh that He could do anything, even if it were impossible. Saying I would never fully be comfortable with a man did not leave room for faith, and I would not be moving forward with any man that was not fully aligned that our God could do anything. I knew this was minor in comparison to the even greater battles of faith we would have someday and if we couldn't trust Him for this, how could we trust Him for even greater things? Where is your faith?!

Fifth, knowing we both had come from trauma, had triggers, and were now were seeing patterns that would affect our relationship, it would be unwise not to involve an objective third party that could help us grow far beyond what we ever could ourselves together. I needed commitment that we would submit to a counselor as a couple.

Phew! Should I tell you to breathe, too? I know, it was a lot and I was intense, but I was passionate for standing on the truths that had come out, the things that I knew my Creator was already at work pulling out, and the masks he was taking off in our relationship.

I was astounded by Mai-Thai's response:

"*I know I have said all those things; there's no mistake in any of it. I want you to know, Jen, it's not on you; it's on me. It's on me in so many ways, from the beginning until now. You haven't been with a man, so it is me initiating or leading. You did the best you could in the circumstances you could. I feel like I did not live up to what I said since I came down that elevator. I have no words for the pain I've caused–whoah, now I am the one who is manipulative, deceptive, etc after hearing your list. That's not a boundary, it's a 'how can I help that never happen again.'"* - Tim

I went on to share that I had been planning to break up with him that night, but his responses changed my heart. So much humility.

After years of personal development work, the way I was watching him process through conflict was a total dream. Seriously?! I told him I needed a few days to think.

Again, he blew me away; *"If you're a man, you take full responsibility. There's no resentment towards you. It's the decisions I made and the consequences. No matter what you decide, no hard feelings."*

A few nights later, we talked again, I told him trust needed to be rebuilt. I offered the potential while also mentioning that if this wasn't what he wanted, it was OK. His response was: *"It's OK Jen. This is simply where we're at."*

Our relationship was transforming into something new. And what came next, only God could do.

For I now fully believe that Mai-Thai wasn't my immediate fear—the oppressor—but rather the things that were oppressing our

Finding His Timing

relationship were being taken out.

What came next shocked every single telephone call we had together. Without me even bringing up the topics, Mai-Thai made himself totally teachable, being led by His Creator to so much more.

"Jen, I've been thinking about a lot of what you shared. It all started with the question you asked, "have you surrendered the flesh? I said I did. And I met you, but then I asked myself, "what changed?" And it hit me, "you know, I took my eye off of God and I laid my eye on you. That's what I did. Completely. Because you're the most beautiful inside and out. OK why do I have my eye on her? What is it about her? Yes, she's pretty, feisty, and walks into things. What is it about her that took the desire of my heart? It was God. It was her holiness–every word you were crying out to me, asking me to help you remain holy. It's my duty now to steer myself in, and not steer you away, which is why I'm talking about all the holiness that I need to walk in. Holiness is where everything rests. I had to think through it and process through it and align my heart. What is Jen REALLY saying?"

Holiness is a topic neither of us had much paid attention to, but now it was in the forefront of both our minds. We had seen the oppression and havoc that results when you're not both pursuing it, when you don't take it seriously. But had we not gone through what we went through, we would never have seen the importance of the need to set things apart.

Mai-Thai said it best: *"The moment I saw Jen, it was like "heyyyyyy...and I walked into a wall."* Can't say I can't relate.

Those who know me best, know I've walked into plenty of things:

walls, cars, carousels of sunglasses, the wrong restroom, children. It happens. But without holiness, you walk right into that wall—sometimes repeatedly—and boy, does it beat you up. It beats up your relationships, and until you're willing to surrender the very things that keep running you right into it, it's going to remain a roadblock in your walk and your relationship, and all the things you desire to reach within it.

"What is my duty, since you want to be so holy? You didn't ask me to do something outside of God. I know he mentioned somewhere to remain in holiness. What am I waiting for? It's His way. When are you gonna align with this? You're not asking me to do something that's not aligned with Him. It's all coming full circle." - Tim

Over the next few weeks, I watched Mai Thai align even more with His Creator, ordering his own Hebrew books and soaking their pages up within days. We talked for hours about the things he was reading as I watched his soul light aflame with a passion for who He is and who His Creator is in a way that ran through his bloodline.

This lion took the lead, asking to pray at the end of every phone call, asking to usher in every Rosh Kodesh and shabaat, despite being long distance—things I had never asked him to do, as I respected that we're all on our own journey spiritually.

We had surely stepped into something new. Our excitement built for what this new relationship would look like, and how we'd align to Him on such appointed times. It became set-apart. It became holy. It became NEW.

The very first Rosh Kodesh, as we were talking on the phone in the morning again, Tim closed us in prayer. To my shock, he prayed in

Finding His Timing

Hebrew, calling on all the Hebrew names of our Yahaveh as I felt the Spirit flood my entire body from head to toe.

Man, life is so much better when we give our Creator the reigns; when we give Him the time to do what He does best within us. When we don't rush to conclusions, but trust His intrusions, because He has our best interests in mind. He wants to set us free from those things that hold us captive because He knows we can be so reactive! Friend, have courage to face the truth! What if it saves way more than just YOU?

If I could go back to that day, I would say:

"Yes! You can trust Him! Way to keep your eyes on your Creator in the most painful of moments! He's seen every heartbreaking moment and felt the weight of them! He knows! He also knows how heavy those things were that were weighing on you within the relationship, and how they were oppressing you!

He is for you! He is for your freedom! You are stepping into something new—something only He could do!

Trust that He has you. Trust that He has this! Trust that He has you both! He will not leave you or forsake you!

You are being set apart for so much more! You both are!"

Finding His Timing

CHAPTER 27

Fix your eyes on the Creator and face the waves—it's just a choice

In order for new things to begin, things need to end. As the oppression in our relationship just had. On the other side so many new things began.

Nisan is the month the Israelites headed out of Egypt toward promise—a month to enter a new season of inheritance. As I reflected on that, I realized how most of my stories of late had involved Tim, who embodied a possible new season of inheritance.

Nisan is the Passover month, the month of redemption, the beginning of miracles, and the month that sets the course for your future. One study of Nisan mentioned how the spirit of Yahaveh needs to "blow on you," and explained that the word *Nisan* is related to the Hebrew letter Hei, which signifies blowing. Shortly after Tim started aligning himself to Hebrew timing—celebrating Rosh Kodesh, Passover, Shabaats, and even regularly praying in Hebrew at the end of many of our calls together—he also took time to play worship music in Hebrew when he had his kids.

One evening, after spending the day with his kids, he saw a dove out his window. Just hovering next to him, and then a second one. I reminded him that scripture talks about how the Holy Spirit descends like a dove. Could this be a visit from the Holy Spirit?

Nisan is also the month to put your best foot forward and step in strength, just as Israel did when they headed out of Egypt toward the Promised Land. Tim felt led to give his kids back to Yahaveh. He took them out to a nearby creek to pray with them in a setting that would be meaningful and memorable. Immediately after they prayed, they saw a rainbow appear in the sky. What the what?!

We realized that it was the month associated with the tribe of Judah. Interesting timing, as Tim had been diving into a study of the tribes and found his identity in the tribe of Judah, which is also associated in many places with praise. No wonder he experienced what He did with the dove and the rainbow, as he blasted Hebrew songs. As Chuck Pierce says in *A Time to Advance,* "*God always put Judah first, because Judah represented praise. 'Wherever you go, let praise go first.' That's great advice for us when we face battles, always begin with PRAISE.*"

But that's not all. As we celebrated the first day of the new Hebrew year together for the first time, Tim and I planned to celebrate Rosh Kodesh together for the first time. We read through the meaning of that next month and the Hebrew tribe chapters together and prayed.

I gasped as he read what Chuck Pierce said about the tribe of Judah: *"The tribe of Judah was the tribe of King David, the tribe of Jerusalem and the tribe of Messiah."* I remembered the prayer I left at the temple wall in Jerusalem in 2019: a prayer that my future husband—whom I didn't yet know—would be of the bloodline of the King. I know, I know, a crazy, bold, and specific request, especially since I was on the hunt for a man of Asian decent. It's a thing (or at least it was my thing), but something deep down told me to be BOLD in my prayers to my Creator that day. What did I have to lose?

I knew that Tim's last name, Saipramuk, meant *"Blood of the King,"* but until that moment I only knew that his family was from Mongolia and he grew up in Thailand. But as Tim was diving into the Hebrew calendar and tribes, he shared how he believed he was from the tribe of Judah—the kingly tribe of King David, and the bloodline of Yeshua. I gasped. My prayer!

The parallels were getting crazy. My Creator was making His timing and design known so I could enjoy the beauty of aligning with it. Why would we choose anything else?

Life is like a roller-coaster. Great, we're gonna puke. At least for me, since I hate roller-coasters. Can't we just ride the merry-go-round? It's peaceful, there's no drama, and you don't go anywhere. Oh…wait. Never mind.

Without the roller-coaster, where would you ever get? So here I go over the roller-coaster again, every time I sit down to write, feeling, *"Do I really want to share this?!"* I am overwhelmed with nausea.

Why? Because once again, it's ugly. But it's ugly beautiful, because that's who our Creator is, taking things from ashes to beauty, if we let

Him. If we say yes to Him and His invitations to cleanse. To vomit out the dark and shameful things, face them, and face the truth.

I share these ugly things because I care about the one who might read this and find freedom. If that's you, you are worth it. You are worth it all.

I have to start by going back to the first few weeks of getting to know Mai-Thai. In our second week of getting to know one another through lengthy, late-night phone calls, we got to the point where I knew it was time to tell him everything: my whole journey, including the same-sex attraction I battled and struggled to leave behind.

I was terrified, not knowing how he'd respond, but he graciously just listened as I shared the whole experience transparently, through many tears—all the mistakes I had made, the regrets, the shame, the questions, and the confusion. All of it.

After about 45 minutes of him just listening to me share, I was shocked by his response. It was beautiful. I felt no judgment, no shame, only acceptance, support, and encouragement. He showed up like a king with total confidence, and I felt empowered. He was so patient listening as I told the whole story. To my shock, it made him love me more. He said things like:

"That's something you had to go through to get you closer to God."

"I'm glad you went through what you went through."

"We wouldn't have met, if you hadn't gotten HERE, if you hadn't gone through ALL of that!"

Finding His Timing

"If people care so much about your past, that's where they're going to be—in your past!"

"I want to nurture and protect that part of you (the struggle and pain you went through to get here) so that YOU can go help the world!"

He surprised me the next day when he told me he had ordered my first book. *"What?!"* I stammered. *"That's what made you want to order my book?"* He replied, *"Well, yea. After you so courageously told me everything, I wanted to read more context of everything you have been through, but I'm not just going to read it. I'm fully aware that your heart is found in the Creator so if I'm going to find you I have to go to Him first, so I'll be praying before I read every chapter, asking Him, "what do you want me to see or hear?"*

I cried. Obviously. What a beautiful gift in response to so much transparency.

As conversations continued, he made it very clear that he was fully aware of what he was "signing up for." He was putting no expectations on me; he was simply here to walk it together. *"Jen,"* he said, *"I'm fully aware and expect that at times you might still find a woman beautiful—and she you—that the waves of that would still come but let me ask you, do you know who stops the waves?"*

"The sand?" I guessed.

"No, a rock! A rock, when you put it in the waves, the waves dissipate and calm...who is the rock?"

Giddily, I replied *"The Creator!"*

"*Yes, exactly,*" He declared. "*It's not my job to stop those waves, it's not even your job...it's His job, and I trust that in time He will help those waves calm and dissipate for you.*"

He was there to meet me where I was and walk forward with me as we navigate it together. What a gift—someone to face it with me, knowing waves were likely ahead.

I remember staring at my own reflection in the mirror processing our many conversations and saying, "*I can't believe this is what you receive when you surrender and choose His design.*"

Here's where it gets really trippy.

I never imagined that, as we faced what I would call the "first wave" many months later, it would be in the timing in Biblical history when the Israelites had just fled slavery in Egypt.

I was preparing for my next monthly Hebrew calendar call, with the first wave splashing around me, when it jumped out at me. In Exodus 15, Pharaoh and his soldiers chased the Israelites into the sea, but the sea fell in on them and drowned them. The pursuers died in those waves!

In my life, my flesh was the pursuer, trying to drag me back into my old life, but I had made my choice, fixed on my Creator. I got chills knowing this is how victories are won.

When we fix ourselves on Him and keep walking forward with Him, as our enemies (the voices battling within us) pursue, we know we will win! He will make a way! And that it is simply a choice. I mean, come on—you just read how oppression in our relationship was also just taken out—the flesh from Mai Thai's battle.

But don't get me wrong, facing my own first wave of serious attraction to another female while in a relationship was not completely smooth sailing. It was my first sail with my new relationship. I hated myself, and my own journey: "WHY does this have to be my journey!?! I hate that I feel this. I hate that I desire this! I hate that I have to still feel this while in a relationship with a man that I already made a choice to choose! This isn't fair to him, either!"

Thankfully, I knew I had to own the feelings happening inside of me. I had to acknowledge them and face them. I wasn't going to bury them, like I had my entire journey. Burying my feelings caused me to hide, feel so alone, trapped, and suicidal.

Never again.

I knew how dangerous that was, but I knew I had to face it, own it, and process through it. I wish I could say I talked about it to Mai-Thai immediately, but I was afraid of hurting him and embarrassed about my own feelings. We had just come this close to breaking up, we were rebuilding. This didn't seem like a good time to bring it up. So it took me a bit to build up the courage to get to the point of surrender, no matter the outcome, with my Creator. I needed to cleanse with my Creator, and HIS (my Creator's) perfect timing determined when everything was brought to light.

I was enjoying brunch with some new friends in another state, when another friend started speaking over me. She didn't even know anything about my situation, she just knew God was telling her to open her mouth and speak.

I'm so glad she obeyed. He saw all the shame I was carrying for being attracted to this female, and He wanted to wash it all away. As she spoke, I felt the Creator's hand ever-so-gently peeling off another layer of shame.

My friend, Cassie said to me:

"We navigate to what's comfortable. When we pray 'help me in this area' and He delivers, guess what? Our flesh doesn't like it. 'I feel inside out, exposed, like this is a full body NO for me and I would rather just give up, because this isn't easy.' He's reminding you, 'Stand up, buckle up. Let's freaking go and FACE these hard things. Where it's hard, lean in. When it gets harder, fall.' You prayed to be in alignment. He says, 'I love you, no matter what society has shaped you to be, pain has brought you, or choices you have made.' When you pray to be in alignment He's going to line you up with His word, which you have spent time in, and He's shedding off the pieces of you that no longer belong to that fullest version of your prayer.

"When that comes, you will know, because you will stand in HIS honor, because honor is YOUR word and you will be sitting in His honor. His honor—not yours—His honor for what He created you to be and for the design that is in your heart. He's shedding off the pain that people told you lies, and all the pain that you witnessed that made you lean a different direction. He's just guiding you, nudging ever so slightly. He says, 'just wait. The like is coming. The love is there now but the like is coming.' As you're learning to navigate and lean into Him, it's shutting off all the stuff.

"There's going to be moments of weakness and embracing old patterns. He's saying 'you're still loved and it's normal. It's human.' That's the battle you have. He knows your heart for the greater good.

Finding His Timing

He sees you in your humanness. It's beautiful. That's what He created you for. That's why Yeshua died for you. He died for all of that.

He knows the draws, instincts, and things that come natural. When you start to question, recognize it is not Him yelling at you. He's saying, 'remember your prayer. You asked me for breakthrough.' Recognize that those nudges are to tell you that's your humanness and He's just gently, with a hand on your back, nudging you.

So when the harshness comes in, recognize that's a battle between your flesh and the enemy. It is not you. The nudge is His love, to see that little uncomfortable feeling in the mix of guilt and uncertainty, that's showing you where your humanness and the love for Yeshua meet.

It's the flesh that we have to drag in this life. That's what you're doing–dragging it, but pursuing Him. It's dragging behind you and you are fixed on Him, because you love Him. You let it behind you and you let it drag. And you say, 'I don't have to live it!'

He just wants to encourage your heart that all of those feelings of yucky, regardless of what it is—your thoughts, your actions, your inhibitions, whatever it is—He's saying to you, 'Keep looking forward. You know the goal. You know where to look—straight to Yeshua.' You say, 'okay, I experienced a little bit that feels this way, and I'm just going to keep walking, forgiving and walking in Your forgiveness. I'm walking in it, and I believe that You died for me. I believe in You.'

As you can imagine, I sobbed, right there at the table. I softly heard His voice say, "Jen, it's just a choice. What do you want to choose?"

It became easy. I knew my choice. I had already known my choice. He was just navigating me through the feelings, helping me own that they existed and deal with the shame, and keeping me moving forward.

Another friend, Brookelyn observed, *"Your Creator is going to bless you beyond what you can imagine for your choices."* I sobbed again.

"He will," she assured me. *"I don't care about the blessing for me,"* I sobbed. *"But what it will be for others, and this is why I have to fight so hard. I have to fight this!"*

I had to fight to leave my Egypt behind—the things that once chained me and kept me from my Promised Land. The things that, if I didn't run after the freedom my Creator offered, would subject to a life of bondage. Did I know what it was going to look like? No, but I knew Him. I imagined the Israelites in their wilderness after fleeing Egypt:

"What if we go the wrong direction!?"

"Wait, do we turn left here or right?!"

"What do we do at this river?"

"Are we sure this is God leading us?"

"Maybe we should go back."

"Why are we doing this again??"

"Where are we even going to end up?"

Finding His Timing

"Are we sure we should be doing this?"

"Is this really Him?"

Even with all that second-guessing and whining, He parted the freaking Red Sea before them, and wiped out their pursuer. He dropped manna from heaven, and brought forth water from a rock. I knew He could be trusted, and there was nothing I wanted more than more of Him.

Thankfully, the female I was attracted to this time, wanted nothing more than more of her Creator, too. She was unbelievably strong, so rock-solid, and full of great faith. She was also an incredible friend, a set-apart human who had taken the time to truly see me as she poured her way through my first book. She saw things about me most people don't see, let alone voice. She saw beneath the pages, and took the time to tell me what she saw. I felt so seen and accepted by her: truly loved. She was so intentional about encouraging me forward in my relationship with Mai-Thai. Deep down, I believed this time things would be different.

As I shared about the first wave, Mai-Thai's responses blew me away. I told him I had chosen him, but there was a wave going on, and I didn't want to hide it, like I had in the past. *"I already knew,"* He smiled. *"I also knew it wasn't a fight in the physical; I knew it was spiritual, and then it was up to the Creator to deliver you. I knew I couldn't fall into the trap of jealousy or attempting to control. You had to face it, and I had to go to the Creator."*

He gave so much support, acceptance, and love. We faced it together. That night we prepared for our first monthly Hebrew call together, and when I read the story about Exodus 15, so much revelation came.

Shame fell away as my Creator reminded me it's not wrong to feel the things we feel, they are simply choices. He paid the price for my shame. What a victory. What a cleansing.

I went through a process where He absolutely scraped my soul clean from wrong (fleshly) desires. How? By my simply facing it and going through it, not hiding it. This revelation turned my world upside down. By facing it, the wave fully crested, capped...and crashed, dissipating on the shore as the rock did what it was designed to do. Deliver. But I had to choose to let it.

The Israelites wandered through a wilderness, not knowing how to get to their destination. You and I are in a wilderness of life, full of life and death realities we have to face.

Adam and Eve felt so many things they were never intended to feel the moment they took bite of that apple. They didn't listen to their Creator's instruction, so they entered shame, embarrassment, and rejection of the Creator's design. Each of us has our own battles to face, but if we listen to His voice in those battles, He will remind us that He is our healer, our provider, and our banner of victory. He worked to cleanse me and direct me as I battled and boy, is He my victory in this one!

Don't be afraid of the waves, friend. Waves come and go and they don't have to overwhelm you. His design for water is to cleanse, let Him wash it all off. Simply come to Him and I promise you, if He can handle me, He can handle whatever you bring Him. What if there's a gift waiting for you on the other side of being transparent with your Creator?

Let your past die in the waves. Let what is pursuing you be taken out, too. Even Yeshua Himself was pursued for His identity, who He claimed to be. If He can die and rise again in victory, I think He's got you. Trust Him to do it! It's who He is.

I wonder if this is why He gave me such an affinity for surfing. In time, He knows I'm gonna ride those waves and surf right over them in euphoria, enjoying victory upon victory He takes me through in life. Every time I surf, it feels like another victory. I am surfing over the waves on the water and in the same way He's allowing me to surf over the waves that confront me in my life. I couldn't help but see the symbolism.

Does that mean I'm fully comfortable with a man? No. But what if there's more to that, too? Without this first wave, I wouldn't have had the conversations or processing that led to the Rock delivering, breakthrough, and new hope in areas that I felt stuck in. There were things I was still super uncomfortable with. For example, I was naive to the fact that my struggle was the flesh until this first wave literally said it to my face. Until then, I had never owned that about myself.

No wonder my previous experience with that other female (the Portuguese Man of War) did what it did: because that was her struggle, too. We were trouble for each other because we had the same struggle. But that's also why it was so "fun." Now that I was in a relationship with a man, this wave was different. Not only because I was in a different place in my personal journey, but because she was so committed to her walk with God as well.

I shared with a friend the frustrations of wishing I had the same desire for a man as I did a female. They replied, *"Jen, maybe that's because the Creator is showing you something different than just the* flesh, which is all you've known. He's giving you a beautiful story. I fully believe it WILL shift for you. Think about how interesting it is that that WAS his struggle, too…the flesh. You almost broke up because of it. BUT, when things do shift for you, and you have those intense feelings for him in that way, it will be explosive in the desire—in the WANT to have it with him because you both have the same struggle in the same way you and the female did. That was explosive. This will be explosive too, but your Creator is taking you on a story to build before you get there! If it started explosive with him, think how hard that would be! Give your Creator time to get you there. I believe it will shift."

I was invigorated with new hope for what was to come as a result of choices, I had made.

A couple of days later, as I was driving, Yahaveh reminded me of the story of Adam and Eve again, how they hid their nakedness. It went all the way back to the beginning! I realized what I needed to do. What if THIS unlocks it all?! I surely wanted to find out.

I asked for forgiveness on behalf of my entire lineage, back to Eve, for any feelings of shame, distaste, or disgust, of the male form, and for rejecting their nakedness as anything but beautifully designed by our Creator!

What if that's all it takes, friend—going all the way back to the beginning with everything.

If I could go back to that day, I would say:

"Yes! He is showing you so much more about His design over time! Keep going back to the beginning with everything!

Finding His Timing

It's where you'll find His design for it all! It's what your spirit craves the most, to be aligned to His design. To walk in it! To receive all the things He has for you...and the world!

There is so much more freedom ahead! So much more cleansing ahead! Embrace the waves! Embrace the Rock! Embrace his work! He is not done!"

Finding His Timing

CHAPTER 28

War for your blessing, your destination

As the first wave crashed on the shore and I stepped onto solid ground emotionally, I found myself noticing His perfect timing again. As we came back around to the Hebrew month of Tammuz, Tim and I recommitted our relationship to holiness before our Creator. Our hearts fixated on setting a new foundation as we prepared to be together again after dating almost a year long-distance. Tammuz is the month that is associated with covenant alignments.

It's also associated with the Hebrew tribe of Reuben. Rueben lost his inheritance, but there was also redemption in his story. Why? Because of how he repented after the choices he had made.

Tammuz was also the month the Israelites chose to worship the golden calf in the wilderness. I can't tell you how many times I have said to myself after reading or hearing that story, *"How could they worship a golden calf!?"* They had just seen their God do incredible things, leading them out of Egypt, even parting a sea in front of them to rescue them! How could they turn their eyes and heart away from Him?! If they would have only looked back on their lives and remembered who brought them out, and who He is. A golden calf... seriously?!

But the more I pondered this story and the timing of this particular month, it hit me how they must have struggled. They didn't know what their inheritance was going to look like. They didn't know where it was, how they were going to get there, or how they could even survive in the wilderness. They had no vision to pursue and no moral compass to guard their hearts and eyes from worshiping other things! The Promised Land was real and waiting for them to receive it, but they had no vision for it.

Another light from the invisible map turned on and this time, I didn't just see the light...I saw the destination. By now I'm sure you're asking the same questions I have asked throughout the discovery of all these lights...where do all these lights lead? Where are we headed? What's the destination?

The destination is a promise, a blessing. It's your inheritance! You just have to follow the leading of the lights, just like the Israelites wandered the wilderness and had to learn how to trust their Creator.

We, too, struggle with not being able to identify with the future He has for us. Where am I headed? What is all this leading to? Am I going to make it? Have I messed it all up? We forget who our Yahaveh is and what He created each of us for before the day we were born. Do you believe it?

Finding His Timing

I fully believe that the challenge is not to get stuck in all the questions, but to remember the truth of who He says He is and the truth of who YOU are!

But don't stop there, friend. So often we stop and cast judgment. *"How could they worship a golden calf?!"* In our disgust and shock we label the choice as sin. We condemn them to death.

Where is the life? Where's the hope? Deuteronomy 30:15-19 says:

"See, I have set before you today life and good, and death and evil, in that I am commanding you today to love Yahaveh your Elohim, to walk in His ways, and to guard His commands, and His laws, and His right-rulings. And you shall live and increase, and Yahaveh your Elohim shall bless you in the land which you go to possess. But if your heart turns away, and you do not obey, and shall be drawn away, and shall bow down to other mighty ones and serve them, I have declared to you today that you shall certainly perish, you shall not prolong your days in the land which you are passing over the Yarden to enter and possess. I have called the heavens and the earth as witnesses today against you: I have set before you life and death, the blessing and the curse. Therefore you shall choose life, so that you live, both you and your seed, to love Yahaveh your Elohim, to obey His voice, and to cling to Him-for He is your life and the length of your days-to dwell in the land which Yahaveh swore to your fathers, to Abraham, to Isaac, and to Jacob, to give them." (ISC)

A blessing and a curse. I don't see a fixation on sin or a casting of judgment, just a presentation of two destinations. Two possible results of the path of your choice. I don't know about you, but that sure sounds like a way better approach in talking with anyone who's struggling with their journey; carrying the enormous weight of guilt, shame, regret, or fear—just as I have—because of the choices they have made trying to figure it all out. What if, instead of casting judgment, we cast HOPE?

Quite frankly, THIS is one of the things that made my decisions in the first wave so clear. I could see all the ruin that would come if I didn't choose His design. I just knew I didn't want to be that human. I didn't want to be the cause of all that destruction and pain, no matter what feelings I was working through. But with the choice I did make, I saw the future blessing; I saw promise! His promises!

Does that mean it was easy? Heck no! I knew the battle that lay before me was within me. But I don't care about the blessing for me, I knew I needed to fight with everything in me to protect the blessing for others. While I didn't know it at the time, that was directly parallel to the Israelites' experience. Did the Israelites just walk all willy-nilly into promise and find everything was all sunshine and rainbows? NO! They had to fight as they entered in! But the Creator had promised He would deliver the land into their hands. They didn't just walk into inheritance, they had to go to war. They had to fight! What are you willing to fight inside of you so you can walk into promise, friend?

That wasn't the only parallel I saw. Around this same time, I took another trip up to California, this time with my incredible mom, so that she could meet Mai-Thai for the first time in person. But that wasn't the only purpose of our trip; we also secretly (well not so secretly anymore) wanted to scope out the land. We wanted to explore northern California (where he lived), knowing at some point in the future it could be my home.

I had known all year that this season was coming, with promise, inheritance, and a new destination ahead and here we were scoping

Finding His Timing

out possible land because of Tim.

Why is that so significant? Why did I see that during this trip? It didn't hit me until after we had returned home. In preparing for my next Hebrew calendar call, I realized we had been in the month of Av. As Chuck Pierce observed, Av is:

> "the month the two spies went in to the Promised Land and brought back samples of the fruit of the land. They said 'this is a wonderful, fruitful land just as God promised'. But ten of the spies added, 'we don't have the strength to take the land.' Two of the spies gave the minority report, 'God can give the land into our hands!' As so often there is a voice of faith and a voice of unbelief. When this happens we have to choose carefully. Av was intented to be the month that Israel entered the Promise Land.
>
> God designed Av to be the month to celebrate entering into the Promise. But instead of believing God the people agreed with unbelief and gave a negative confession. They said, 'The enemy is too strong for us we will all die!' They TASTED the fruit of the land but refused to enter. They held back in unbelief, and by doing so put themselves under a curse.'"

Woah! I realized it had just been me and my mom who went to scope out northern California...two people. Could it be this literal? This parallel?

Then I saw something that erased any doubt. Mom and I were running through the San Francisco airport when I happened to glance to my right (trying not to miss our flight), and there on the wall was a giant picture of none other than ORANGE BIRD. In San Francisco, not Orlando. This is a Walt Disney character, the one that defines the beginnings of the park in Orlando. Remember? Why is it in San Francisco, of all places? This character entered my story a year prior, six months before I found Tim. The orange had been a huge part of my family legacy. Yahaveh had spoken so much through it, led and nudged me forward with it, even to this unique detail with this specific character...and here it was as I was leaving THIS land.

Could He be leading me yet again, giving me a TASTE of His promise of the land ahead? I surely believed so, as I reflected on the parallel of what the two spies brought back from the promised land— FRUIT! I saw the fruit of this land. I could see His nudge leading me forward again with perfect timing. His timing. His fruit. His promise!

That was the month the 2024 Paris Olympics started. During the opening ceremonies, the story blasted all over the media of outrage as what appeared to be a mockery of certain faiths: the representation of what some deemed the Last Supper, but with all sorts of LGBTQ characters. It was blasted everywhere, with comments of *"How could they?!"*

A parallel to Biblical history jumped right out at me: the worship of self versus the worship of the Creator, in the month of the golden calf.

I don't know your journey, friend, and by now you've read the guts of mine. I know the struggle of confusion. I know the desperate cries for clarity. I know the things you may be feeling and the importance of voicing them, even (experiencing things) at times, to work through them. If you're like me, thinking at any point that you have to have walked the journey perfectly to get there, I'll be the first to tell you that's now how I got there. I made plenty of mistakes and did things for which I felt deep regret and shame. But your Creator died so that you don't have to pay the price for it, or even carry it. What if you had to experience the pain in your journey to get where you are today—to find your answers and to get closer to the one who loves you more than anything?

Don't carry it. Lay it at His feet! Let Him envelope you with the truth of who you are and who He is! Entering promise is not about doing it perfectly. I challenge you to open up to Genesis and read the story of Reuben! There is so much redemption in his story because of repentance.

What is that promise? What is that inheritance? It's PEACE! CLARITY! HOPE! Establish your identity in the Creator and how He sees you! How He created you. You are designed to be a display of His splendor!

The more you see yourself the way the Creator sees you, the more peaceful your life will become! That's who He is! That has been my journey as I discovered His timing and who He is—a journey to more peace, clarity, and hope than I ever could have imagined.

That is my hope for you, friend.

I hope by this point you've seen enough evidence of this invisible map I've found and where it leads. While seeking out His timing is what made it surface, it wasn't about finding His timing, but rather finding Him in the moments that were appointed for us to meet. I would have missed Him if I hadn't dove in.

Friend, dive in. He has the same kind of appointments for YOU.

I think this life has the potential to be more FULL of everything

He desired and designed for us to experience, all the way back in the beginning of time itself.

I can't wait to hear YOUR stories, and I hope you reach out and let me know as you begin your own hunt with Him! We'd love to have you on any of our "monthly hunt for gold" calls, where we share stories just like you've read in this book every single month.

I wonder what else He might have out there for us to discover. We've found His voice, His timing...what might be next?

I, for one, can't wait to see what He reveals next about who He is and everything He so perfectly designed.

OTHER BOOKS BY JEN

"Finding His Voice"

Available on Amazon. Scan QR Code:

Finding His Timing

WE'D LOVE TO HEAR FROM YOU!

Have a testimonial from reading? Please share it here;

www.amazon.com/Finding-His-Timing-Jen-Horling

Then scroll down to the bottom where it says *customer reviews* on the far right and click **"write a customer review".**

Email us at:
info@theovercomersmovement.com

www.theovercomersmovement.com

Find us on Social Media:
Facebook: @WeBelieveInYourStory
Instagram: @Overcomers_filledwithgold

Finding His Timing

EXPERIENCE MORE WITH JEN

BREAK FREE. FIND CLARITY. BUILD YOUR BRAND.

7 MONTHS of coaching & training in an
ELITE GROUP EXPERIENCE.

Are you ready to step into what you were designed to do, gain confidence in your story, and build something that truly represents YOU?

The Gold Track Experience is a transformational
7-month experience designed to help you:

+ Uncover your story and break free from what's holding you back.
+ Clarify your vision so you can step boldly into your future.
+ Launch your personal brand—complete with a logo that represents your unique identity.

**Here are just a few people who
have been transformed by The Gold Track:**

"I've never slowed down enough to answer 'who am I?' What does that mean? No one else gets to determine your value, because they didn't go to the cross for you, yet I realized I'm listening to all those people. I am just so grateful for Jen. She was obedient to putting this together because

Finding His Timing

I don't know where else I would've hear this, share this, and empower me! God made me to do what He designed me to do. He didn't make me like this or that other person but golly I spent a lot of years trying to be like someone else, to have their speaking voice, or their impact on their audiences. And then there's Jen with this incredible program and REALLY... GIRLFRIEND...this has been life-changing. She is raising up an army of us. Empowering us, and I know it's downloaded to her. Romans 12 says offer your bodies as living sacrifices, and she is offering her life, time, and energy, to write her book, be transparent, to write all these worksheets every single week in this program! She had to start somewhere, and was willing to do that for people she didn't even know when she put it all together! And that made me realize, all that I'm going to do going forward is going to make an impact because He's designed me to do that. So I won't have to fear what my identity is, because I'm going to be in HIS design! This was so huge for me."

"Because of this experience, I believe my story is so much more exciting and is going to resonate with a lot of people!!"

"There's been so much breakthrough. Just going through it made me realize how much I need to cover YOU in prayer because of the program. You are putting yourself in the gap for us. You are leading us through the valley. I'm allowing myself to go to places I don't normally go. I feel safe here. It's a spiritual journey. Jen you are brave enough to have paved the road so I'm covering you in prayer more intensely and intentionally."

ONLY 4 SPOTS AVAILABLE FOR EACH 7-MONTH EXPERIENCE.
APPLY NOW;

www.theovercomersmovement.com/accountability

HELP US HELP OTHERS

Overcomer Kits

Sent to families who have lost
someone they loved to suicide

Submit a name

Donate & help us
send more kits

FREE DOWNLOAD

Cheat Sheet to Overcoming the Next 12 Months

Submit Email

www.theovercomersmovement.com

FREE GROUP

Monthly Hunt for Gold

Find us on Facebook!

Join Here

FREE DOWNLOAD

Cheat Sheet to Overcoming the Next 12 Months

Submit email

www.theovercomers.com/your-cheat-sheet

FREE GROUP

Monthly Hunt for Gold

Find us on Facebook

Join here

www.ingramcontent.com/pod-product-compliance
Lightning Source LLC
Chambersburg PA
CBHW011521070526
44585CB00022B/2487